PORTFOLIO
WHERE WILL MAN TAKE US?

Atul Jalan, forever on the lookout for the next exciting idea and the next exciting thing to do, is an entrepreneur who is always on the move.

A childhood interest in technology transformed into a lasting love—life–technology intersections—through which he now explores how the technology man built is transforming him and the institutions he has created. What interests him the most about this merging of biology with technology is the fact that there is no end to it. There is always something new, something exciting, something surprising around the corner.

When not peeking at how technology impacts life next door, Jalan likes to travel—preferably on the bicycle he's built himself with the aid of a few tech tools he is testing.

A science storyteller and futurist, Jalan is the founder-CEO of a pioneering AI venture, Manthan, by day. It is his fourth successful venture as an entrepreneur, and there is no knowing where he might take us next.

WHERE WILL MAN TAKE US?

THE BOLD STORY OF THE MAN
TECHNOLOGY IS CREATING

ATUL JALAN

PORTFOLIO
PENGUIN

An imprint of Penguin Random House

PORTFOLIO

USA | Canada | UK | Ireland | Australia
New Zealand | India | South Africa | China

Portfolio is part of the Penguin Random House group of companies
whose addresses can be found at global.penguinrandomhouse.com

Published by Penguin Random House India Pvt. Ltd
7th Floor, Infinity Tower C, DLF Cyber City,
Gurgaon 122 002, Haryana, India

Penguin
Random House
India

First published in Portfolio by Penguin Random House India 2019

ISBN 9780143446934

Typeset in Adobe Garamond Pro by Manipal Digital Systems, Manipal
Printed at Replika Press Pvt. Ltd, India

www.penguin.co.in

MIX
Paper from
responsible sources
FSC® C016779

To

Papa,
For teaching me to think and then giving me the freedom to do so

Madhuri,
If you had not let me be, this book would never have been

Yash, my son,
May you live to see all that I dream of, here

Zineb, my muse,
May you inspire me to do much more

Manthan,
For all that you have given and taken from me

Tony Lawrence,
You should have been co-author; thanks for the thought partnership
and help with the writing

Contents

Prologue

ONE FINE DAY, ABOUT 400 million years ago, a fish (let's call her Wanda) decided to crawl out of the sea. We do not know why her ancestors, happy swimmers all, had over generations developed the four fin-feet that would help her crawl up the beach. Indeed, we do not even know what gave Wanda the gills to believe that she could indeed survive outside water.

We do not know what Wanda was thinking that day or whether fish think at all, but we do know that it was a good day— for that tiny crawl for Wanda was a great leap for mankind.

Fast forward many million years, to say about 3.2 million years ago, and we have Wanda's descendant, Lucy. Lucy brings us the earliest evidence of a hominid opting to walk rather than swing from the trees.

While Lucy fossilized a few million years ago, debate on what made her descend the tree is yet to die down. And the debate on why she chose to walk. It is possible that our hominid ancestors had to cross large swathes of grasslands between shrinking patches of forests.

What we do know today though is that chimpanzees expend 75 per cent more energy while walking than we do. Which proves that Lucy's descent was great for our ascent—bipedalism is a distinct advantage.

We do not know why Wanda crawled out of the sea, why Lucy climbed down from the tree or why we stand precisely where we are today, 4.5 billion years after this planet was born. Evolution could have gone a billion different ways. But what it has done is lead us to this stage where we indiscreetly call ourselves Homo sapiens—wise man.

But let's put the hubris behind us and look at where we stand today.

I consider this day as important and significant for this planet as the day Wanda crawled up and Lucy climbed down. Because while we got here on the back of natural selection, what takes us forward will be, in all probability, artificial selection. Man has neither the time to allow natural selection the few generations it needs for a change in heritable traits nor the patience to accept random mutations.

We believe we know what we want to do with ourselves and we are developing the tools to do it.

I consider myself very lucky. To have grown up reading Isaac Asimov, Arthur C. Clarke, Philip K. Dick, Robert Heinlein and Douglas Adams and then, as an adult, to see some of those worlds come alive. Maybe it is this childhood love for both technology and sci-fi that has kept me interested in life–technology intersections.

With every passing day, the biology we inherited all the way from Wanda is merging with the technology we have created—changing us as a species. This is a tiger we cannot get off and I wouldn't recommend that we do.

I like to call ours a Gutenberg moment. As Johannes Gutenberg looked at his first proofs, did he for a moment think that he was flagging off one of the golden ages of mankind? Did his neighbours know that we would be speaking of that day in (almost) the same breath as Wanda and Lucy? I don't think they did. They would have been more concerned about the price of fish in Strasbourg.

We are witnesses to a similar moment in history, when mankind takes another giant leap. One that will elevate man again—to a species infinitely more sapient. And much like Homo habilis evolved into Homo sapiens (via many other Homos), we might evolve into a new species. A new man altogether.

The technologies we have invented are merging with our biology—giving us control over pain, disease, ageing and maybe soon, even death. This, makes us our own gods. From here on, we can no longer be content with being mere humans.

This realization and this unbelievably exciting time is what *Where Will Man Take Us?* is all about. We should not make the same mistake Gutenberg's neighbours did.

Where Will Man Take Us? looks at how all of this is coming about. It looks at the drivers of change—artificial intelligence (AI), nanotechnology and genetics. At how this is impacting us as a society. At how the new-found powers of science and math might help us solve some of man's greatest mysteries. And, of course, at this new species that we might evolve into.

If we look at our history as humans, we see two distinct abilities and their consequences running together—our ability to invent stories and our ability to turn these stories into technology. Both, in turn, reinvent us.

Wheel to steam engine to electricity to telephone to Google—all are our inventions that have reinvented us. Each of them changed our life so much that those of us who have lived through any of these epochal changes cannot remember how life was before this. I struggle to wonder how I managed before mobile telephony and Google arrived at the scene.

This time around, the technologies reinventing us are AI, genetic engineering, nanotechnology and quantum computing.

Everything around us, I contend, can only get better with cognification. And that makes AI the next electricity, the next driver of human reinvention. But what I find even more exciting is that in our quest to bring humanlike cognition to AI, we are forced to examine ourselves and our brains a little more closely—what is it to be human? What is self-awareness? What is consciousness?

While these questions are man-old and have been pertinent since the time we started gossiping around a fire, it is only now that science has acquired the ability to bring us some pertinent answers. What could only be answered by philosophy and religion in the past can now be viewed and analysed through quantitative, algorithmic and scientific lenses.

AI's ability to crunch infinite amounts of data and math's ability to find patterns could also help us unravel some of our greatest mysteries: astrology, alien life and the secret to eternal happiness.

Where Will Man Take Us? also looks at advancements in genetics. With the ability to edit the genome, we really are heralding an end to natural selection. The end of randomness in human evolution truly marks the beginning of man's next avatar.

With all of this happening around us, societal change is inevitable. And that's where the book spends most time. Much of what defines us as 'man', as well as some of our greatest ideas and institutions, is directly impacted by these transformations and transformational times. Love, sex, marriage, jobs, currency, privacy, democracy—all of these are changing around us.

Sometimes I wonder if social media is making democracy more direct—where every citizen believes they have (and need) a direct say in the creation of laws that impact them—as opposed to the representative form where we restrict ourselves to voting our representatives to power.

When it comes to employment, machines will definitely change our idea of work. As automation becomes the new immigration and we start creating greater growth with lesser jobs, we will be faced with a new problem. Will this lead to discontent or will it lead to a new era where people are free to pursue their passions? The answers to these could change our ideas on work, earning and money.

All these years, we have spoken about the ideal mate, knowing fully well that no two humans can make an ideal pair. But we stand at the threshold of creating an ideal partner—with all our likes and dislikes programmed in. But we also live in a society that believes same gender relationships are not natural—how will we accept a man–machine relationship?

Speaking of society, our thinking is getting narrower by the day. L'affaire social media and algorithms, which keep showing us what we like, are driving us into smaller and smaller echo chambers. The result of what diminishing views, smaller minds and fake news can do we know from the last US elections.

These islandizations are not restricted to people alone. Having realized the power of data to control populations and their behaviour, nations are going all out to keep their data within their borders. Iran's halal Internet and the Great Firewall of China are good examples—keep our data in, keep other data out; keep ourselves well-informed, keep our people ill-informed.

Nations are watching their people as well, all nations. The amount of data nations have access to, on their populations, would make the surveillance states of yore go mad with glee. If he wants to, Big Brother can keep an eye on when you wake up, when you eat, how much you walked, where you went, what you watch, your preferences, your pulse through the day, who you spoke to, wrote to, what you spoke, wrote, every single thing about you. Should we worry about this? Or should we look at how this data can be used for public good?

These are changes most of us see happening around us. The book connects the dots and helps us look at what lies ahead. The future will question much of what we consider fundamental and common knowledge today.

Every age changes the pillars the previous age stood upon, kills a few gods and invents new ones. Like Neil Gaiman says in *American Gods*:

> Gods die . . . Ideas are more difficult to kill than people,
> but they can be killed, in the end.

The hunter–gatherer needed to worship nature, the farmer needed a pantheon, civilizations needed monotheism and an Industrial Revolution called for socialism. What will this new human ask for? What new god will we invent? What new saints will we summon?

If the first man was clay (and that is definitely more poetic than Wanda crawling on to land), the new man will be data. *Where Will Man Take Us?* attempts to catalogue this rewiring, this redesign.

Albert Camus once said:

Man is the only creature who refuses to be what he is.

We crawled out of the sea. We climbed down from the tree. But we are not going to stop with that. No, we won't.

SECTION I

THE DRIVERS OF CHANGE

A look at the defining technologies of today.
And what their confluence is making of us.

A Requiem for Alan Turing

I STARTED OFF LIFE WITH many heroes. Thanks to my grandparents, I had enough and more from Hindu mythology. And then, of course, there was Hercules. Then I grew a little older, became monotheistic and concentrated all my worship on Alan Turing.

The pattern of the monomyth or the 'hero's journey' is always the same—mysterious adventures into supernatural worlds, supernatural encounters, fantastic victories and, of course, they all come back with the superpowers to help common folk like you and me.

And by this definition, Turing is among the greatest heroes this world has ever seen. He ventured into mysterious worlds that most men of his time had not even imagined, made some phenomenal discoveries and laid for us the foundations of this world that we live in today.

As an analytics practitioner, it is impossible for me not to acknowledge the founding contributions of Turing. But then when I think about it, there isn't a discipline of science that Turing has not left an impact upon.

A Tormented Existence

Turing's was an uncommonly tormented life. His childhood was consumed by the pain of living apart from his parents. His adolescence witnessed the pain of an unspoken love (and the agony of losing that soulmate). With adulthood came the ignominy of being hounded as a homosexual and the trauma of forced chemical castration.

On 7 June 1954, Turing was found dead in his room, with a half-eaten, cyanide-laced apple next to him. The coroner believed it to be suicide; but many still believe that he choked on an ignorant world.

But in this pain, the beauty is unmissable. In forty-two tormented years, this man asked more questions than any of his genius brethren. Questions on logic, mathematics, computing, theoretical and mathematical biology, metaphysics, the list is endless.

And the questions he asked went on to become the foundation for a lot many more, those that practitioners in all fields would ask later.

> How does the mental mind arise out of a physical brain? How does language relate to thought?
> Where does knowledge come from? How does knowledge lead to action?
> What are the formal rules for drawing conclusions? How do we reason with uncertain information?
> How can we build an efficient computer? How should we make optimal decisions?

I really do not know if Turing was referring to himself when he said this:

> Sometimes it is people no one can imagine anything of,
> Who do the things no one can imagine.[1]

But if he did, it was true then and it is true now.

The Turing Machine

Mechanical or formal reasoning was debated on and developed by philosophers and mathematicians in antiquity. Aristotle, and later Socrates, had developed syllogism—deductive reasoning leading to a conclusion based on two or more propositions assumed to be true.

After that, a lot of tautology followed—debates, propositions and demolitions—until Turing came along. He argued that when human knowledge could be expressed using logic with mathematical notation, it would be possible to create a machine that reasons,[2] that an ideal computing device would be capable of logical reasoning by performing mathematical computations that could be represented as an algorithm.

Turing's theory of computation suggested that by shuffling symbols as simple as 0 and 1, a machine could simulate any conceivable act of mathematical deduction. This is what we know today as the Turing machine.

This theory raised the capabilities of machines from simplistic, predictable operations to a level of complexity that could produce insights and innovation. This is what has led to all the intelligence that we cannot live without today.

The Boxes Never Stopped Opening

Once we were enabled to conceive of a machine that could attempt logical reasoning, the next inevitable step was to model the machine on the mind—what we today refer to as AI, both the strong and weak varieties.

Turing's revolutionary ideas and concurrent discoveries in neurology, information theory and cybernetics led researchers to seriously consider the possibilities of an electronic brain—the first step towards AI.

The idea of a machine that modelled itself on the mind was just the beginning. It led us to delve deeper into psychology, philosophy, linguistics, neurosciences and biology. The world was waking up.

Bliss was it in that dawn to be alive.[3]

In a paper titled 'Computing Machinery and Intelligence', Turing posed his famous question:

Can machines think?[4]

His proposition was that if you were interacting with multiple subjects and could not distinguish if one of them was a computer, then that computer was an intelligent machine. A machine deserved to be called intelligent only if it could fool you into believing it was human.

Turing's path to AI was to construct a machine with the curiosity of a child—and let intelligence evolve. He was optimistic that machines could possibly in the near future exhibit intelligent behaviour and learn, to the extent of being able to 'think' like humans. (He was aware too of the standard philosophical and scientific objections that prompted some to reject his views.)

A sunset, the scent of a woman, a chilled Chardonnay—while a computer might still not be able to completely comprehend 'human', it is capable of a vast range of complicated responses that mimic the human mind. And, it has the ability to learn.

The Mechanical to the Metaphysical

At school, Turing developed a friendship with another talented student called Christopher Morcom. Christopher's death, many believe, is what led to Turing's obsession with deconstructing the nature of consciousness.

He longed to understand what had become of the essential aspect of Christopher: his mind.

This led Turing to delve into every subject that could be of relevance: biology, philosophy, metaphysics, even mathematical logic and quantum mechanics. And unlike philosophers and scientists before him, Turing was not compelled to keep the divine, the physical and the human mind wholly separate from the material universe. He could actively consider a mechanical explanation of the mind.

As If Man Didn't Have Enough to Think about . . .

In an era where natural selection, creationism and intelligent design were still being actively discussed, Turing argued for the chemical basis of morphogenesis,[5] which now serves as the basic model in mathematical biology. Many say that this is the very beginning of the chaos theory.

Having said all this, we still haven't spoken about Turing, the cryptographer, the man who created the 'bombe' that cracked messages enciphered by the German Enigma machine during World War II, an act that helped end the war sooner and saved thousands of lives. Ralph Waldo Emerson was right:

When nature has work to be done, she creates a genius to do it.[6]

The Two Apples

So here was a man, vilified by societal mores, who best exemplified Bertrand Russell's words:

Mathematics, rightly viewed, possesses not only truth but supreme beauty, a beauty cold and austere like that of sculpture.[7]
—words from the Alan Turing memorial

In 2009, the Queen officially pardoned the man convicted and hounded for homosexuality. But more beautiful than this belated pardon for the man who first visualized this world we live in is this lovely urban legend about the half-bitten apple next to the dead Turing.

Many believe that the Apple logo is a Jobs–Wozniak tribute to the man who laid the foundations for modern-day computers and for pioneering research into AI. It apparently is not.[8] But I would like to believe it is. What better tribute could there be to a man who had bitten off more than his share of the forbidden fruit of knowledge.

The Philosophy of AI: Beyond the Mechanical Machine

SHOULD THE TITLE OF THIS chapter have been 'The Technology of AI'? Or maybe 'The Science of AI'? The jury is still out on this but I chose philosophy because when we discuss AI, we are talking about intelligent machines. In all fairness then, we have to go beyond the mechanical nature of machines to look at the nature of their knowledge, their reality and their existence. Hence, philosophy.

For a while now, machines have been transcending their mechanical form to take on a new role in our lives. As a teenager, I first read Isaac Asimov as science fiction and to me, the Three Laws of Robotics in 'Runaround' were just that, science fiction.[1] But in 2007 the South Korean government set in place a Robots Ethics Charter, with regulations for both users and manufacturers. Asimov's Three Laws of Robotics played a role.[2]

Words like robotics and psychohistory[3] that Asimov used in his fictional creations are now used in real life. That's how much the world has changed in the past couple of decades. What in my youth was sci-fi, is 'sci' in my middle-age.

Where Did All of This Begin?

Every time I take a flight, I marvel that we have evolved to a stage where we can take to the skies and soar without even thinking about the idea of 'flight'. Something that for our forefathers—

from the dawn of man until just 110 years ago—was just a dream. For us, it's just technology between meetings.

In the past few years we have built supercomputers and the Internet, mapped the genome, smashed atoms at near light speed and peered deeper into the universe.

All of this has been achieved by this three-pound masterpiece of design, this tiny storage space for our intelligence and consciousness—the human brain. It is the single reason we are where we are—right on top of the food chain.

But the construct and working of it still remains our greatest mystery. Like astrophysicist Neil deGrasse Tyson said:

> Everything we do, every thought we've ever had, is produced
> by the human brain. But exactly how it operates remains one of
> the biggest unsolved mysteries, and it seems the more we probe
> its secrets, the more surprises we find.[4]

Some of our earliest recorded questions and musings have been about the brain. Both philosophers and biologists have pondered about the mind, self and body. For millennia, we have tried to understand how the amorphous mind and consciousness develop in the physical brain. Is the brain an organic analogue of computer hardware and the mind, of software? Why do we think and behave the way we do?

It is not surprising then that developing the theory of human intelligence and consciousness has occupied our brightest minds.

The First Steps to an Intelligent Machine

It was in the appropriately named Ratio Club[5] in London that Alan Turing and Grey Walter first traded ideas about intelligent machines (the club was named 'Ratio' as that is the Latin root that means 'computation' or the faculty of mind that calculates, plans and reasons).

Around this time, Turing came up with his famous question: 'Can machines think?' He followed this up with the Turing Test[6] which benchmarked the intelligent machine—one that could fool a human into thinking the machine was also human.

Turing also came up with the Universal Computing Machine—a hypothetical machine that can process any algorithm.[7] All of these advanced the thought that not just biological organisms, but non-biological systems might also be capable of experiencing intelligence.

The term 'artificial intelligence', to refer to non-biological systems that could perform tasks that otherwise required human intelligence, was coined by the likes of Marvin Minsky, John McCarthy, Allen Newell and Herbert Simon.[8]

Marvin Minsky, often called the father of AI, believed that every aspect of intelligence could be precisely described and that then, a machine could be made to simulate the same (incidentally, Minsky and Carl Sagan, according to Asimov, were the only two people whose intellect surpassed his own).[9]

Minsky was so convinced that human intelligence could be replicated by a machine that he once famously said that 'a man is nothing but a meat machine'.[10]

In the 1950s, these discussions on AI by scientists, engineers (and science-fiction writers of the day) were energizing a whole lot of other fields of science. The philosophers, the mathematicians, the computer scientists, the psychologists, the linguists, the neuroscientists, everyone was excited. Out of this were born new sciences like cognitive science, genetic algorithm, A-life, cognitive psychology, emergence, cybernetics, expert systems, robotics and more.

When we have so many excited scholars and so many diverse fields working on the same problem at the same time, we usually have multiple, headstrong opinions. AI, therefore, saw two paths— the computational theory of mind and the non-computational Theory.[11]

The Computationalists and the Non

The proponents of the computational theory, led by Minsky and McCarthy,[12] believed that the mind operates like a computing machine. And that there is no mind, only a brain and its mechanical functions.

Believers of the non-computational theory, like John Searle, Hilary Putnam and Roger Penrose[13] contended that the mind is more than a syntactic system and is open to creative functions that can't be predicted. They argued that the human mind has the capacity for language and use of meaning in a communicative situation—a function that a mind that is purely syntactic cannot perform.

These two opinions, absolute contradictions, led to equally contradictory approaches to the design of intelligent machines.

The group led by Minsky favoured a top-down approach—programming a computer with the rules that govern human behaviour. Minsky saw the brain as a machine whose functions could be deciphered and replicated.[14]

The other group preferred a bottom-up approach—where neural networks simulated brain cells and learnt new behaviours. These computers would learn from the ground up (from data).

In the brain, synaptic connections between pairs of neurons grow stronger or weaker depending on our own trials and errors. With a reward and punishment system, we train our brain to choose the right action.[15] The bottom-up theorists believed that an artificial neural network could do something similar. The intelligent machine would not need to be programmed with fixed rules, they contended. It would rewire itself and reflect patterns from the data it absorbed.

Overpromise: AI's Gulag

These were heady times and there was a lot of excitement in the air. In 1957, American computer scientist and economist Herbert Simon proclaimed:

. . . in the visible future—the range of problems they (intelligent machines) can handle will be coextensive with the range to which the human mind has been applied.[16]

But 'the visible future' was still far away.

Minsky and McCarthy had prevailed with their computational and top-down logic and were able to get substantial funding from the US government, who hoped that AI might give them an upper hand in the Cold War.[17] But the attempts that followed were at variance with the hype.

Like the frenzy that followed the launch of Sputnik, making the Russians the first into space ahead of the Americans (marking the beginning of the 'space war'), the Americans laid their hands on some Russian scientific papers.[18] At the time, it was thought that a rules-based system could easily translate these papers into English.

All that was needed, after all, was a simple syntactic transformation based on the grammars of Russian and English; a word replacement from an electronic dictionary. The machine, however, came up with marvels like 'the spirit is willing, but the flesh is weak' becoming 'the vodka is good but the meat is rotten'.[19]

But when you think about it, every technology goes through a hype cycle and this has been amply illustrated by our experiences with technologies in recent times. We always overestimate the benefits of technology in the short term and underestimate its power of transformative change in the long term. Our visions get trapped 'in the visible future'. And this happened with AI as well; exiling it to a long Siberian winter.

It was a long and cold winter. The expert systems that were created during this period were way less ambitious than the plans of the early glory days. These expert systems focused on narrower tasks, as opposed to creating general intelligence. They also failed to imitate biology.

There were victories, of course, like IBM's Deep Blue which in '97 defeated Garry Kasparov. The machine was capable of evaluating up to 200 million positions a second. Some hailed this as the coming of age of AI, but all it was brute force at work on a specialized problem with clear rules.[20] AI looked like it had lost its way.

The Second Coming

But you can't keep a good man down for long. In the mid '90s, almost like it was destined to happen, the universe conspired to bring together various factors that gave AI a second life.

It proved, almost ironically, that the evolution of technology is like the evolution of biology. It is probabilistic, without predetermined direction and shape—allowing environmental factors to give it form. There were many determinants for this second coming.

1. Data

Data created in the wake of digitization, Internet, social media and mobility became fodder for the bottom-up approach to AI. These data are what train the neural nets of the artificial brain, with machine learning mimicking the way our brain functions. Think autocorrect.

2. Rising computing power

The recent past has witnessed an exponential growth in computational power of systems and an incredible drop in corresponding price. Think smartphones—it would embarrass the supercomputers of old, power-wise and price-wise.

3. Ability to sense and measure

With Internet of Things (IoT) and sensors everywhere, everything is getting cognified and quantified—from your heart rate to emotions to DNA. Life is reducing to a data flow, making us info-organisms—not just bio-organisms.

4. Neuro, genetic and other emergent sciences
The merging of technology with our biology unleashes unimagined potential from both machines and humans, in a manner that they can complement each other.

5. Better, more sophisticated algorithms
Machine learning, based on neural networks that are inspired by the human brain and the nervous system, has seen quite some progress. Artificial neural networks are mathematical systems designed to analyse an enormous amount of data.

6. New beneficiaries, new investors
The greatest beneficiaries of the Internet, social media and mobile computing have been the likes of Google, Facebook, Amazon, Apple, Baidu, Tencent and Alibaba. Initially, Google used AI to better their search. Today, they use search to better their AI— which will help them create more solutions and hence, greater revenues (and greater control over our lives).

These companies are becoming more powerful than nations, spending more on AI than governments would or could.

7. The number revelation
In the beginning, computers were nothing but calculators—they added, subtracted, divided and multiplied to get new numbers. Then came the realization that every piece of information could be represented as numbers. That changed everything. Now the computer that was used to process numbers is being used to process all types of information—your voice, your photograph, everything.

While a whole lot of advancements are happening, we still have no general theory of artificial intelligence. Much as we do not have a general theory of human intelligence. We are still a long way from creating machines capable of thought, consciousness and emotions. Let us take a quick look at where we are.

Based on its calibre, AI can broadly be classified into three categories. Artificial narrow intelligence (ANI), artificial general intelligence (AGI) and artificial super intelligence (ASI).[21]

Artificial Narrow Intelligence

Also called weak AI, ANI is machine intelligence that equals or exceeds human intelligence or efficiency at one specific thing. At this stage in the evolution of ANI, the human mind is still incredibly smarter than the smartest machine.

The term 'augmented intelligence' is also used for this type of AI. And that is exactly what it does, supports our decisions.

The aim of ANI is to develop theories of human and animal intelligence and then build working models to test these theories. So for weak AI, the model helps understand the mind; for strong AI, the model is the mind.

ANI concerns itself with the degree to which we can explain the mechanisms that underlie human and animal behaviour. Crucially, this capacity is narrow and specific. Today' AI produces a semblance of intelligence through brute number-crunching force but still has nothing approaching the human's fluid ability to infer, judge and decide.

ANI extends human mental capabilities in one narrow area of its application. But even this degree of success has made AI critical to our everyday lives. Think smartphone again—GPS, image recognition, natural language processing applications like Siri, Cortana, Alexa, language translators, spam filter, smart replies to emails. We cannot live without these!

Today, the world's best checkers, chess, scrabble, backgammon, and Othello players are all ANI systems.

Housekeeping must have been farthest from the minds of AI's founding fathers. But with relatively simple sensors and minimal processing power, the Roomba is the first and best housekeeping robot.[22] Roomba also ushered in a new era of autonomous robots, focused on specific tasks—like surgical robots in operation theatres, autonomous weapons in theatre of war, humanoids for elderly care and even companions for love.

AI is integral to our lives today—it has effortlessly baked itself into our daily life without us having to acquire any new skills to use these life-changing applications. They have made themselves simpler for us—killing our awe of technology. As McCarthy once said:

As soon as it works, no one calls it AI any more.[23]

Artificial General Intelligence

At the AGI stage, also called human-level AI, the computer will be as smart as a human, across the board. The machine will be able to perform any intellectual task that a human being can.

I personally like to call this stage of AI, artificial 'I'. Because AGI is when the machine talks likes me, walks like me and, maybe, is a better version of me. Can AI multiply two ten-digit numbers in a split second? Yes. Can AI beat any human in chess? Yes. Can AI map every road across the world for me, in real time? Yes. Can AI read a paragraph from a six-year-old's picture book and not just recognize the words but understand the meaning of them? No. The day machines figure how, we shall move on from ANI to AGI.

Tough stuff that involves computing—like calculus, financial market strategy and language translation—are child's play for an intelligent machine. But what we humans do without thinking— like vision, motion, movement and perception—are insanely hard for the machine.

Ironically, AI has succeeded in doing everything that requires 'thinking'. But it has failed to do most of what people and animals do without thinking.

At the ANI stage, humans are a whole lot smarter. By the time we reach AGI, machines would have caught up with us and would be more intelligent at specific tasks and as intelligent at a general level.

Artificial Super Intelligence

At this level of evolution, I have good reason to expand AI as alien intelligence. We call it ASI when the intellect of machines is much better than the best human brains in practically every field, including scientific creativity, general wisdom and social skills.

While at the ANI stage humans are smarter, at the ASI stage we see a role reversal. At the ASI stage, the rate of progress triggered by AI would be infinitely more than what we have experienced over the last couple of decades, in the digital era.

Yuval Noah Harari believes this is when Homo sapiens will transform into Homo deus (do read his book by the same name). More conservative folks call that world the 'post-human era'. This will be an era where our capabilities will go beyond our biological range.[24]

Post-human evangelists believe that in this era, we would not only be cloning our biology but would have developed ways to distil consciousness into a chip. And maybe save it on the cloud. That the mind will clone itself and remain in unity with its clones and maybe achieve immortality of consciousness by migrating from platform to platform.

This features in the TV show *Altered Carbon*, where three centuries in the future consciousness can be digitized and stored and bodies exchanged (they call the body a skin). Death also becomes a temporary feature, a state you can resurrect from.

These utopian (or dystopian) worlds are not too far into the future, say many. Futurists like Ray Kurzweil believe the singularity[25] is almost upon us.

The singularity or 'technological singularity' is the theory that ASI will trigger runaway technological growth, leading to change we cannot measure or understand now. According to the champions of singularity, an upgradable ASI system could get into a runaway reaction of self-improvement. This would lead to newer and more intelligent generations of machines appearing more and more rapidly, leading to an intelligence explosion—super-intelligence that would surpass all human intelligence.[26]

This sounds crazy all right. But then, so did Asimov's three laws in my youth. Driverless cars were the stuff of comic books and facial recognition, sci-fi. If someone had told me then that the whole world would be mapped or that I would be figuring my location on a global positioning system that rests on my phone, I would have either called the man a liar or worshipped him.

Why I Love AI

When we speak of AI, what we speak of is the intelligence of machines, of the artificial. But what truly excites me about AI has nothing to do with the machine.

What truly excites me about AI is that in our quest to replicate our intelligence, we will ask ourselves some really profound questions. If the goal of AI is to make the machine capable of thought, consciousness and emotions, then we are forced to look at how these work in us humans.

We have tried, without success, to understand the brain. What is consciousness? What is self-awareness? Ramana Maharishi once asked:

> Who am I? Not the body, because it decays; not the mind,
> because the brain will decay with the body; not the personality,
> nor the emotions, for these also will vanish with death.[27]

We still do not know what it is to be human.

We can no more limit ourselves to just understanding the biology of the brain. In our quest to perfect AI, we have to understand the construct of the mind as well. We have to look at the neuroscience behind how our brain stores, retrieves and processes information. We have to understand the architecture of human intelligence.

We have, since the dawn of history, conveniently palmed these questions off to philosophy and religion. But now, we have the ability to look at these very same questions from quantitative, algorithmic and scientific perspectives.

Very soon, we will have a lot more to say about artificial intelligence. My greatest joy is that we will also have a lot more to say about ourselves. I might know what it means to be human better.

The Technology of AI: The State of Play

I READ SOMEWHERE RECENTLY THAT in 2016, 'AI' was not among the top hundred searches on Gartner's website but by 2017, it was ranked at number seven.[1]

What I like about this little factoid is the interest AI is generating in the tech and business worlds (remember this is Gartner and not Google). Suddenly everyone is interested in AI and its applications in their businesses and developers are bending over backwards to incorporate AI into their products (or at least talk about it).

This degree of hype and hullabaloo does lead to what we have discussed earlier in this book—overpromise and under-delivery—and so this is a good time to take stock of where we are with regard to the technology of AI.

While talk surrounding AI is practically mirroring science fiction, the fact of the matter is that we still are at the ANI stage that we discussed earlier—artificial narrow intelligence. It can today equal or exceed human intelligence at one specific thing, which in itself, one has to admit, is remarkable.

At the time of this writing, human intelligence theories are being developed and working models are being built to test these theories. Today we can create an appearance of intelligence with AI's number-crunching ability, an ability which is best demonstrated in games. The human cannot beat the machine at chess, scrabble, backgammon, checkers, and even GO (a game of infinite permutations and combinations).

One might therefore wonder, why games? What is this deep link between games and AI?

I believe that AI's success at games that are considered benchmarks of human intellect and intuition is a great indicator of its capabilities and constraints. So let me take a couple of thousand words to discuss how games can tell us the progress AI has made until today.

Let's Start with a 'Török'

If we are awestruck today by machines that can beat us at games, imagine folks in the eighteenth century being exposed to a machine that could beat everyone at chess. They would have found it divine (or demonic, depending on which side you look at it from)!

A Török or The Turk[2] was a mechanical chess player created by a Hungarian, Wolfgang von Kempelen, to impress Empress Maria Theresa of Austria. In 1770!

The Turk could beat human opponents at chess (including Napoleon and Benjamin Disraeli, one of the brightest minds of his time). It could also perform the knight's tour, which is where the player moves the knight to occupy every square on the chessboard exactly once.

It attracted much attention in its day, with the eastern connection of the 'turk' adding its own exoticness. But the truth is that while it was referred to as an automaton (a self-operating machine), reality was that the machine was built to conceal an experienced chess player inside. Kempelen employed some of the best players of the day to hide inside it and play. The Turk won most of the games it played across Europe and the Americas over eighty-four years and continued to be thought of as an automaton until its destruction in a fire in 1854.

While the story of the Turk is not an AI story (and is a hoax), it does say something about how the power of a machine to defeat a human in a game captures the imagination.

From the Turk to the Russian

In 1996, the inimitable Garry Kasparov played a series of six games against Deep Blue, a supercomputer designed by IBM.[3] In the first game, Deep Blue defeated Kasparov. But he came back to defeat the machine in three games and drew the next two, thus beating the machine.

In 1997, man and machine played another six-game series. If you ask me, this was the best one-on-one ever, beating Ali's Rumble in the Jungle against Foreman, beating Carl Lewis vs. Ben Johnson at the Olympics.

What came in '97 for the rematch was a heavily upgraded Deep Blue (but the same Kasparov). This fight is the subject of many books and films—which again indicates our fascination for the man vs. machine play. The fight was billed as 'The Brain's Last Stand'[4] (a little too dramatic, if you ask me). Deep Blue won this rematch 3.5:2.5

This was a watershed moment in AI's history, the first time a computer had defeated a world champion under standard rules—an indication of where the machine was going. Deep Blue was a top-down, rules-based expert system (a concept covered in the 'Philosophy of AI'). It had a knowledge base and an inference engine.

The knowledge was represented in a set of 'if-then' rules and the inference engine used logical rules for deduction. These fixed rules were preprogrammed from the play of many past grandmasters. Which means that for every move that Kasparov played, the machine could—almost instantly—analyse the outcome and counter it.

The machine could, with brute number-crunching force, look further ahead than any human ever could or can. (I have always wondered how Kasparov managed those scorelines.)

But when it comes to vanquishing man, this was not AI's big moment. That was yet to come.

After the Turk and the Russian, Ancient China

Ever since Deep Blue defeated Kasparov, the machine's ability to beat man in games that are benchmarked as measures of human intellect became acknowledged. Except at Go.[5]

Go, which originated in China about 2500 years ago, is a two-player game in which the aim is to surround more territory than the opponent (I rein in my comments on contemporary China here). Go is incredibly more complicated than chess. It is played with polished stones on a 19x19 grid (361 squares to chess's 64) with one stone for each square (361 to chess's 32). While the rules are relatively simple, Go is a game of profound complexity. While in chess, there are on an average 35 possible moves at any point, in Go there are 250. And each of those 250 could have another 250. And similarly, going forward.

I don't know who calculated this but apparently, there is an astonishing 10^{170} possible board configurations.[6] Disturbing, when you compare with the number of atoms in the universe: 10^{80}.

Players make moves based on the general appearance of the board, not by analysing each move. It is played, therefore, primarily through intuition and feel—qualities one does not usually associate with a computer. Which is why when AlphaGo, a system developed by DeepMind in Great Britain beat Lee Sedol, many believed it to be one of the major breakthroughs of AI.[7]

Here was Lee Sedol, a 9-dan professional without handicaps—the Roger Federer and Michael Schumacher combined of Go—getting beaten in a five-game match!

Go is a bottom-up game. You begin with an empty board and you build the game, with multiple, simultaneous battles. What AlphaGo (later acquired by Google) developed was a bottom-up AI approach—that is data-driven and leverages deep learning techniques.

DeepMind created a collection of moves from expert players (about thirty million) and trained the system to play on its own, which logically would create a machine that is as good at Go as human masters. But then, DeepMind matched their system against itself—this led to the machine generating new moves that it used to train itself to beat humans. (This is ironic because Go is seen by many as man vs. self, embodying a quest for self-improvement.)

DeepMind's machine learning approach, which combined deep learning with reinforcement learning and others, heralds a future where robots can learn to respond to their environment.

Machine Learning and the Intelligent Machine

A lot of the advancement we see in AI and robotics today is driven by machine learning, the two most popular forms of which are deep learning and reinforcement learning.

Deep learning runs on a combined network of hardware and software—called neural network[8]—that approximate the networking of neurons in the brain. The neural network does not believe in brute force, instead it analyses large sets of data to 'learn' a task. Image recognition is a task neural networks have already 'learnt'. Feed it enough images of cars and it will start to recognize cars. It might not understand cars as humans do, but it will recognize the object.

So after being trained on millions of human moves and having visually 'seen' millions of board positions, the DeepMind neural network has evolved to predict a human-like Go move 57 per cent of the time.[9]

Reinforcement learning focuses on how an intelligent machine should act to maximize its rewards—it is inspired by extrinsic motivations, much like how the brain learns and works. When it does something that turns out to be right, it earns points; when it does something wrong, it is penalized. This ensures that the machine is perpetually being motivated to be correct—a reward–punishment approach that is steering the success of projects like autonomous cars.

In the case of AlphaGo, it initially developed its skills by practising against thousands of amateur players. It now hones its skills by practising and playing against different versions of itself. Each time, the machine learns and remembers the move that brought it its Go reward, which is maximum territory on the board. The machine is learning from its mistakes with every single game and its neural network is getting stronger. This reward of every win creates an unbeatable virtuous cycle.

So when you look at it, AlphaGo has acquired mastery in the game much like humans do, by watching, playing and practising—with human-like reinforcement learning and strategy derived from match experience. This 'learning' is what makes DeepMind's AlphaGo one of the greatest breakthroughs in AI in recent times.

We have moved ahead from the brute force of Deep Blue to the 'learning' of AlphaGo. According to Demis Hassabis, the founder of DeepMind:

> It is all pattern-matching, and that is what deep learning does very well.[10]

Coincidentally, like most state-of-the-art neural networks, DeepMind's system runs atop machines equipped with graphics processing units (GPU). These chips were originally designed to render images for games and other graphics-intensive applications.

As it turns out, they're also well-suited to deep learning. So the same chips we used to conjure up imaginary worlds for gamers now helps computers understand the real world through deep learning. Games and AI seem to have a deep cosmic connection.

Games Are a Microcosm of the Real World

Games can provide simulated worlds that replicate the real world. It is a lot less expensive, in every which way, to create these and can be used to test various hypotheses, models and approaches.

I am a great fan of Nat Geo and Animal Planet and can watch their videos endlessly. Ever noticed the cuteness of the cubs of predators at play? Or pups at home? Ever noticed how they are always attacking each other, simulating the hunt or the fight for domination? What they do is learn the tricks without the cost, or the consequence. They are trying out concepts, reasoning, judgement and decision-making—in short, embodied cognition.

With a games-playing approach, that is what AI is doing as well, studying embodied cognition. Evolution, in the case of the lion cubs, did not have the assistance of computers to arrive at this process.

But the fundamental point of such activity is that it prepares all players—cub and computer alike—for the greatest game of all: reality.

AlphaGo Shows Us Where AI Is Today

Very soon, we won't be programming computers. We will be training them, like you do with your pups at home. Because intelligent machines are increasingly acquiring cognitive capabilities—they can sense, learn, reason and interact.

AlphaGo has given us a clear indication that we have moved ahead from the top-down brute force of the Deep Blue days. It played moves that were inventive and, according to seasoned Go players, some moves were practically 'divine'.[11] Which means that the machine is developing some approximations of intuition and creativity through deep learning and reinforcement learning.

For humans, intuition is easy, but tough to continuously access. But if intuition is implicit knowledge that can be acquired through experience, then machines can soon get better at it than us, as AlphaGo demonstrated.

Similarly, the logic can be applied to creativity—that it can be operationalized as an ability to synthesize knowledge to produce something original.

Remember the Infinite Monkey Theorem[12] that stated that a monkey hitting keys at random on a keyboard for an infinite amount of time will almost surely type a meaningful and creative text such as the complete works of Shakespeare?

I think soon we won't need the monkey. Machine learning could well create the next Shakespeare.

But until then, AI is at a 'learning' stage.

Nanotechnology: Nano Is the Next Big Thing

IN TAOISM, THERE IS A maxim that greatness and smallness are always relative.[1] And that becomes so true when you consider the magic of nanotechnology. Some of the greatest advancements in the next few decades will have the tiniest stamp on them—the stamp of nanotechnology.

To begin with, I would like to give you an idea of size. Ever tried to imagine how incredibly tiny a nanometre is? Well, try imagining a billionth of a metre. Or if that is tough, try this—it is $2,54,00,000^{th}$ of an inch.

Okay, I will make it simpler. It is $1,00,000^{th}$ the width of human hair or if you were to think of the Earth as a metre, the nanometre is a marble. Even the wavelength of visible light is larger than a nanometre!

It is nanotechnology that will change our lives in the years to come.

'Surely You're Joking, Mr Feynman!'

This is what Richard Feynman called a collection of his thoughts that he released in 1985. And the reason he called it this could well have been the number of times he might have received this response, after all he was among the first to discuss nanotechnology.

In his talk at Caltech in December 1959, titled 'There's Plenty of Room at the Bottom', he hypothesized:

> Nature has been working at the level of atoms and molecules for millions of years, so why do we not?[2]

During this talk, he imagined a day when huge amounts of information could be compressed into progressively smaller spaces—miniaturization. He confessed:

> I don't know how to do this on a small scale in a practical way, but I do know that computing machines are very large; they fill rooms. Why can't we make them very small, make them of little wires, little elements, and by little, I mean little?[3]

While many debate the extent to which Feynman dictated the rise of nanotechnology, it is universally accepted that this talk was the seminal event that laid the conceptual foundations of nanotechnology—and led to Feynman being hailed the father of nanotechnology.

Incidentally, Feynman never used the term 'nanotechnology'. The closest he came was to call an updated version of his original talk 'Tiny Machines' (in California's Esalen Institute in 1984).[4]

But in the mid-'70s, Professor Norio Taniguchi of the Tokyo University of Science coined the term nanotechnology, and it stuck. He used the term in his explorations of ultra-precision machines to describe semiconductor processes on a nanoscale. Nanotechnology, according to him, consisted of the process of separating, consolidating and deforming material by one atom or molecule at a time.

We are talking about sizes so minuscule that even microscopes needed to see things on a nanoscale—like the scanning tunnelling microscope that could see individual atoms—were invented only in the early '80s. Often, it is the visualization of an object or a process that leads to a scientific breakthrough. So, understanding how things work on a nanoscale is a very recent phenomenon.

Very, very recent, in fact. The 2017 Nobel Prize for Chemistry[5] was awarded to Jacques Dubochet, Joachim Frank and Richard Henderson for developing the cryo-electron microscope which can freeze biomolecules mid-movement to visualize processes that man has never been able to see before.

What nanoscience now shows us, when we look at it from 'a level of atoms and molecules', is that materials when reduced to a nanoscale show very different properties compared to what they exhibit on a macroscale. For instance, opaque substances like copper can become transparent. Solids like gold can turn into liquid at room temperature. An inert platinum becomes a catalyst. Stable materials like aluminium become combustible. And an insulator like silicon can become a conductor!

In short, matter begins to behave very differently and sometimes in a diametrically contrasting manner on the nanoscale. This is a technique nature has perfected, because everything we see around us is manufactured at a molecular level—including us.

So, much like nature, if we are able to put atoms together on a nanoscale, we can manufacture anything! As the Nobel laureate Horst Störmer said, the nanoscale[6] is the first point at which we can assemble something—and it is not until we start putting atoms together that we can make something useful.

The Ancient and Nanotechnology

Although the light microscope and the study of nanotechnology are very new, nanoscale materials have been in use for a while.

In fact, William Illsey Atkinson starts his book on nanotechnology, *Nanocosm*, with this quote from the Upanishads:

The wise man looks into space and does not regard the large as too large nor the small as too small, for he knows there are no limits to dimensions.[7]

One wonders whether these guys were really on to something or whether they were sharing a joke. But the fact remains that practical use of nanotechnology has been around for a while.

Heard of Damascus steel? Swords made from Damascus steel were reputed to be tough, resistant to shattering and could be honed to a sharp, resilient edge. (For a *Game of Thrones* fan, that would be Valyrian steel. 'Nothing cuts like Valyrian steel', says Grand Maester Pycelle to King Joffrey.)

This Damascus steel—the scourge of the crusaders—was made (most probably in Damascus) from steel ingots called 'wootz' that came from India.[8] These ingots might actually have contained carbon nanotubes that grew when impurities in the ore catalysed the growth of carbon from smoke in the forges. But how the Indians manufactured wootz is technology that is lost to us—steel that reputedly could:

> . . . cut through a rifle barrel and would shear in half a human hair that fell on it.[9]

Another great example of nanotechnology in olden times is the beautiful stained glass windows that we see in medieval churches. The artists back then might not have known nanotechnology but they created these breathtakingly beautiful windows by trapping gold nanoparticles in a glass matrix to create the rich ruby reds. And trapping silver particles for those deep yellows. 'They know not what they do',[10] but they ended up creating awe in the believers' eyes.

If you are keen, you can also search the Internet for Deruta Ceramics (from Renaissance Italy) and the Lycurgus Cup (from fourth-century Rome). Legend also has it that the sword of Tipu Sultan, in more recent times, was made of Damascus steel.

Nanotechnology in Nature

There is nothing around us that is not composed of atoms—the food we eat, the clothes we wear, the houses we live in and our own bodies. With nanoscience and nanotechnology, we now have the ability to see and control these individual atoms and molecules.

This means scientists today can deliberately create materials on the nanoscale to take advantage of their enhanced properties such as higher strength, lighter weight, increased control of light spectrum and greater chemical reactivity (than their larger-scale counterparts). Nature, of course, has mastered the art. And mimicking nature's nanotechnology is big business today.

Scientists have turned to the common house lizard and mussel, to develop adhesives that stick to dry and wet surfaces alike. Lizards have nanofibres in their foot hair, which allow them to cling upside down on inclined surfaces. And mussels use nanoscale structures to 'glue' themselves to underwater rocks despite the surfaces of these rocks being wet.

The surface of a butterfly's wings is composed of multilayer nanoscale patterns. These structures filter light and usually reflect just one wavelength which shows us one bright colour—because the multiple layers in these structures create optical interferences.

Scientists are using the same method in laboratories today to analyse the colour of light.

The moth's eye has hexagonal-shaped bumps on its surface, a few hundred nanometres in size. Because these patterns are smaller than the wavelength of visible light, the moth's eyes can absorb more light. We are using similar nanostructures today to enhance the absorption of infrared light (heat) in thermo-voltaic cells.

The same carbon nanotubes that probably created Damascus steel are being used to create sheets that are incredibly strong. A stack of 100 sheets (which will be thinner than 1 mm) can stop a bullet![11] Making for a thin, ultralight bulletproof vest.

Carbon nanotubes are also being used to create a material that looks like black paper but can store energy at temperatures ranging from 100–300° Fahrenheit.[12] Roll it up and keep a few in your pocket, this could soon be charging most of your devices.

As Störmer said, if we start putting atoms together, we can make some really useful stuff.[13]

A Million Breakthroughs Now

Today, much like in our discussions of AI, there's a lot of hype and hyperbole surrounding nanotechnology. And in the initial days of every emerging technology, we also pass through phases where the lines between science and science-fiction are blurred.

Much of what is being debated may sound unreal, but it is clear that nanotechnology's applications and potential, so far as it relates to the advancement of science, are unlimited.

In 1986, inspired by Feynman's concepts, the American engineer K. Eric Drexler proposed the idea of a 'nanoscale assembler' in his book titled *Engines of Creation: The Coming Era of Nanotechnology*. This assembler would be a device that would be able to guide chemical reactions by positioning reactive molecules with atomic precision. It would also be able to build copies of itself, much like ribosomes.

While the assembler has gone into science-fiction in a wide variety of atom-manipulating roles, there also is some real action happening on that front—the Engineering and Physical Sciences Research Council in Britain funded the development of an assembler in 2007. They are hard at it as you read this.

The idea of these microscopic vessels, as magnets or robots, is opening up more and more doors across disciplines of science. We stand on the verge of scientific breakthroughs in nanotechnology that will benefit mankind in every aspect of life.

One area that will be deeply impacted by this technology is medical science.

Nanotechnology and Man

As we have discussed elsewhere in this book—in chapters on genetics and also on our eventual upgrade to gods—nanotechnology has a huge role to play in our future biology.

As we advance with computers and biotech on a nanoscale, it is clear that very soon the lines between computers and biology will become fairly thin. The idea of a biological singularity where biotech and nanotech merge is not alien or fanciful any more.

In the near future, nanomachines could soon patrol your circulatory system. They could, in your blood, detect specific toxins or chemicals to give you early warnings of organ failure or tissue rejection. They could also keep track of biometric measurements to monitor your general health.

These tiny robots will soon be able to attack cancer cells, bacteria, viruses and all other disease-carrying agents. They will also be able to communicate wirelessly and download new software when new pathogens arrive in your system.

There already are several ideas to treat cancer that are at the pre-clinical and clinical trial stage. One involves targeted chemotherapy that delivers a tumour-killing agent called tumor necrosis factor alpha (TNF) to cancer tumours. It hides behind a gold nanoparticle to prevent attack from pathogens, as it sails through our bloodstream (this may sound unbelievable, but it is true).[14]

Another targeted cancer-killing technique involves nanoparticles called AuroShells that absorb infrared light from a laser and then convert it into heat to kill cancer cells.[15]

Nanotechnology can also work on metabolic diseases like diabetes. Tiny robots in your system could maintain the optimal levels of everything you need in the blood, including nutrients— supplying the right doses of the right chemicals in the right places to keep your engine running perfect.

To me, this sounds much like the elixir of immortality that the gods and demons churned the ocean for in Indian mythology— the 'amrut manthan' (what my current venture is named after). Or the Greek elixir of life.

From treating diseases to conserving the planet's natural resources to not having to depend on fossil fuels, nanotechnology and our new ability to put atoms together in new forms is recreating our future.

The Next Big

While we have acquired the ability to manipulate material on a nanoscale, we still are some distance away from nanobots and 'molecular assemblers' that can replicate themselves and even repair themselves atom by atom.

But the fact is that there already are many products around us that have benefitted from this science—sunscreens, clothing, paints, cars and much more. And with every passing day, the digital revolution is advancing with our ability to make chips with nanoscale features.

In many ways, I find this ability to manipulate material and life, molecule by molecule, very God-like. It brings us both the ability and desire to create. And as the fine Mr Feynman pointed out, the principles of physics do not speak against such a future.

Quantum Computing: Figuring the Small Stuff Out

WE ARE A REALLY SMART race and we have figured out the big stuff. Planetary motion, colliding galaxies, the dynamics of the expanding universe, we know all about these. What we haven't figured out yet is the small stuff.

We haven't really been able to use the laws of classical physics (and general relativity) to describe nature at its very smallest, at the subatomic level. These wee, unexplained, unruly particles are what make up the quantum world—a world where none of our rules apply, a world that is beyond our definition.

The best way to understand this quantum world and the conundrum it poses is to look at a problem we face today.

We have watched computers become smaller, as they become more powerful. One of India's first computers, the Hollerith Electronic Computer-2M, imported from Britain in 1956, measured 10"x7"x6"—with a phenomenal 3KB of memory. It was installed in a specially constructed air-conditioned room at the Indian Statistical Institute.[1] My computer fits into my back pocket and stores up to 464GB.

All of this happened thanks to the invention of the electronic transistor in the 1940s. Since then, transistors kept getting miniaturized and we kept creating highly complicated electronic circuits using them, to the extent that today we can fit 4.3 billion transistors into a chip[2] as large (or small) as the tip of your finger. The miniaturization of transistors has helped shrink industry, commerce and governance into our hand. And also stream pornography in HD.

But Houston, we have a problem.

We Can't Get Any Smaller

We can't shrink the transistor any more. At 1 nanometre, we have already created the smallest transistor switch.[3] This is atomically small—atoms range in size from 0.1 to 0.5 nanometres.

The reason we can't get any smaller is because at these tiny sizes, electrons start behaving weirdly. At subatomic levels, the laws of classical physics that apply to objects at a macroscopic level are not relevant any more. Here electrons start following a completely different set of laws—laws that exist only in the quantum world.[4]

In the quantum world, particles flow easily through barriers that in our orderly, macroscopic world they cannot pass through. This phenomenon is cutely called quantum tunnelling.

Now, this poses a problem. With unpredictable (a classical physicist would call it lawless) phenomena like tunnelling we cannot have transistors in subatomic sizes. They will not behave the way that respectable 1-nanometre transistors work.

It does look like Moore's Law[5]—which predicted that the number of transistors per square inch will double every two years—has come to an unpredicted end.

Therefore, if we need to make our computers even smaller (and even more powerful) we need to look beyond transistors, we need to look elsewhere.

Quantum Mechanics

I am sure it must have been a classical physicist who said that atoms are never to be trusted. Because they make up everything.

And he wasn't too wrong. Classical mechanics operates on well-defined, easy-to-understand laws. Look at Newton's laws of motion, for example. Properties of objects—like position, velocity and momentum—have specific values at any point in time. But when you get to the subatomic level in quantum mechanics, none of these laws apply. Everything gets blurred.

Which is why quantum mechanics has a reputation. It defies all logic, but it is the best theory we have for describing our world. Quantum mechanics is how the universe works, which we smart folks have not yet been able to comprehend.

For centuries, we had a very clear notion of a continuous, deterministic universe that deals in certainties—where every cause is linked to a specific event. Quantum mechanics replaced that world with one that deals in probabilities—where events at a subatomic level happen in quantum leaps with multiple possibilities. These really are mind-bending ideas (and not just for laymen).

Particles behave weirdly; like the fact that they can exist in a dual state, as both a wave and a particle. That is, until they are measured. The very act of measuring however influences the nature of the particle! Particles again, until they are pinned down, are neither here nor there, but are both here and there at the same point in time—which means that each quantum state can have a range of possible values instead of one specific value.

This simultaneous existence of multiple possible values of a property is called a 'superposition'.[6] Particles maintain their state of superposition as long as you do not 'look at them'. For the moment you do, if you try to observe them, they immediately collapse into any one position—pick one value from the range of possible values and settle. It truly is as if they live in a world of their own and have no intentions of letting you in on their secret. (If this is mysterious, do take the time to check out the double-slit experiment online.)

Particles are also uncannily linked to each other in a phenomenon called entanglement,[7] a condition where any change to one party in an entangled pair is instantaneously felt by the other.

Imagine you are a photon, a tiny blip of energy travelling through the universe on your own. But you have an entangled twin who is intimately connected to you from the moment you were born—who shares the initial source of energy creation. This twin could be anywhere, right next to you or in a different galaxy altogether. But regardless of what distance separates you, any change in you is felt immediately by your entangled sibling. At a speed that logically should be faster than that of light.

Spooky? Not to worry because it spooked Einstein as well. According to Einstein and the fundamental laws of physics, light travelled the fastest. But here were particles, communicating instantly across cosmic expanses. How is it possible? Are they using wormholes—a hypothetical passage that bends space-time rules to create shortcuts for long journeys across space? Quantum entanglement spooked Einstein and he called it 'spooky action at a distance'.[8]

Our future truly is spooky. And the only way we can create exponentially greater processing power to answer the questions that the future will throw up is by turning to quantum mechanics.

How the Quantum Computer Works

We are not very sure how quantum physics works. But fortunately, we don't need to fully understand a phenomenon before we start using it. Og didn't know about friction when he invented the wheel. Nor did the Chinese understand antibodies when they began inoculating people against smallpox a good 600 years ago.

A quantum computer differs from a conventional computer in that it does not use transistors. The conventional computer requires data to be encoded into binary bits, each of which can have only one of two values, 0 or 1. The fundamental difference in a quantum computer is that it is not limited by these two options. Quantum bits (qubits) can exist as 0 or 1, as a point anywhere in between or, wait for it, as both 0 and 1 simultaneously (superposition).

Now that, truly, is earth-shattering. Because a conventional computer can only work on one computation at a time; we can increase speed only by making multiple components work on separate tasks simultaneously. But the magic of superposition gives quantum computers the ability to work on a billion computations at once! The possibilities are frankly, unimaginable. Sergey Brin of Alphabet illustrates the possibilities nicely in a letter to his investors.[9] He says that the first Pentium II computers that Google used could perform a 100 million floating point operations per second. The GPUs they use today have a capability of 20 trillion operations. Their TPUs (tensor processing units), are capable of 180 trillion floating point operations.

But all of this pales in comparison to what quantum computing is capable of. According to Brin, if they are successful with their 72-qubit prototype, its computing ability would be equal to that of millions of conventional computers. And a 333-qubit quantum computer would offer a 10,000,000,000,000,000,000,000,000, 000,000,000,000,000,000,000,000,000,000,000,000,000,000, 000,000,000,000,000,000,000,000,000,000,000x speed-up.

Count the zeros, if you feel like it.

This mind-boggling capacity is also thanks to quantum entanglement. Let me illustrate with an entangled system of two qubits. When you measure one qubit, it 'chooses' one value. But it also gives you the value of the other qubit, because they are correlated. When you add more qubits to the system, these correlations get complicated and start growing exponentially. For 'n' qubits, there are 2^n correlations. But for you to explain a system of 333 qubits, as we just saw, you need more zeros than you can count.

And that's just the point. While these numbers are beyond what we could ever record with a conventional computer, a quantum computer might help us do that, crunch unfathomably large amounts of information.

Satya Nadella of Microsoft illustrated the potential with the example of a maze.[10] If a conventional computer has to figure a way out of a maze, it will approach the maze the traditional way—start down one path, hit an obstacle, backtrack and then start down the next. And keep at it until it finally finds the right path. But a quantum computer would approach every path in the maze simultaneously. 'That,' he said, 'is the power of quantum'.

Quantum Mechanics and Life

Now, as we just realized, atoms make up everything. (I would have loved to share more atom jokes but the best ones argon.) Everything around us, including us, is made up of protons, electrons and other particles (and quarks, but honestly, you don't want to go there).

Which means that the bizarre rules of quantum mechanics should apply to us as well. Shouldn't they?

Erwin Schrödinger's (yes, he of the probabilistic cat fame) book *What Is Life?* discussed applications of quantum mechanics in biology. Other quantum pioneers like Niels Bohr, Pascual Jordan and Max Delbrück also agreed with the idea of quantum mechanics being fundamental to all life sciences.

In their book, *Life on the Edge*, molecular geneticist Johnjoe McFadden and theoretical physicist Jim Al-Khalili[11] discuss that quantum effects are decisive in biology. They believe that the science of the small has a big impact on life.

They take the case of the European robin as an example. Every autumn, these robins migrate from Sweden to the Mediterranean. We know migratory birds can navigate, obviously, but how do they do that?

The theory is that the eye of the robin contains a chemical which, when it absorbs light of the right energy, shuffles its electrons around. This shuffling creates a system that (spookily) exists in two forms at once, each of which leads to a different outcome. Which outcome dominates is influenced by the angle of the Earth's magnetic field, which is how the robin figures out whether it is heading towards the equator or away from it. If only the robin knew.

Another example, closer home, is photosynthesis. Every middle-school kid knows photosynthesis. Yet, none of us do.

So what is it that we know? We know that a photon, having travelled millions of light years through space, collides with an electron on the corner of a leaf of the money plant that your mother planted.

The electron, excited by this burst of energy, starts bouncing around until it is able to make its way through a tiny part of the leaf's cell and pass its excited energy to a molecule that can fuel the plant. That's simple.

Now, the less simple part. According to the laws of physics, the excited electron should take some time bouncing off obstacles before it is able to find its way out of the cell. But that doesn't happen, it doesn't take much time. Also, strangely, the electron seems to lose absolutely no energy from all this bouncing around. Everything is too perfect to be true.

Recent insights have physicists as excited as the electron. Superposition, the ability to exist in several places at once, may explain this speed and energy efficiency of the electron. By quantum exploring multiple potential routes, the electron might be able to find the shortest, most efficient route, without bouncing around for too long. Physicists claim to have solved photosynthesis, although some biologists are yet to see the light. And where else would we move on from here but to the brain. The fact is that we are nowhere closer to an understanding of the brain than we were, say, about a century ago. Despite all our advances in neurobiology. Even if we were to map all the neurons, synapses and neurotransmitters in the brain, it is unlikely that we would have a clear idea of how the brain works.

We still have not been able to apply our knowledge of physics to the brain, leading David Chalmers, the Australian cognitive scientist and philosopher, to claim that consciousness might be a property of nature that exists outside of our knowledge of physics.[12]

This brings the British physicist, Sir Roger Penrose, into the story. Sir Roger believes that we need to go beyond the neurosciences, to quantum mechanics, to understand and explain the brain.[13] He goes back to superposition to explain how the brain behaves—multiple quantum states existing simultaneously before collapsing into one (almost instantaneous) calculation.

Then along came Stuart Hameroff, the American anaesthesiologist, with the argument that this quantum process happening in the brain was the result of microtubules—tubular structures inside the eukaryotic cell that play multiple intra-cellular roles—in the brain.[14]

Our brain might be a quantum computing device. Neurotransmitters and synaptic firing could be creating quantum coupled networks, just like a quantum computer would. Quantum mechanics might be doing its jiggery-pokery in the brain. Particles in superposition might be clicking into outcomes as we read each word. The fact is, we can speculate but do not know for sure.

It is clear, though, as the theoretical physicist Richard Feynman pointed out, that life and nature are not classical:

> Nature isn't classical, dammit, and if you want to make a simulation
> of nature, you'd better make it quantum mechanical, and by golly
> it's a wonderful problem, because it doesn't look so easy.[15]

If we intend to understand all this—life and nature and the quantum world—if we are to untangle the inexplicable knottiness of life, then we need a different kind of computer—the quantum computer.

We do have a wee problem.

Genetics: The Story of Our Lives

'But then, in all honesty, if scientists don't play God, who will?'[1]

THIS WAS HOW DR JAMES Watson (who with Francis Crick discovered the structure of the DNA) responded recently to critics of genetic engineering. But even in this day and age, many view this as an extremely arrogant statement.

Prince Charles, holding forth against GM (genetically modified) food, stated recently that scientific rationalism has undermined the sacred trust between man and God. He argued that if nothing was held sacred, then scientists would turn the world into a great lab where science is allowed to run rampant and unchecked.[2]

Richard Dawkins stated, immediately, that he was 'saddened' by this idea of scientific rationalism as the arch enemy of environmental protection.[3]

That we are still having this debate is shocking. Or blasphemous, depending on which side you are on.

Today we can design, create and transfer new genes into humans within months. We can create new chromosomes within months. In short, what has evolved over millions of years can now be reformatted and redirected by science. Which, if you ask me, is the power to play God.

To me, it appears that we are living in a world of magic realism. A rational world with a whole lot of magical elements revealing themselves with every passing day. A world that a Marquez or an Allende would revel in.

But before we get to playing God and quoting magic realism, let us take a quick look at the very brief history of the genetic sciences.

Gregor Mendel: When Biology Met Math

Humans have known that progeny resembles the parents for tens of thousands of years. This is the reason why people, the moment they see a wrinkled newborn with totally unrecognizable features, have to coo that it resembles the parent(s).

Man has intuitively known of genetics for long. In agriculture, this goes back to the time man became a settler and cultivator. The humble potato, for example, has been undergoing selective breeding in South America for millenniums.[4]

But while the farmer and the animal breeder guessed at the logic of inheritance, they could never pin down the science of genetics.

Before Gregor Mendel, the theory in use was one of blending inheritance,[5] that each parent contributed fluids to the fertilization process which blended to produce the character of the offspring.

Even Darwin spoke of 'gemmules',[6] imagined particles of inheritance that would mix during reproduction.

Mendel's training in mathematics (Christian Doppler, of the Doppler effect fame, was his peer), helped him bring a mathematical lens to biology.[7] Mendel's leap (of discovery) was the statistical analysis of his experimental data; obtaining connections between the peas he bred and conceptual models of how these peas were related.[8]

Mendel performed a series of experiments to show that the traits inherited from parents were not just blended versions of those of the parents, but the result of 'discrete inherited units'.

Today we understand these as the genes that reside in the chromosomes.

While Mendel was not the one to coin the term 'gene', he came close with 'discrete inherited units' that lead to 'observable physical traits'.

Mendel's work, like that of the proverbial artist, went unsung in his own time (but he had laid the empirical foundations for a science that would soon benefit from a confluence of developments in other sciences in the twentieth century).

Schrödinger: When Biology Meets Big Physics

When he witnessed the successful testing of the atomic bomb in New Mexico, Robert Oppenheimer, the head of the Manhattan Project, quoted the Bhagavad Gita:

Now I am become Death, the destroyer of worlds.[9]

This painful, intimate, responsibility for what was then the most destructive force known to man was carried by many physicists who were involved in the project, along with others whose research had led to that destructive cloud. But even those working on the Manhattan Project realized that while the atomic bomb was the destructive side, the benevolent side of the research would eventually change biology and medicine.[10]

One of those disillusioned by the horror of Hiroshima and Nagasaki was Erwin Schrödinger. Pained at the sight of physics as the science of death, he turned the other way.[11] He looked at the application of the structure of atomic sciences to the biological sciences—if one could go subatomic in physics, why not go subcellular in biology? He believed that looking deeper at the physical aspects of the living cell could help us understand life better.

What followed was *What Is Life?*[12], the compilation of a series of lectures at Trinity College, Dublin. Schrödinger warned attendees that:

> . . . the subject matter was a difficult one and that the lectures could not be termed popular.

The lectures focused on how events happening within space and time boundaries of an organism could be explained by physics and chemistry.

It was in *What Is Life?* that Schrödinger touched upon the idea of an aperiodic crystal that contained genetic information in its configuration. He argued that this carrier of information contained a code-script that impacted:

> . . . the entire pattern of the individual's future development and its functioning in the mature state.

In a way, the men behind the 'science of death' had given the 'science of life' a big, fat clue. This was key to Watson and Crick's work on the structure of the DNA—the double helix.[13]

Watson and Crick: When Biology Became Big

Schrödinger's work (and that of others) led to the greatest revelation of our times—Watson and Crick's transformation of biology with their understanding of the structure of the DNA, the 'molecule of life', in 1953.[14]

It's a common misconception that Watson and Crick discovered the DNA. The DNA was discovered in the late 1860s by Swiss chemist Friedrich Miescher. And in the years that followed, other scientists like Phoebus Levene and Erwin Chargaff revealed additional details about the DNA molecule.[15]

What Watson and Crick discovered was the structure of the DNA. And as they pointed out:

> It has not escaped our notice, [that the double helix] immediately suggests a copying mechanism for the genetic material.[16]

The double-helix model cracked the code for how genetic information is passed from an organism to its offspring.

Very simply put, they discovered that DNA consists of two chains of alternating phosphate and sugar groups, twisted around each other (the famed double helix). The two chains are held together by four organic bases—adenine (A) with thymine (T), and guanine (G) with cytosine (C). ATCG are the 'binary codes' of our life. The biological code that makes each of us who we are, is written by a combination of these alphabets.[17]

Each of us then is just the execution of a programme that is written using these four alphabets in a single, 'universal' machine language. This understanding that permutations and combinations of these four compounds can determine everything from our physical appearances to our risk of being born with a devastating disease was one of the biggest revelations of the last century.

And this put man in total command. Because it was all of this that laid the groundwork for genetic modification, the Human Genome Project (HGP),[18] the first cloned animals, synthetic biology . . .

What Watson and Crick brought to us is the ability to play God. They showed us that we are info-organisms and information can be computed and combined with the power of Big Data analytics. We can now churn this information to reveal more about ourselves. And we can reveal patterns, trends and associations that otherwise were hidden from human intelligence.

In short, with the discovery of the double helix, biology had become Big.

The Possibilities: Big Biology Meets Big Data and Big Money

As is the case with most sciences, genetics has also benefitted from the confluence of sciences and technologies that we witness today.

Genetic sequencing is so advanced today that labs can read millions of letters of DNA from a single gob of spit.

The possibilities are staggering—in theory, this can help scientists cure genetic disorders and identify gene targets for combating HIV. (It actually makes chemotherapy sound incredibly medieval.)

The HGP, launched in 1990, with James Watson as one of the primary drivers, attempted to identify and map all the genes of the human genome from both a physical as well as a functional standpoint.

The world's largest collaborative effort, the HGP can help us understand diseases, mutations linked to cancer, the design of medication and much else.

HGP will also impact agriculture, animal husbandry, anthropology, evolution, practically everything around us. Another outcome will be the commercial development of products based on genomic research—a multibillion-dollar industry. These are not just possibilities; look around and you see a lot happening in this space. Companies like 23andMe and many others are offering direct-to-consumer genetic testing, reading every letter of the 22,000 genes in your body for a few hundred dollars.[19] This is a personalized DNA service that provides information on everything from your ancestry (you can figure what percentage of Neanderthal you are), athletic ability, how much coffee you are likely to consume and much else that does absolutely nothing to change or improve your life.

But then, they also tell you of your predisposition to more than ninety traits and conditions ranging from baldness to blindness. Whether you are carrying genetic variations related to diseases and could possibly pass them on to your children. This became controversial and the Food and Drug Administration (FDA) clamped down on such services for multiple reasons— including the fact that people might misinterpret the results and seek treatment they might not need. But as of writing this, FDA has allowed 23andMe to forecast susceptibility to Alzheimer's, Parkinson's, Celiac and seven other inheritable genetic traits.[20]

People are taking susceptibility seriously today. Angelina Jolie's double mastectomy made news. Genetic tests showed she was carrying a dangerous mutation of the BRCA1 gene. The test forecasted an 87 per cent probability of her developing breast cancer in fourteen years' time.[21] While at that point in time Jolie did not have cancer, she eliminated the actualization of the probability with her double mastectomy.

All of this news in genetics is attracting big money—from traditional pharma companies to governments to Silicon Valley billionaires with moonshot projects. Quite a bit is being spent on moonshots and as is to be expected, overpromise and under-delivery are at their perpetual game. Optimism is high and breakthroughs are regularly reported with great enthusiasm.

But the hope is that soon we will be able to comprehensively understand the genetic components of major diseases that ail us— and that we might be able to prevent, predict and eliminate them.

We Are 'Rewriting' Our Future

CRISPR (clustered regularly interspaced short palindromic repeats), a technology that will play a decisive role in genetic engineering, had an innocuous origin. Scientists at Danisco were trying to control the viruses that destroy good bacteria in yogurt and cheese. As part of their attempts, they isolated the DNA of the bacteria and read its sequence. They figured (to everyone's surprise) that bacteria carry mug shots of viral codes that have attacked them in previous generations. The moment the DNA faces a new attack; it identifies the mug shot and deploys CRISPR to defend itself. CRISPR identifies the malicious virus, cuts it out and replaces it with some harmless code.[22]

Simply put, CRISPR is like molecular scissors that can chop specific stretches of genetic code. Genome engineers have now programmed this bacterial defence system to target and edit mutations at precise locations in the human genome to eliminate genetic causes of disease at the DNA level. In short, a genetic McAfee.

The most amazing video I have seen in recent times (amongst many cat videos) is one by Kanazawa and Tokyo universities that uses a technique called high-speed atomic-force microscopy to capture a CRISPR-Cas9[23] system at work, editing inside a molecule! While it is one thing to change our environment by deliberate selection and breeding to promote unnatural selection, developing the ability to engineer life code and 'rewrite' it for our specific purposes should rate as man's single greatest achievement![24]

When future historians discuss science, they will most probably refer to the pre and postgenomic eras. A pregenomic era, where we saw ourselves as bio-organisms and a postgenomic era where we are info-organisms. Where the chemicals in the cell are the hardware and the information encoded in the DNA the preloaded software. The interactions between the chemicals become akin to the constantly changing states of processing and memory chips.

Once we understand cells in this manner, it becomes possible to understand an assemblage of cells—like you, me, your orchid or your pet dog—with completeness.

In his book *Regenesis*, American geneticist and molecular engineer, George Church, explains how synthetic biology will reinvent nature and humans. And driving this reinvention will be humans. And as we walk that path is a good time to ask this question—having decided that we are in charge of evolution, what will we do with these God-like powers?

Ethics: The Big Question

Juan Enriquez and Steve Gullans have this eerie vision of our near future in their book *Evolving Ourselves*:

> The questions driven by and the powers granted by our increasing ability to decode, encode, and engineer life forms will challenge religions, corporations and governments. Each will seek to earn our trust and help guide us as we face some thorny issues. In turn, each of these core institutions will also need to adapt and evolve existing dogma; each will have to re-earn its legitimacy to provide guidance on some truly complex options and dilemmas.

While genomics evolves from sci-fi to reality (with huge implications for our future), there come to the fore a whole lot of concerns. Should the same technology used for treatment also be used for enhancing ourselves? For modification or alteration of our appearances? For adaptability, intelligence, character or behaviour?

Should bereaved parents be able to clone a lost child? Or a widow her departed husband? Should the rich be able to pay their way to becoming supermen? Or design superkids?

Very soon it should be possible for you to ask for a child who can run like Bolt, look like Sean Connery and talk like George Carlin. But then, should he be allowed into the Olympics to participate with the, well, humans?

All this while, it has been natural selection that has driven evolution—where random mutations rise in the genomes of individual organisms, which could be passed on to the offspring, called natural selection because it happens on its own and cannot be influenced. But we stand at a point in history where we will soon have the power to eliminate the word 'random' from natural selection. Where we decide what needs to be carried forward and what not. This means that evolution tomorrow will be planned and deterministic, not natural and probabilistic. This changes us as a species.

James Watson was right. Scientists will be the ones with the ability to play God. What remains to be seen is if we will have the humility, consistency and impersonal randomness of God.

THE NEW SOCIETY

New technologies are creating a new man.
And this new man is creating a new society.
Everything about us and around us is changing.

The Filter Bubble: Many More of Me

I CAN THINK OF A thousand reasons for being thankful to comic books. But none more so than for introducing me to the eminent *kūpamanduka* and the equally distinguished *kumbhamanduka*— the frog in the well and the frog in the pitcher.

From the Kasika (a commentary on Panini's *Astadhyayi*),[1] the kūpamanduka and the kumbhamanduka best symbolize what Homo sapiens is slowly evolving into. Both these fictional frogs believe that the well and the pot, respectively, to be the whole world and having seen it all, become pompous—for they believe they know all there is to know about the world and everything in it.

That's our future then—frogs in a well that, strangely, is expanding with knowledge. This is the tragedy of our generation and I fear, the next. We really are beginning to believe that we know it all, and that our thinking and our analysis on matters that interest us is spot on. And better still, all the other frogs in our well tend to agree with us. We are living in a very unhealthy, paradoxical and knowledge-driven ignorance.

Why is something so alarming happening with us in this day and age, when there are infinite possibilities for enlightenment? Well, the answer is that the Internet has become personal. The algorithms have become so good that they have begun to reinforce our personal, preconceived biases when the Internet shares information with us.

In addition to this, we are spending more and more time on social media with people who agree with us—which is but a natural human tendency. So, between search engine algorithms and social media platforms that parse information in the same manner, we are beginning to see only what we like.

We are unwittingly cutting out every view that does not agree with our own, making our wells and pitchers smaller . . . and smaller. Each of us is creating an echo chamber for ourselves—in which we only see and hear like-minded thoughts and voices.

Since Eli Pariser, CEO of Upworthy and also an author, probably did not read about the kūpamanduka in his childhood, he called this phenomenon 'the filter bubble' (in his book by the same name).[2] He defined it as a state of intellectual isolation that results from personalized searches where algorithms choose information that information-users would like to see ('approve of' is a better term, honestly). This selection is made by algorithms based on the knowledge they have of the user; like search history, location and click-behaviour.

To add to this, Facebook and Google tailor your news and friends' status updates so that you like what you see and hence, keep returning to them. Every time you 'like' something shared by a friend, some search engine somewhere is adding one line of code to its definition of you.

As Pariser says:

> Your computer monitor is a kind of one-way mirror, reflecting your interests while algorithmic observers watch what you click.[3]

In essence, with every passing click, we are digging our own wells. Now that's regretful, isn't it? This was not the way it was meant to be.

The Irony of the Internet

I am old enough to remember what the information revolution was meant to be. The Internet started off as this 'anarchic autobahn'—this revolutionary world of infinite information—accessible to all. It set out to create this better-informed, utopian knowledge meritocracy where everyone with an opinion could engage in free, uninhibited exchange of ideas. As the famous Berners-Lee Declaration went:

> This is for all![4]

But, thanks to personalization algorithms, instead of being the mainframe of knowledge, it is gradually becoming a messenger that confirms personal biases. Even the wisest among us is, at some point in the day, relying on his filter bubble to prove his point, to confirm his biases.

This becomes even scarier when you think of the post-millennials. For them, this is the world—for them, it is tough to even understand or see the bubble they were born into. They will:

> . . . lead lives of quiet desperation and die with their song still inside them . . .[5]

in a techno-dystopia, never having known any better.

This, in my mind, is the irony. From oneness, the Internet is taking us to what Pariser calls the 'web of one'. The Internet has become so bespoke, it looks like each of us might be seeing our very own, personal web. What was meant to unify, is now dividing.

Until recently, I thought that the best example of irony is the fact that the Bible is the most shoplifted book in the US. I would not say that any more.

We Need Our Wells and Our Pitchers

I think genetically we were all engineered to be journalists, every other profession we engage in is just random stuff we stumbled upon. For, man loves to report; we always want to be the first to share something interesting.

Think about all that you keep sharing daily. How much of it happened because you decided to study a subject, sat down, did your homework and then decided to share it with friends you knew would be interested in your findings?

Chances are, none.

You were in a cab, you were waiting for a meeting, you were in the metro or (most likely) you were procrastinating when you picked up your phone and started scrolling. And whatever caught half a fancy of yours you shared, randomly.

We are rabid information-seekers and the Internet is just godsend. Our brain is a gratification-seeking monster, it seeks dopamine.

Dopamine is released by rewarding experiences like sex, food and drugs. Replace these fixes with information-seeking and you have just hit a gold mine. We are in a dopamine loop.

Aiding and abetting this suicidal loop is that evil genius—the smartphone. Look at how important the phone has become in our lives. In our pocket, right next to our bed, next to us on the couch.

It has replaced every other affection of ours. The average Indian millennial spends 2.2 hours with the phone every day while their American equivalent spends more than 4! We can't take our eyes off it, we live in aching expectation of that notification tone and that gratifying little glow. This reminds me of E.E. Cummings:[6]

> Lady, i will touch you with my mind.
> Touch you and touch and touch
> until you give
> me suddenly a smile, shyly obscene.

We are walking deeper and deeper into the web.

Life Inside the Bubble

When the results of the 2016 US elections rolled out, there was utter dismay (and silence) across the liberal world. Everyone (and their friends) took a while to recover from the shock (and by the time they did, we were already into the inaugural attendance controversy).

If I were to look at my newsfeeds across channels, I would never have believed that Trump would win. Nor for that matter did the machine inform me that the BJP would win India with such ease in 2014. Nor did I expect Brexit to happen.

Now, where did I go so horribly wrong in my analysis of trends? From all that I saw, the pundits broadcasting to me got it horribly wrong as well. The truth is that I was isolated from divergent views in my filter bubble, and frankly, so were the pundits.

The Internet was designed to bring all knowledge and opinions to one place, made accessible to all. But the fact is that while it is accessible, algorithms have ensured that they are not visible, unless I expressly search for them. According to Pariser, today's Internet is not designed to bring differently minded people together to engage in debate. In these elections, all of us only foresaw what we hoped would happen, what we would have liked to happen.

This, by the way, is also what went wrong with the Hillary campaign. The entire backbone of the campaign was an algorithm called Ada (named after Ada Lovelace, the British mathematician who worked with Charles Babbage on the mechanical general-purpose computer) which played a vital role in every campaign decision. The problem was that Ada retained the biases her creators had programmed her with.[7] Instead of generating recommendations to collect new data that might have contradicted and falsified her premises, Ada kept showing what her creators had wanted to see. Ada's creators were convinced that Pennsylvania, historically and otherwise, was safe. And Ada mirrored that as well. As it turned out, Pennsylvania wasn't safe.

What is worrying is that our media is also trapped in a filter bubble of their own making. Instead of driving down and talking to people in the teashops and to garage mechanics, they fly around and stay in fancy hotels and publish stories from within their respective filter bubbles. Or worse, they believe that Twitter is a good microsample of a macroworld.

In a process now called cyberbalkanization,[8] the Internet is dividing people into like-minded subgroups each cocooned in the warmth of their own virtual communities. Remember John Donne?

> No man is an island,
> Entire of itself;
> Every man is a piece of the continent,
> A part of the main.
> If a clod be washed away by the sea,
> Europe is the less.[9]

This should make us cry today (and not just because of Brexit). Cyberbalkanization will make us islands—will make us opinionated, absolutist islands and perfect, dangerous arseholes.

Smaller and Smaller Islands

I have a little experiment for you. Ask Google 'Is Trump popular?' On another tab, type 'Is Trump unpopular?' Take a look at the results.

Ideally the results should give you a clear, unbiased idea of Trump's popularity. But those two keywords, 'popular' and 'unpopular' are a sign of your preconceived biases and have completely thrown the machine into a quandary. The results reinforce your biases as a consequence of how the algorithm parses your question. To add to that, the algorithm also takes into account everything that it knows about you and your surfing habits, and frankly, all your preferences. So your results will be different from what I get if I were to try the same questions.

Google is trying to fix this by training its search engine to recognize intent rather than literal syntax. But I think that refinement is a long way off.

I want to put together what two of the leading men in the business said, in different contexts. Marc Zuckerberg once said:

> . . . a squirrel dying in your front yard may be more relevant to your interests right now than people dying in Africa.[10]

He was of course, trying to impress upon the world Facebook's insistence on relevance being the critical criterion to what users see.

Now take a look at what Bill Gates said about social media, that it:

> . . . lets you go off with like-minded people, so you're not mixing and sharing and understanding other points of view.[11]

You put the two together and it ends up painting a pathetic picture. Of not just an island but a really small, lonely island. People who are isolated from the rest of the world, who only see and hear what their like-minded friends have to say, about their squirrels and their yards.

Now, given the fact that for most of our youth the Internet is their sole window to the world, this isolationist view could have disastrous consequences for all the pillars that hold up our fragile existence—communities, governments, democracy. And truth.

But, Hey, We're Lovin' It

All of us got sucked into this situation unintentionally. Personalization, on the face of it, is a beautiful value-add.

I am not a conspiracy-theorist to believe that this was a deliberate ploy—that Internet giants and their algorithms purposely divided people into subgroups that would become isolated and insulated so they could weaken the very ideas of diversity that our unity is built upon.

But as far back as 1995, Jaron Lanier,[12] the computer philosophy writer, was warning the world about 'intelligent agents' (AI-powered personalization engines) that would customize for you and thereby, make you lesser beings!

We might have come into it unwittingly, but we love it! And we believe in the power of the Internet. We really believe that by sharing an article (that we agree with), we will change public opinion when what we end up doing is only reinforcing opinion within our subgroup.

In his interestingly named book *The Net Delusion*, Evgeny Morozov rips apart this universal, utopian, emancipatory image we have of the web. He argues that behind our awe of technology is an innocent ignorance that misrepresents the Internet's power and potential.

Social media believed that Twitter could foment revolution in Iraq in 2009, when all Twitter had in Iran, on the eve of the elections, was 20,000 users. In democracies across the world, we do tend to overestimate social media's capabilities. If Twitter is to be believed, India is a state in eternal strife—torn between conservatives and liberals. But we often forget that this is the opinion of about 26 million people in a population of 1.2 billion.

Which is why stepping out into the streets once in a while helps. It gives us a good dose of vitamin D and reality.

I Believe I Am Right

The effects of the filter bubble are beginning to show. We see this more often now on social media, the unwavering belief that what we say is right. And not just a subjective correctness but an informed, objective veracity. But we also know this, that 'pride goeth before destruction, and a haughty spirit, before a fall'.[13]

Overconfidence is one of the primary signs of what is known as confirmation bias. Confirmation biases are errors of cognitive reasoning marked by a tendency to seek out or only remember information that confirms your hypotheses, or to interpret information in a way that suits your opinions. It is time to watch out when we start believing our personal truths to be universal truths.

Very soon, you will start quoting ambiguous evidence to bolster your position. With time, the degree of ambiguity of the evidence increases. The more emotionally charged you are about an issue, the greater the bias and its effects. The problem is that these biases will eventually lead to extremely poor decision-making in political and organizational contexts.

As we ensconce ourselves more comfortably in our filter bubbles, our biases find approval among the other kūpamandukas and our belief in our own omnipotence increases.

Within the bubble, we also have the danger of groupthink—a phenomenon where groups exhibit a temporary loss of rational, moral and realistic thinking. When every member of the group views the same confirmatory information, this could lead to extremely irrational behaviour—in the faith that the behaviour is purely rational.

In group-think situations, people start taking ridiculous risks, become intolerant of other views, see everyone with a different opinion as an enemy, push others to conform and become extremely optimistic about their views. In short, individuals begin to believe that they are right and everyone else is wrong. Think about your own social media interactions. Haven't you seen this happen? Don't you see it happening every single day?

Groupthink is also evident in how dominant societies show greater degrees of confirmation bias. Countries like India and the US truly believe that democracy is the best solution for all people on the planet. Many of us believed that authoritarianism could easily be replaced with democratic thought in Iraq and Libya, didn't we? Now we say the same about Syria. But we were proved wrong in Iraq and Libya, weren't we?

When China brings the baton down on the Internet, we believe it is an assault on freedom of speech. But when a European nation does the same, it is to protect the eyes and minds of their youth who are being exposed to offensive content.

Another issue we face is that our biases are beginning to creep into our machines as well. How does AI learn to take decisions? By looking at historical data. And what does that imply? That it has the potential to perpetuate existing biases hiding within that historical data.

Recently we had the situation where Amazon had to scrap using AI to vet job applications.

What did historical data, in this example, in a male-dominated technology industry do? It created a machine that penalized any applicant that had say, attended a women's college. It also turned out that the AI was biased towards buzzwords. Amazon killed it.

As Morozov argues, we are not yet 'cyber-realists'. We really do not have the ability to make the Internet an ally to achieve an objective.

Confirmation bias becomes an even bigger issue when we have to fight our next monster—fake news.

Fake News Gets Faker

We touched upon Trump's inaugural attendance controversy. A few days after his inauguration, sales of George Orwell's *1984* saw a 9500 per cent increase.

The reason for that was the phrase Kellyanne Conway used to defend Sean Spicer's lie about Trump's inauguration attendance numbers. She defended it as 'alternative facts'. It truly did sound like it came from *1984*:

> If all others accepted the lie which the Party imposed—if all records told the same tale—then the lie passed into history and became truth.[14]

But this is not a dystopian tale any more. This is the world we live in. A world where our truth changes depending on who states it. In an innocent world, just ten years ago, fake news referred to parodies presented as mainstream journalism (theonion.com). Not any more.

Today fake news refers to deliberate misinformation being spread on social media. Such information often gets picked up by lazy researchers and seeps into mainstream media as well. How many times in the recent past have we seen mainstream media get caught in a fake news spill?

I don't know if you have heard this old tale in which a person has a disagreement with his neighbour and then goes around maligning her character. Later he repents and confesses to the village priest and asks what he can do as penance. The priest asks him to climb the church belfry with his pillow and once there, to empty all the down in it and then return. The man does that, watches the feathers float across the village and heads back to the priest. 'Now,' says the priest, 'pick up every single feather and put it back in the pillow.'[15]

Fake news has a tendency to spread like wildfire. But clarifications travel at a snail's pace. Fake news spreads like greased lightning across social media networks. A study on fake news by MIT, published in *Science*, showed that a fake story can reach 1500 people six times faster than a true story.[16] Six times faster than truth!

The study, which analysed every major contested news story across Twitter's life (that is 1,26,000 stories over ten years tweeted by 3 million users), clearly showed that truth is no match for fake. In fact, it looks like humans may prefer to share fake news. As the study showed, falsehoods were 70 per cent more likely to get shared. Bots, in the same ten years that were analysed, were as likely to share real news as fake news.

This is not surprising because fake news is often more exciting and interesting than the truth as they tend to evoke the right (actually, wrong) emotions in a filter bubble world. The study found that fake news elicited words associated with surprise and disgust, definitely more provoking than what real news elicited—sadness and trust.

It is a fact that the top twenty fake stories about the 2016 US elections had more engagement on Facebook than the top twenty stories on the election from nineteen media majors; this clearly means that more Americans read fake stories leading up to the election that influenced, one presumes, their choices. (Pew Research—62 per cent of Americans get their news from social media!)[17]

What is it that leads to fake news? There are multiple reasons for this phenomenon. The first, of course, is a deliberate attempt to mislead public opinion which is then picked up and spread amongst like-minded people across the world. This is a deliberate attempt to redefine propaganda in a way that would have made Goebbels ecstatic.

The other reason to create fake news is to increase advertising revenues generated from increased activity. Sensational headlines are deliberately planted to get people to click and share. The organizations that create them then get users to click on links that lead them to pages with ads.

Almost all of the fake news stories are generated by anonymous websites which makes it difficult to prosecute them for libel; jurisdiction also becomes a complex matter.

Additionally, the lines between the fake and the accurate are also blurring. In a very Rashomon kind of scenario, we are facing alternative truths. We did laugh at Kellyanne Conway's 'alternative facts', but the fact is that one objective truth is giving way to many subjective truths in a complex world.

Where Fake News Treads upon Freedom of Expression

Let us look at the story of a website called Right Wing News.[18] The site has, over the past years, created many pages and accounts on Facebook under multiple fake names.

After Christine Ford testified in the Justice Kavanaugh case, Right Wing News swung into action. It posted several fake stories about Ford and then used the profiles it had previously created to spread the news. With 3.1 million followers, Right Wing News could really amplify misleading content.

Now this is not the Russians trying to pull a fast one. This is Americans trying to polarize opinions among Americans. Politics has never been about absolute truth and one could argue that slightly shaded versions of the truth could be passed off as freedom of expression.

Practically everything we hear today from politicians is shaded, to the extent that we have convinced ourselves that there is no one, absolute truth. We are open to 'perspectives'. We have compromised. We are in our little bubbles listening to the White House press secretary and the counsellor to the president talk 'alternative facts'. We are in a situation where we cannot identify an opinion from a fake story. Who do we believe? What do we believe in? What do we do? How do we burst the bubble?

Is AI the solution?

There are many solutions being talked about that can help us come out of the bubble that we are in. Technology may not have created the bubble deliberately but it does seem to aggravate the problem.

There are soft solutions for us to get around this. We can make it a point to deliberately follow people on social media who have contrarian dispositions. We can, deliberately again, seek feedback from them on our point of view and try to develop empathy with their beliefs. These solutions require an open mind but that, precisely, is the problem we are fighting: we are closing our minds as if the Huns are at the gates.

There also are simple tools like EscapeYourBubble[19] and HiFromTheOtherSide[20] that actually enable the soft options we discussed above. They help us connect with people who differ in opinion and thus try and give us a balanced view of realities we are faced with.

Researchers from Helsinki and Rome have collaborated to see how technology can burst the bubble.[21] The algorithm they have created ensures social media users are presented with views that they do not agree with.

It works by simulating a network with people and their connections, as if they are interacting with each other. The algorithm then clusters different perspectives to find two opposing viewpoints. It then shares these viewpoints with influential users who have a balanced view along with a large number of connections/followers. The idea is that the sharing of a balanced view on polarizing issues could help dispassionate, rational thinking.

The success of ideas like these depends on the collaboration of social media platforms who have to take the lead to provide access to information about who reads and shares what information, which, er, they seem a little reluctant to do.

Fake news is also getting a lot of attention from AI. And I really do believe that AI could play a huge role in segregating fake from real news, that with big data and automation, we could push emotion and unreliability out.

This is practically our existence that we are fighting for; so many approaches are being tried out. West Virginia University is using an approach that analyses text and then uses machine learning to give it a score that indicates its likelihood to be false.[22]

Another approach is to look at multiple factors in the headline, the subject, the geolocation and the body text and match it against how mainstream media is handling the same story.

Facebook had, in 2015, filed a patent for a 'sophisticated system' that identifies inappropriate text and images and removes them from the network. But whether Facebook is balanced and neutral is now under question. In multiple fora, Marc Zuckerberg has accepted that the filter bubble and information accuracy (a nicer way to say 'fake news') are areas of worry. Precious little, however, has been done.

The solution, wherever it comes from, requires the parsing of massive amounts of information in real time—a task definitely cut out for AI. The advantage with AI is that, unlike people, it never gets political or emotional—it just addresses the problem. As long as, of course, we ensure our biases don't leak into the system.

We need a solution and we need it fast. As with every passing day, our truth is getting blurred.

Who Am I?

In the Old Testament, Moses asks God whom he should tell people he represents. And rather grandly, God replies, 'I am that I am.'

Which is fine when you are God. But when you are a twenty-first-century man, the answer is a little complicated. Who really is the real me? The real physical me or the profile that exists on social media.

Often, we are in a situation where we are trying to fine-tune our real selves to match the glossy virtual selves we have created. For, sometimes, we do fall in love with our virtual selves. As Junot Diaz said:

I think one of the paradoxes of writing fiction is when people enjoy it, they want it to be real. So they look for connections.[23]

The sad reality of the kūpamanduka is that he sincerely believes he knows and understands reality when what he lives is fiction.

Smartphones and social media are rewiring our brain as we seek dopamine fixes, making us scrolling automatons who are fast losing their grip on reality. While we walk around with a blue glow lighting up our faces, our worlds and our minds are diminishing and becoming more isolated.

We have to open our minds to more opinions. To quote Donald Trump:

We have to go see Bill Gates and a lot of different people that really understand what's happening. We have to talk to them, maybe in certain areas, closing that Internet up in some way.

Somebody will say, 'Oh, freedom of speech, freedom of speech'. These are foolish people. We have a lot of foolish people.[24]

We cannot afford to be foolish, can we?

Matchmaking: Is Data Science God's Own Match.com?

'. . . AND THEY LIVED HAPPILY EVER after.' I just got done with a compilation of 200 Italian folktales by Italo Calvino,[1] and this is how every single one of them ends. This ubiquitous finale to all our folk and fairy tales is what someone like Nicholas Taleb might have rightly referred to as the impact of the highly improbable.[2]

The Improbability of Compatibility

The perfect match? Life-long compatibility? Theoretically, this should be more in the realm of fantasy than reality—for both love and compatibility are dependent on context.

Most of us, when we first fall in love, are just infatuated with physical charm (ah! beautiful days), followed by a youthful companionship that is often blind; ruled more by blood than by reason.

As people and relationships mature, they are confronted with a large number of circumstances that seriously challenge long-term compatibility; they are confronted with the realization that needs and desires from a relationship are in constant flux.

Perfect compatibility therefore demands two individuals waltzing in perfect harmony through an entire lifetime of changing circumstances, much after the orchestra has packed up and gone home. It is a fairy tale, yes. If it makes you feel any better, no one's got it right. The First Matchmaker saw Adam frolicking about, alone, and the poor guy ended up losing a rib.

The question is—could data science have created a better Eve? I'll need to double-check with the Mrs, but I really believe it can—that analytics is our best hope for compatibility. Or if you wish to be more poetic about it, love.

Which prompts a larger question. Can data science help in improving romantic outcomes? Here again, I think it can.

Now that I am out on a limb, let's step back a bit and look at matchmaking down the ages.

From Barbers to Coders

Matchmaking has been around since, well, Eve. But what we often get wrong is that matchmaking isn't always about the couple. (Of course, there are blind people falling in love, but that was and continues to be extremely rare.) Matchmaking had a completely different purpose.

Matchmaking's primary objective was to bring two families together, to ensure the survival of a good bloodline; to ensure that wealth accumulated and stayed in the right hands. It wasn't so much about the couple's idea about compatibility as much as it was society's.

In most cases, like the Shadchan among Jews, matchmakers knew both families and used socio-economic statuses, beliefs, outlooks and backgrounds to justify a match.[3]

In China, a matchmaker would be assisted by an astrologer to determine compatibility (and happiness). The charts, based on a person's birth and animal symbol would permit an insight into various aspects of a potential mate's character that otherwise might have remained hidden.

In India, until recently, it was the Brahmin priest or the barber who played matchmaker. Once the families were identified, horoscopes were matched for compatibility. A set of factors were given numerical values that added up to thirty-six; score eighteen and bingo, you were set to tie the knot![4]

Now when you think about it, this was a problem awaiting a data scientist. If you could map attractiveness, character, preferences and compatibility, you could then use statistics and probability to create a match made in heaven.

Part of this is what Jeff Tarr and Vaughan Morrill accomplished at Harvard in 1965. (That they had run out of other ways to hook up with women adds a special poignancy to the discovery.) Jeff and Vaughan called their idea Operation Match and computer dating was born.[5]

Now This Sounds like a Good Idea

In the Western world (and increasingly in the rest of the world as well), people are expected to identify their partners on their own. While this sounds dreamy, it is in reality a pain as most of us would know. It is an effort that involves significant time, ambiguity and often, extreme excitement followed by extreme aggravation. So it is not surprising that Operation Match was soon followed by a whole set of competitors, each with their own secret sauce—their unique matchmaking algorithm.

Today there must be a few thousand sites and apps that help you connect. Connect with people you know, people you knew and people you don't know from Adam. While this spells doom for the Shadchan and the Brahmin, online dating and matchmaking are superior to conventional matchmaking on several levels.

Instead of relying on a finite set of probable partners that the matchmaker knew (and on the intuition of parents and relatives), singles today have access to a practically infinite set of probable partners. All other factors being equal, access to many instead of a few considerably increases the probability of the right match. Online matchmaking, therefore, has increased reach.

But reach is not the primary reason that online dating is superior to the traditional matchmaker. The new ways we communicate have a significant role to play as well.

Texting, Sexting and Emoting

First it was texting. Then Facebook and then WhatsApp. And then of course, the tyranny of the emoticon. These have completely changed how we communicate and have created what can only be called a new digital idiom. This digital idiom is an English alien to my father. And sometimes, to me as well. This is communication that is a lot more spontaneous, instinctive and with a lot more urgency, passion and intent. Only this idiom, I feel, could have invented Snapchat. A more deliberate generation like mine cannot conceive why you would want to send out a timed-to-self-destruct 'snap'.

Aziz Ansari talks in his book, *Modern Romance*, about computer-modulated-communication that has created a phenomenon where two people who get introduced today could, over a few hundred texts overnight, feel like they have known each other for ages.[6] People who haven't met each other might find it awkward to speak to one another. But texting feels perfectly normal. Even at the rate of one every twenty seconds.

This brings a certain immediacy to things. Ansari writes in *Modern Romance*, a probable girlfriend's failure to respond to his insouciant text within a couple of minutes could send him into a:

> tornado of panic and hurt and anger.

This flood of information and emotion alters every parameter we had of 'getting to know each other'.

Every conventional way of matchmaking involves people getting to know each other—for better or for worse—much after they have met. Computer-modulated-communication reverses convention. It allows you get a fairly good idea about the person way before you decide to take the interest a step ahead into an actual face-to-face meeting.

This considerably increases the chances of a romantic outcome as you are connecting with a person who has the maximum number of attributes that you wish to see in a potential mate.

Algorithms—Sound Unromantic but Are Not

While algorithms have clearly improved romantic acquaintance, the jury is still out on romantic outcomes. As a data science practitioner and someone with a more-than-keen interest in matchmaking, I have reasons to believe that improved romantic outcomes are on the way.

In the journal *Psychological Science*, Eli J. Finkel and his colleagues show how a long-term relationship depends on three variables—similarity between partners, a category that includes religion, education and music and a critical third variable—how partners collaborate day-to-day and react to stressful events.[7] So how does technology impact this?

The fact is that most of the matchmaking models currently in use are from the early days of the Internet. We are still in the realm of surveys and data honesty of the user. The possibilities, though, are immense.

Tanzeem Choudhury and Alex Pentland discussed the sociometer,[8] a wearable sensor that measured face-to-face interactions between people and could help many disciplines— organizational behaviour, social network analysis and knowledge management applications.

Imagine what the sociometer could do for relationships! It could help you continuously see how your behaviour is impacting your partner—becoming a telemetric monitor for a relationship's health.

Based on this, in 2005, Anmol Madan created an ahead-of-its-time app, the aptly named Jerk-o-Meter.[9] When it sensed your interest flagging in a phone conversation, it would helpfully advise you to 'stop being a jerk' (with of course, other more helpful suggestions as well).

Dr Helen Fisher and Sam Yagan are talking about apps that use what we know from evolutionary psychology, linguistic studies and body language—to provide a deeper understanding about who you are connecting with.[10]

In a live interaction, we spend time evaluating people by body language and how they talk. An app that contributes that information brings online matchmaking closer to reality, with a better forecast of future compatibility. We will soon see enhanced opportunities for interactions through videos, virtual environments and social networks. We could see the creation of knowledge networks based on other interactions of the people in question. Enhanced networks will also discourage digital dishonesty as it becomes increasingly tough to maintain a façade.

The closer we can get to live interaction, and the more algorithms there are that can sense how people will react to situations, the better will our chances be of finding compatibility and a better romantic outcome.

Technology and Happier Couples

Sure, depending on algorithms to find a mate sounds a lot less romantic than bumping into 'the one' at a concert. But when you look at the possibilities of billions of people having to bump into their 'the one', technology makes a lot more sense.

Let's face it, an overwhelming majority of people actually go through an entire lifetime without meeting that significant someone. If you have, consider yourself lucky.

Technology has provided greater access; technology helps you get to know the person better before you decide and soon, technology will help you get an honest understanding of how the person is likely to behave in a relationship. Does this not make data science the holy grail of relationships? When it comes to romantic outcomes, data science will soon make the Black Swan the norm.

And not just romantic outcomes, data science will soon be helping us decide on business partners, friends, social circles. But for now, I would like to restrict my thoughts to matchmaking. As an eternally romantic data scientist, I would like to work for a world where everyone can truly live happily ever after.

Electoral Math: The Voter As Consumer

IF YOU WERE A TEENAGER growing up in Calcutta with Cold War fiction, the streets of Berlin were never far. (Yes, that Calcutta is very different from this Kolkata.)

In the Calcutta of those days, the Cold War was not an affair across the globe. It was the air you breathed, it was the smoke curling up from the *para*s in the morning, it was the shadow that lurked around every corner. You were never a boy walking across to buy milk, you were our man in Havana, or on a really good day, George Smiley OBE.

Free Soviet propaganda on the one hand and Graham Greene, le Carré, Richard Condon, Ian Fleming and Ludlum on the other, left us a little confused as to who the real good guys were. But we grew up with incredibly fantastic plots to destabilize evil empires—anarchy, assassinations, undermined currency, the works.

In those days a plot where Russia manipulates US elections would have been fiction gold! Which is why I find this entire Facebook-Cambridge Analytica episode such a bummer.[1] All it took was a social media platform?

We can debate till the cows come home about the extent of Russian involvement and whether that really did play a role in the 2016 US elections. But the fact is that we need to accept that the way we understand the idea of democracy and elections has changed.

Elections are still about numbers but not numbers as we understood them. There is a difference I will elaborate upon shortly and this was most dramatically visible in 2016. It seems that this has been happening for a while now, unbeknownst to us. Let us take a look then at what lies in wait.

Cleisthenes to Trump—Some Journey!

Take a step back, to 500 BC, to see what got us here. At a forum in Athens, Cleisthenes,[2] the founder of the Athenian democracy, gathers his robes around him and asks for calm. In the nervous silence that ensues; he tells the crowd that the era of autocrats and aristocrats is over; that every citizen has the right to determine who will run the state. Thus began democracy.

What Cleisthenes and his fellow Athenians founded that day is direct democracy, a purer form where every citizen decides on practically every action that the state (or city-state) takes. We are not direct democracies any more as that would not be practical.

But we have taken the basic idea forward—government of the people, by the people and for the people—into representative democracy.

In Cleisthenes's time, the math was very simple. But as we have progressed with representative democracy, the math has become very complicated. In fact, the math has become technology.

In 2012, the primary decision maker in Obama's campaign was Narwhal.[3] Narwhal was not a grey-haired Democrat who had the experience of many elections behind him. It was a data-platform, named after the 'tusked' whale that inhabits the Arctic waters. Narwhal served as the backbone for Obama's campaign operations—integrated data for functions such as customized emails for fund-raising, identification of likely-voter clusters and using them via social media as influencers. The core task was to build as personalized a campaign as possible. It was Narwhal who determined what direction the campaign should take.

Not to be left behind, the Republicans had Orca,[4] so named because it is the only known predator of the Narwhal. Orca was a mobile application that would be used by 37,000 Republican volunteers in the swing states to track known Romney supporters on polling day. Through the day, they would use Orca to spot voters who were not turning up and then would keep pushing calls to them.

Unfortunately for them, Orca crashed on Election Day. Narwhal won, marking the success of one of the first and largest technology-backed, voter-as-customer campaigns.

This indicated that when it came to election decision-making, a politician's gut had given way to his data-platform. Electoral math was not as simple as it was in Cleisthenes's day. Or Kennedy's.

Developing an Affection for Elections

Like I said, I grew up in Calcutta. And it would have been surprising if I had *not* developed an affinity for elections and electioneering. As a young student, I was fascinated by the pure reds of socialism and the pure whites of the then unassailable Jyoti Basu.

As young students, we marched for causes domestic and international, relevant and irrelevant. For Nelson Mandela, for Bishop Desmond Tutu, against imperialism, capitalism, fascism and many other -isms. (And then, I grew up and started shaving.)

We marched because we believed elections to be decided by defining causes, by the zeitgeist of the political moment, by charismatic personalities, strategic manoeuvres and of course, by the power of rhetoric. We believed that elections hinged on the motivations of millions of individual human beings and their views.

They still do. Elections are still driven by the sense-of-purpose of millions but how we reach out to those millions and influence them has changed.

Let's look at what happened in the 2016 US elections, for example. (At least, this is the story that came out in public.)

It all started with Michael Kosinski and David Stillwell, psychologists at Cambridge,[5] who had developed apps like myPersonality for Facebook (in which users were rated on five personality traits).

Dr Aleksandr Kogan[6] (who, strangely, also called himself called Dr Spectre) saw the potential in this and replicated it. Then, pretending that it was for research, he managed to get 3,20,000 people take this test on Facebook. Each of them unwittingly also gave Dr Kogan access to their friends (approximately 160 each).

Do the math. That's data on over 50 million users! Over a third of the active Facebook users in North America and almost a quarter of the American voting population! When Kogan sold this data to Cambridge Analytica, it was worth its weight in gold. With this data, Cambridge Analytica built an algorithm that could analyse individual Facebook profiles and determine personality traits linked to voting behaviour.

With this, the campaign could actually identify possible swing voters and craft messages more likely to resonate with them. (That 75 per cent of news snippets American voters followed on Facebook were fake is another can of worms entirely).

Look where we are going with our democracies. Data is driving our motivation and our sense of purpose without us even realizing it. We believe we are informed but honestly, we aren't.

Math and the Magic It Plays in Elections

Congressman Jerry McNerney says:

It's not a science yet. It's an art.[7]

But the potential for mathematics and data in politics is growing and will soon be science. We should have realized that when analytics came into sports; the next stop would be the next most-watched event on TV, politics.

Michael Lewis's 'Moneyball',[8] chronicled Oakland Athletics's Billy Bean and the use of sabermetrics in the first known use of data and statistics to evaluate baseball players. Today you see guys with iPads, churning numbers, in every dugout of every game.

Fans love data too, and websites and apps like fivethirtyeight.com provide baseball fans their numbers. (To prove my earlier point about the politics–sport association, fivethirtyeight.com also predicted the eventual outcome in forty-nine out of fifty states in the 2008 US elections.)[9]

When Lincoln believed that a substantial percentage of the North would back him on the abolition of slavery, that was just his gut. His gut and those of other grey-haired eminences who believed their call were right; their moral instincts were proven right.

But today's average politician is armed not with instinct but with behavioural psychology, social media strategies and randomized experiments with voters as guinea pigs. He is surrounded by men with numbers who can predict who will vote for them even before the voters themselves know.

Today's support team is full of data scientists, using math and statistics to predict the behaviour of various segments of the populace. And thanks to the information we keep putting out about ourselves—on social media and otherwise—data scientists can continuously gather data to keep themselves in tune with every tiny swing in the public mood. This helps them decide everything from candidate selection, to ideological stances, to campaign ideas, to personalized targeting to predicting voter turnout.

The analytics-backed politician knows exactly who to target and with what. Going into the 2016 US elections, we knew that a substantial 31 per cent of voters were non-whites (of other racial or ethnic minorities). But what the politician also knew is that millions more older, white, working-class people voted in 2012 than members of the aforementioned 31 per cent.[10] With these numbers before him, the analytical politician knew that a wall at the border could get him more voters out on voting day. Enough to outweigh the 31 per cent. Once politicians have their segmentation in place, they turn their attention to what the segment likes to hear.

Inane 'Likes' and How They Influence Elections

For most of us, 'likes' are just a way to acknowledge something interesting we have just seen. Sometimes, we do that just to make others feel happy.

But beneath its tranquil nature, 'likes' are a truly dystopian manipulation tool. The kind that no one thought of in Cold War fiction, unfortunately. The algorithm that led to the Facebook breach is a truly sinister being that trawls 'likes' that users casually click as they go through Facebook. From these harmless 'likes', it gathers sensitive information about race, gender, orientations, intelligence and much else.

With a few dozen 'likes', the algorithm can predict significant clues about you, your life and in this context, who you are likely to vote for. Of course, if you had ever liked any post from a political campaign, you had hoisted a flag on your roof.

Michael Kosinski and David Stillwell had seen the dangers of this and raised concerns. They said that:

. . . the predictability of individual attributes from digital records of behaviour may have considerable negative implications, because it can easily be applied to large numbers of people without their individual consent and without them noticing.[11]

They noted that both marketers and governments could use software to infer attributes about you, attributes that, as an individual, you might not desire to share. But by then, the harmless 'likes' had gone ahead to acquire a Machiavellian life of their own.

When you think about it, all of this is not so surprising. Politics is just round the corner from popular culture and if you can influence culture, you can influence politics. To these ends, data and social media have incredibly powerful roles to play. If you make socialist culture cool, you make socialist politics cool. And unlike in the days gone by, you can now do this in just weeks.

Is all of this nefarious stuff the gift of US 2016? Not really. In 2012, this is exactly what President Obama's team and Narwhal were up to.

Their database was created by asking individual volunteers to log into their site using their Facebook credentials. This meant that with just that log-in, the user was consciously and more often otherwise, handing over a treasure trove of information and more importantly, their network of friends, to Narwhal. The legality and ethics of it just didn't make headlines then.

The Politician As an Analytics-Driven Marketer

The voter has always been a consumer and the politician has always been a consummate marketer. The analogies have always existed except that now data science and analytics-led consumer marketing are making them equivalents, not mere analogies.

Today every political party, like any toothpaste, looks carefully at branding, market research, voter segmentation, use of imagery, personalization tactics, targeted and personalized communication, and the emotional quotient of the voter when crafting each appeal. What we are seeing (and what politicians saw way before us), is a coming together of cognitive and behavioural patterns that have always coexisted in the consumer as citizen and the citizen as consumer. The average Joe in an advanced economy spends most of his time thinking of himself as a consumer. It is but natural, then, that these thought processes would spill over into other compartments of his life that contribute to his decision-making.

This is why political parties now opt for branding consultants. How many of us can deny the role played by Shepard Fairey[12] in 2008? Fairey's 'Hope', 'Change' and 'Vote' posters were the defining images of President Obama's campaign.

The *New Yorker* called it:

> . . . the most efficacious American political illustration since 'Uncle Sam Wants You' . . . [13]

And President Obama, in a letter thanking Fairey, acknowledged that:

> The political images involved in your work have encouraged Americans to believe they can change the status quo.[14]

The marketer also knows where to continuously look for the opinions generated by tracking the changes in behavioural psychology of the contemporary consumerist-voter.

Engaging Your Consumer. Er, Voter

> The key is what you offer them, and how you make it stick.

This is not a brand marketer talking about a launch. This is Alex Black, of CSC's Enterprise Intelligence Practice, talking about micro-targeting voters for Obama re-election campaign.[15]

The Obama Big Data team identified converted advocates and used 'affinity ratios' for matchmaking—linking people with the same lifestyle and life-stage details to drive action. They were building on the age-old 'people like us' theory of social behaviour, but with the aid of technology.

How different is this from anything that a marketer does on a daily basis?

What the marketer offers a customer is choice, so that the customer is capable of taking an informed, *individual* decision. What elections offer a citizen is a responsibility. A responsibility that in many ways goes beyond the individual and becomes *collective*.

In the consumerization of the voter, is citizenship being eroded by selfish, individualistic choices? Wouldn't we rather have 'citizen behaviour'?

In some ways, in these 'informed' social media days, with every individual also being an active social media participant, we are in some ways heading back to Cleisthenes's times, to direct democracy.

While direct democracy sounds idealistic, it is neither practical nor perfect. It may be so for a tiny city state, but not for complex democracies. With Brexit, all of us just saw what a referendum (the simplest form of direct democracy) can do to a contemporary (though monarchical) democracy.

After Voter As Consumer, What Next?

Where will this lead to, tomorrow? The possibilities are well, infinite. Take for example legislations. Today what we see, more often than not, is voting along party lines. With, of course, whispers of lobbies and lobbying.

But there is a whole lot of data available now about voting on legislations. And there are firms that now process relevant data to predict the voting patterns of legislators. One of these firms can predict, with an accuracy of 95 per cent, the outcome of bills in the US Congress and state legislatures.[16]

When you place this fact alongside the immense information available on each legislator, campaigners know how legislators have voted in the past and their stand on specific causes. This gives campaigners a clear idea of which legislator to target their communication at and what tack to take before the bills come to be discussed.

This is one of democracy's paradoxes. While the citizen's responsibility in a democracy is collective, a legislator's responsibility should ideally be individual. Will we soon see politicians voting on each bill according to their conscience's whip and not the party's? Idealistic, but a possibility.

All of this will pose a whole lot of uncomfortable questions in the days to come. Many of us worry that elections will eventually become a data and social media game. For them I have a word of comfort—they who live by Twitter, will die by Twitter.

Let us hope that we will soon understand technology well enough to be truly 'informed' and that soon elections will go back to being decided on the informed motivations of the masses.

Blockchain and Cryptocurrency: The Face of Money Is Changing

FOR MOST OF US, THE Silk Route was that ancient network of routes that linked East and West. Along this route, much trade, culture, myths and romance travelled as well.

It was 2013 that marked the end of that innocence. It transpired that Silk Route[1] was also the name of an extremely enterprising enterprise on the Dark Web. On this site drugs, women, children, arms and illicit services were trafficked.

This was the first time many of us were hearing of the Dark Web. And it was also in this unfortunate context that many of us heard of a beautiful invention called bitcoin.

Bitcoin is about as decentralized, universal and pure as the concept of currency can get but it was being heard of, for the first time, in the unfortunate context of gunrunning and human trafficking.

Did Ross Ulbricht—the chap who ran the Silk Route—really consider himself a people's hero? The hero who created a truly egalitarian marketplace that exploited the true, decentralized universality of bitcoin?

He called himself Dread Pirate Roberts. I find that choice of alias very interesting because there have been numerous occasions in history when the line between pirate and patriot has been extremely thin (Sir Francis Drake being a notable example).

However, Dread Pirate's efforts to create a marketplace free from authority resulted in exactly the opposite! What the Silk

Route bust managed to do was give agencies like the Federal Bureau of Investigation (FBI) unrestrained rights to snoop, under the guise of preventing cybercrime.

What the Silk Route bust also did was to get governments into bitcoin.

Journalist Nathaniel Popper wrote in *Digital Gold*:

> The unmistakable irony of these wild days, was that a technology that had been designed, in no small part, to circumvent government power was now becoming largely driven by and dependent on the attitudes of government officials.[2]

So, how did an Internet drug peddler lead us to these discussions on ideal money and freedom?

The Idea of Money Has Changed with the Times

Many believe that the idea of compensation is an invention as significant as the wheel. Alongside language, it enabled man to solve issues of cooperation that other species could not—like reciprocal altruism, kin altruism and the alleviation of aggression (the day the chickens figure out barter, they will be just a couple of 1000 years away from reaching the top of the food chain).

As the idea took form, money carved out for itself four primary functions. As medium, as measure, as standard and as store.

We can argue about whether these functions complement or conflict with each other. For example, money's role as a medium of exchange is at conflict with its role as a store of value—while one requires that money should circulate, the other requires that it should not. But the fact is that this invention, with its inherent contrasts, has served us well.

For it to perform all these functions, money needed value. After a few initial experiments, man came up with coins, where the metal itself was the value. For example, it was the quantity of silver in the silver coin that provided the value.

Paper money first made its appearance in the China of the seventh-century Tang dynasty (as promissory notes)[3] when people could hand over their silver or gold coins to a trustworthy party to receive paper denoting the value of the coins they had deposited. This reduced the need to carry large quantities of heavy coins around. Especially when trading in large values.

In 1717, the then master of the royal mint (you will be surprised at the name), Sir Isaac Newton put Britain on the gold standard.[4] With the gold standard, a country's paper money was assigned a value directly linked to a fixed amount of gold.

Adoptions followed and the gold standard continued in various forms until 1971 when President Nixon nixed the gold standard. Since then the US has been operating on a system of fiat money: money not linked to any commodity but called into existence by government (hence by 'fiat').[5]

This frankly, my friend, means that what you have in your pocket is just paper. Which in times like the sub-prime crisis is worrying. J.P. Morgan meant much when he once said:

Money is gold, and nothing else.[6]

It was the fear that there was too much illicit paper floating around and hiding in the wrong places that led the Indian government to demonetize five-hundred and thousand-rupee notes on 8 November '16. With that diktat, the paper denominated for these amounts ceased to have value.

What used to be good, solid, reassuring metal is now just electrons, whizzing all around the world at speed, open to loss, theft and misappropriation at every stage.

In this day and age, should there not be a more secure, more reliable way to transact business? One that does not further maul a concept that has been central to our progress?

Which is where more and more right-thinking folks around the world started talking about ideal money—to salvage the idea of money.

John Nash—Only a Mathematician Could Conceive Ideal Money

After World War II, international currencies went through a whole lot of fluctuations and crises. The Bretton Woods International Monetary System was the first to come into existence—where the dollar was made the global reserve currency and all major currencies were fixed to the dollar and the dollar fixed to gold.

But in 1960, American economist Robert Triffin spotted an inherent conflict in Bretton Woods that was called the Triffin dilemma. He rightly argued that the dollar's role as a reserve currency led to a fundamental conflict of interest between domestic and global economic objectives.

Besides, there were a number of post-war societies that needed global lenders but had unpredictable rates of inflation that kept lenders at bay.

It was to address the Triffin dilemma and stabilize international currencies that mathematician John Nash proposed the idea of 'asymptotically ideal money', which was:

. . . intrinsically free of 'inflationary decadence', a true 'gold standard'.[7]

Asymptotically ideal money focused on the fluctuations and long-term perceived value of money, with an ideal inflation rate as close to zero as possible.

The simplest definition of Nash's ideal money would be money that is stable over long periods of time. In his own words:

Our observation, based on thinking in terms of 'the long term' rather than in terms of 'short range expediency', was simply that there is no ideal rate of inflation that should be selected and chosen as the target but rather that the ideal concept would necessarily be that of a zero rate for what is called inflation.[8]

If you look at the fundamental aspects of bitcoin's economic nature, it truly represents Nash's work. His insight was that we should evolve a true form of money that can be used as a true measuring tool comparable to the watt, the hour or the degree; that solves the Triffin dilemma and also is stable due to zero inflation. All of this is what bitcoin turned out to be.

Bitcoin by design is disinflationary. The bitcoin protocol is limited to 21 million. Which means that no more can ever be created. No central bank of any government can come along and 'print' more bitcoins when it suits them. The inflation rate of bitcoin asymptotically approaches zero as we get closer to its currency limit of 21 million units. This disinflationary nature alone will make the bitcoin grow in value.

Which Brings Us to the Bitcoin

In 2008, a certain Satoshi Nakamoto published a paper[9] in which he unveiled bitcoin—a cryptocurrency and digital payment system that is peer-to-peer, which means that transactions are direct between users, without an intermediary. It was the blockchain that made this lack of intermediary possible—administrator or repository—making bitcoin truly decentralized.

Satoshi turned out to be the Banksy of the cypherpunk world—no one knows who he is. (Now, isn't this getting interesting!) Many believe that Satoshi is not one man but a group of cypher-altruists[10] who have created a universal, decentralized currency that can actually be our way forward with money.

Many also believe that it was John Nash's 'Beautiful Mind' that led to the creation of bitcoin. While even his greatest fans (and you can include me here) would not argue that Nakamoto is his alias, it is his math and his work (as we just read) that lives on in the monetary policies built into the bitcoin protocol.

Hal Finney,[11] the first transaction recipient of bitcoin, is also considered by many to be Satoshi or one of the Satoshis. And just as Finney is credited with optimizing the math and cryptography behind bitcoin technology, John Nash can be seen as an integral, (even if) indirect component of the decades of research that led to the invention.

The Bitcoin Revolution—Bloody and Otherwise

Bitcoin was created so that transactions could be peer-to-peer and could avoid an intermediary or intermediaries which would increase transactional costs.

In Satoshi's own words in his 2008 paper:

I've been working on a new electronic cash system that's fully peer-to-peer, with no trusted third party.[12]

While he made no direct reference to the 'third party' being governments or banks, the idea of 'trust-less' contains the seeds of anarchic sentiment.

By design, bitcoin is trust-less and borderless and its adoption in its original form can truly destroy centralized control by governments and banks—it truly puts money back in the hands of the people.

This makes it a financial weapon that can take on corrupt, entrenched systems.

The time of its creation was not a coincidence—bitcoin technology was revealed in 2008, just after the financial mess of 2007—when the lid came off extensive banking fraud, fiat inflation and the nasty political machinations to cover up.

The system was broken and needed a fix.

Unfortunately, bitcoin found early adopters like Dread Pirate Roberts. This decentralized 'ideal money', thanks to its open, borderless nature, became ideal for drug-peddling, hiring hitmen and all sorts of monstrosities in the veiled markets of the dark web.

When the FBI finally caught on to it, the Silk Route had generated 9.5 million worth of sales in bitcoin (approximately $1.8 billion), which is enough for any aspiring buccaneer to turn coder.

No Government Will Ever Love a Decentralized Currency

Soon, governments, banks, mainstream investors and entrepreneurs were looking to cash in on the bitcoin boom. And this was not just in the United States; China was casting a baleful eye as well.

As Sterlin Lujan wrote:

> In reality, Bitcoin was meant to function as a monetary weapon, as a cryptocurrency poised to undermine authority. Now it is whitewashed. It is seen as a polite and unassuming technology in order to appease politicians, banksters, and soccer moms . . . However, no one should forget or deny why the protocol was written.[13]

But it is not all dark. There are sunny stories of economic freedom as well.

In 2016, we heard the depressing story of a hungry mob in Caracas that broke into a zoo to eat a horse.[14] One of the reasons for the food crisis was that government currency control was making it incredibly difficult to import food products.

Venezuelans are now bypassing this barrier by buying in bitcoin from global e-commerce sites (Amazon is delivering!). Bitcoin also helps them bypass the high import tariffs and other taxes imposed by the government.

And true to the dream of the founding fathers, it is also making transactions and businesses in Venezuela incorruptible. This is thanks to the blockchain, a unique architecture that can never be tampered with—a solution to the weak institutions we are faced with in many parts of the world.

Is it just electronic money with a fancy pedigree? Is it the foundation for smart contacts and electronic shares? Is it underground and subversive? Will it challenge governments, or will it integrate into mainstream finance?

If you know the answers to any of these questions, there may be many lucrative opportunities awaiting you in the bitcoin space. For, bitcoin is still a cutting-edge experiment in technology and economics. And like the World Wide Web in 1995, its potential and its myriad purposes and applications are yet to be discovered.

Which Brings Us to the Hero of This Story: Blockchain

All of this became possible thanks to the blockchain, the most disruptive technology of recent times. It could (and will, eventually) completely change how we do think of transactions, records and transparency. And how we see the idea of authority.

What structures the bitcoin system is the blockchain—the protocol that holds the entire network together. It is nothing but a distributed public ledger of accounts which keeps track of every transaction ever made in the network and ensures that each transaction is verified and timestamped. This is how the blockchain works. Across the world, thousands of specialized computers have been built to 'mine' bitcoins and in the process validate transactions and protect the system. Every few minutes, mining computers collect a few pending transactions and convert them into a mathematical puzzle. The first miner with the solution announces it to the rest on the network. The other miners then check if the fund-sender has the authorization to spend the money.

Once the right quorum of miners give their approval, this set of transactions (a 'block' and hence blockchain) is added to the ledger cryptographically and the miners move on.

After another ninety-nine blocks have been added to the ledger, the miner who found the solution receives his reward—in bitcoin. And the cycle repeats itself. This reward ensures that miners are always keen to participate in the system and validate transactions.

Every transaction on the blockchain is completely transparent and accounted for. Anyone can see the public keys of any transaction but there are no names associated with the transaction (which is what worked for Silk Route). You can go all the way back and check out the first-ever transaction, if you want to. This by the way is, very originally, called the Genesis Block.

Blockchains are the latest examples of the unexpected fruits of cryptography. Mathematical scrambling is used to convert an original piece of information into a code, known as a hash. Any attempt to alter the nature of the information is immediately apparent, because the new hash thus created won't match the old one. This is a paradox—cryptography, the science that was created to keep information secret has also now become the source for transparency. Different blockchain configurations use different consensus mechanisms, depending on the type and size of the network. But across configurations, both the databases and the consensus, are distributed.

What Satoshi's blockchain did is to find a solution to the double-spend problem (also more interestingly called the

Byzantine General's Problem),[15] a long-standing computer science paradox.

The network protects itself against someone spending a bitcoin twice by verifying each transaction. The blockchain ledger ensures that each transaction is confirmed by miners. This confirmation makes each transaction unique and legitimate. If someone tries to duplicate the transaction, the original block's functions change, immediately showing the network that it is a false transaction.

With bitcoin and its timestamp, you can now avoid a third party to timestamp transactions. Therefore, you don't now need a 'trusted' intermediary like a bank to complete a good transaction.

In the bitcoin scenario, the blockchain is public and permission-less, everyone can participate and contribute to the public ledger.

The Blockchain Outside Bitcoin

It is becoming increasingly clear (to people and to governments) that Satoshi's invention has a lot of potential outside the bitcoin. And with a lot of, well, consequences akin to Silk Route.

Bitcoin might be the greatest invention since Luca Pacioli created the double-entry system[16] of bookkeeping for accounting transactions. For the first time, two people can exchange a piece of digital property, without any prior relationship, and in a secure way, over the Internet.

If you were to think beyond bitcoin, the blockchain is a fantastic secure ledger for any kind of data. The secure nature of the blockchain design, and because it enables decentralized consensus, makes the blockchain ideal for the recording of all kinds of events, transactions and contracts as well as for activities such as identity management and documenting provenance. This means that all records could someday soon become secure, transparent and decentralized.

It simplifies record keeping, reduces transaction costs and, most importantly, keeps data true. This makes it ideal for thousands of applications in commerce, finance and potentially, politics.

It enables people who do not know each other (enough to trust each other) to interact and coordinate directly. For a network like Airbnb, it could create a secure, tamper-proof system for managing digital credentials and transactions. It could become the platform for distributed power generators and individuals to interact and manage transactions (e.g., compensation by the grid to individuals generating energy from nonconventional sources).

It could become the final say in property records and transactions. Keeping records on the blockchain could also reduce admin costs and in many countries, corruption.

When it comes to securities trading, Goldman Sachs estimates:

> . . . the industry could save $11–$12 billion in fees, OpEx, and capital charges globally by moving to a shorter, and potentially customized, settlement window.[17]

For the finance industry, data stored on a blockchain could help finance firms to easily and instantly do a KYC (Know Your Customer check) on new customers. In short, anything that requires maintenance of records and transparency gets a boost. What I envision is a near future where entire companies and governments operate in a distributed, automated, secure fashion.

All this implies that the legalities of blockchain need to be understood and codified.

The Power of the Distributed Ledger Is in Distributed Use

The power of blockchain really reveals itself when you use it across institutions and organizations. Let us look at your Uber driver's example.

He is a good driver and gets consistently good ratings from customers. He wants to buy a refurbished high-end car but has funding issues.

In a smart economy, it is very easy for a Toyota to explore new avenues to increase their business in the used-car business. What if they were to look at alternative models for car buying and leasing? What if they decide to create a smart contract with Uber to underwrite loans for qualified drivers?

When our man applies to buy a new Toyota, the smart contract application process uses multiple contextual checks. The government attests to his identity, the department of transportation attests that he is certified to drive the vehicle he is applying for, Uber certifies that he is employed with them and confirms his earnings, Uber also confirms his high ratings, Citibank confirms his ability to repay and his repayment record and, last but not the least, Toyota attests to the service history of the vehicle.

With all this information available, an algorithm is run on the data and a decision arrived at on the terms our man should get. Metlife, his insurers, also have access to his employment details, his driving history and the vehicle's service history to arrive at the precise insurance quote.

As organizations coordinate and use this distributed ledger, the speed and efficiency of every kind of transaction improves substantially.

From the perspective of the government and you, there's built-in safety because your driver clears criminal background checks, has a valid license and has a clean driving history. You can also see that the Toyota he is driving is safe and well-maintained.

Minting a Brave, New World

It is for sure that a brave new world lies ahead. But where blockchain will lead us is a guess I am not willing to make.

In theory, blockchain is potent technology. A technology that is shared and trusted. A transparent ledger which everyone can inspect, but no single user controls. Imagine a currency that is safe from the machinations of government and international politics, free of the Organization of the Petroleum Exporting Countries (OPEC), free from the consequences of war and free of control by a central bank. In a sense, such freedom gives power back to the people. Imagine being able to trust anyone across the world because the platform or system enables trust. We are looking at an open world. While the hero (or villain) today is bitcoin, the true champion is blockchain.

Blockchain truly will change us. Hopefully not how Dread Pirate Roberts imagined it, but the way John Nash did.

Personal Data Ownership: Own, Complete, Monetize

ON 10 APRIL 2018, MARK Zuckerberg appeared before forty-four members of the US Senate's commerce and judiciary committees to discuss data privacy and ownership after the Cambridge Analytica furore.

Gone were the tee and the hoodie. Here was a man definitely not used to facing committees, blinking through a series of questions ranging from the incisive to the ridiculous.

Very uncomfortable in the defendant's chair, Zuckerberg admitted that a vampire app had mined information on 87 million Facebook users and sold it to Cambridge Analytica.[1] Even though only 2,70,000 people had agreed to share their information with the app. The company had benefitted from a Facebook feature that allowed apps to access your data as well as the data of all your friends.

Then more facts came out: that Facebook could track you even when you were logged out and that it could track you even if you were not a user. The days that followed revealed a lot of skeletons in the cupboard. And it had a lot of people worked up about a lot of privacy and ownership issues. People felt violated. People felt robbed.

The good news is that we now know what Facebook is doing, which means regulators can find ways to stop those practices of theirs that undermine privacy. We are also recognizing what the boundaries are when it comes to privacy and what is inevitable (knowing what is inevitable could also help us figure how to make the best of the situation). Zuckerberg stated that Facebook collects:

> . . . data of people who have not signed up for FB.[2]

for security reasons. Facebook hasn't stated what those security reasons are or what it does with that information. Now that we know, we can regulate whether a private corporation can gather non-user data for security reasons.

All of this has had people in quite a tizzy; worked up about their privacy and the ownership of their data. My request is that we put this behind us and see how each of us can best benefit from our data; how each of us can profit from this juggernaut that is rolling ahead, whether we want it to roll on or not.

Face It, the Faustian Bargain Is Made

In the German legend of Faust, young Faust's boundless desire for knowledge leads him to a pact with the Devil.[3] The Devil has to provide Faust all that he asks for, for twenty-four years. In return, Faust pledges his soul.

I am reminded of this quite often these days. We have signed our souls away to devils, big and small. To Facebook, to Amazon, to Netflix, to Google, to our banks, to our ISPs, to app developers, to the state and to many others. Our personal data is not private, not any more.

Now please wait a minute, I am no doomsayer. Much like Faust, I appreciate what the Devil has brought me. I cannot live without Google or my credit card or Netflix. They really have taught me to chill. But in return, they have taken my privacy.

I am neither naive nor reactionary to argue that an asset as important as personal data should be locked away. It can and should be used to the advantage of society, corporations and the economy. But, under the strict supervision of the individual, the true 'owner'.

Like Faust, we have signed up. All I am looking for now are ways and means to a more equitable future.

My Data Is Not Mine. And, It Is a Conflicting Mess

I am a gentleman and I do not renege on deals, with the Devil or with anyone else. In return for the goodies I receive, I have agreed to hand out personal information about me in ways that are both implicit and explicit.

I am not asking for my data to be returned to me. All I am asking is that I have some degree of control and more importantly, ownership of what is supposed to be my 'personal' information.

Every subatomic activity of my life is being recorded by someone or the other. I am surrounded by sensors, IoT, cameras. My smartphone, my credit card, my browser, my car; why, even my toothbrush, are all traitors—leaking data about me. They are whispering to the world every location I have visited (real and virtual), every conversation I have had, every movie I have watched, everything I have bought.

My heart is pumping out data, my neurotransmitters are leaking data, the electrochemical activities in my brain are EEG-ing data. I have become a walking-talking data source. Every click, every tap, every swipe of mine adds to this growing digital avatar of mine, adding to a huge bank of data that already exists.

But, as we speak, what does this data say of me? Some know of my sexual preferences, some know what I read, some know what I watch, many know what I eat and many know what I am buying. Some know my political inclinations, some know of my ideological affiliations, some know of my religious leanings.

Everyone knows something about me, but no one knows the whole Atul Jalan.

Because each of these definitions and descriptions of me are from different contexts; all reside in silos across the world. They are creating a very fragmented and, in many cases, lop-sided view of me.

There is a whole analytics and data industry that is trying to get an approximation of me and frankly, that is all they are getting—an approximation.

I don't like it. For the simple reason that today, my personal data resident on the cloud is who I am. This digital model of me, my cyber avatar, is for all practical purposes the real me. And I would expect this to be complete and perfect, not an approximation.

What we have here therefore—ironical, in an era defined by data—is personal data that is inaccurate, incomplete, fragmented and owned by everyone except the real owner of the data.

Who Does This Model Work for?

This inefficient model serves its masters well. It suits Facebook, it suits Google and the other owners of my personal data. They might be better served with a more holistic version, but it works for them in its fragmented form because what they are catering to is just that particular fragment of me.

The current model does not help advertisers either. Recently I considered a holiday in Vietnam with my girlfriend. We went, we photographed, we returned. But many months after, I am still plagued by online ads on and about Vietnam. Recently I was helping my son with his school project on 3D printers. It was just a school project, but 3D printer manufacturers are still spending good advertising dollars targeting me.

This happens because TripAdvisor, Airbnb, Google, Emirates and 3D printer manufacturers don't talk to each other. If they could, and if I had a way to tell them of my needs, both our purposes would be better served—the advertiser's and mine.

Right now, my personal data is fragmented, incomplete, does not benefit me or advertisers and is not available to newer players who would court me with better and more products. My data and I are the raw material that fuel today's economy. But the same machine-learning algorithms that are making these companies understand me better are not making me smarter about myself or my actions.

Isn't It Fair to Seek a New Model That Works Better for Everyone?

Let's begin with a little sharing. I want Google to share what it has learnt about me. I want Facebook to share what it knows about my social activities and interactions. I want LinkedIn to do the same with my professional network and interactions. And I want everyone else including my doctor, my school, my bank and my geneticist to do the same.

In fact, some of them do provide this data in parts. But in different formats and forms. Not in a form where data can be ported between providers. I want interoperability between services. So that I can create a holistic, complete version for the world. Of who Atul Jalan is. And then, build the Me Model.

The Me Model

With all fanfare and drumrolls, let me announce here the Me Model—a unified, holistic, digital model of myself, created from the billions of bytes of data that I generate. That would be a true 360° profile of myself.

This Me Model would be a multidimensional, organic profile that has all my data from everywhere—the bar I frequent, my bank, Facebook, Google, Amazon, Netflix, my Fitbit, my hospital and everything else. All stored in one single repository that uses rich machine-learning algorithms to keep developing an organic digital 'me'.

The first advantage of the Me Model is that it belongs to me. It is entirely up to me where and with whom I wish to share that data. And most importantly, what I wish to share.

The second advantage with the Me Model is that it addresses the inefficiencies of the current system. It creates the perfect model of me which is critical today, because as we mentioned earlier, my data defines me. Our digital future begins with this realization—that more than me, my data defines me. (I generate data, therefore I am.)

The third great advantage (which is where monetization comes in), is the fact that the Me Model is bidirectional. While in the current unilateral model, platforms can sell and use my data to their benefit, the Me Model works for me.

So how do we build the Me Model? To me, that is not so complex as long as we can get the few players involved to collaborate with each other.

We need a tool that can assimilate data from different sources—as diverse as Facebook, Uber and my school. The tool also needs to keep collating data so that my digital avatar grows with me. To store these, we need secure vaults that can guarantee security. All of this can be enabled only if governments bring in policies that ensure all current owners share my data with me, in a prescribed form.

To complete the loop, we have data exchanges that act as staging points for my advertisers. The exchanges also need to be able to monitor and monetize all content that I create—if I create a meme or a story that social media channels use, I need to be compensated for it. Much like YouTube pays content creators.

The Me Model can make life easier, more efficient and more profitable for all concerned.

How Does the Me Model Work for Me?

The Me Model can actually pitch my data against, say Google, to advertisers. Why would an advertiser pay Google big monies for fragmented data when I am willing to sell them holistic (and more accurate) data about myself?

Why would a car manufacturer pay Facebook and the newspapers in the hope of hitting pay dirt when they can get access to data on who exactly is in the market for a car? Then rather than spend their monies on reaching me, car manufacturers can spend on convincing me why I should buy from them.

This works for me and works beautifully for platforms and advertisers who use my data to propel their multibillion-dollar businesses. They can have a clear view on who Atul Jalan is and his needs—creating a more harmonious ecology of data producer, advertiser and platform.

Imagine matrimonial sites performing a match based on this data as opposed to the limited and inaccurate data available now. Imagine the Me Model being used for job hunting. If my prospective employer so wishes, my Me Model could share a Myers–Briggs[4] type personality indicator as well.

The Me Model could give me and the healthcare industry a clearer view on my health and my healthcare needs. To add to that, if we also use this model to contribute to genome sequencing, we really could get to the bottom of some serious health issues that affect the race.

The Me Model also makes for a less monopolistic environment where new entrants could access my data directly from me on a level playing field, rather than struggle for data in a hostile, locked-in environment. Which means that current giants will have to work that much harder to retain my loyalty.

All the better for me, isn't it? I get to own my data, I get to monetize my data and I get better service from all concerned.

Trust, the Me Model and a Better Life

The biggest issue with data privacy is that we do not trust corporations. Or the government. Or society. If that trust could be engendered, we could start seeing it as less of a Faustian bargain.

The Me Model comes with ownership and trust. If I owned all the personal data of Atul Jalan and I had the right to share whatever needs to be shared, with whomever I wish to share it, I (and the world) would be able to truly unlock the true potential of personal data.

While many have talked about data being the new oil, it was Meglena Kuneva, the European Consumer Commissioner who got it right. She said:

> . . . personal data is the new oil of the Internet and the new currency of the digital world.[5]

I really believe that what she said is the next truth. We have no idea what our personal data is being bartered for, absolutely not a clue. But imagine if we could build the Me Model and you could monetize your (more accurate, holistic) data for say, about $1000 a year. Now look at a 7-billion population doing that and we are talking about $7 trillion. That, I guess, is big.

The $1000 I talk about come from sources both direct and indirect. Among others, it includes what data exchanges will pay me for information, what advertisers will pay, the discounts that manufacturers will pass on to me (what is now marketing spend), what I could make from being a sample for researchers and what I could be paid for creating content for the web.

I like it that the model also helps content creators monetize what they create—all those wonderful men and women who create those memes, videos and content that makes the online world such a lovely place to be in. Similarly, it will compensate the labour and investment of media companies which have been struggling to monetize the value of their output.

Give Me My Fair Share

The truth is that whether we like it or not, we are a data economy and there are two facts about it that we have to accept: the first, that your data out there defines who you are; the second, that to make the best of this data economy, we have to share our personal data.

Unfortunately, we have transferred our data ownership rights for a few colourful beads. That needs to be corrected.

Our current state of affairs reminds me of a Bishop Desmond Tutu story—as poignant as it is funny. He once said that when the Europeans came to Africa, they had the Bible and the Africans had the land. They requested the Africans to close their eyes and pray, which the Africans did. When they opened their eyes, they had the Bible and the Europeans had the land.[6] Like the African's land, my data is my new source of wealth.

Right now, we are split between two groups. A first, that doesn't care about the value of personal data, and therefore, doesn't consider the possibilities and the repercussions of sharing the data. Then there is a second that is too worried about the repercussions to think about the possibilities. What we need is a meeting point that both can trust.

The problem is that I have created a few million bytes of data today but instead of it showing in my bank account, it is just floating in someone else's data lake. The Me Model creates a more equitable and efficient ecosystem that helps me monetize the value of my personal data in what will be the next economic revolution.

All of us know that this is where the next fortunes will be made. Everyone and his uncle, except me, is monetizing my data. All I am asking, as Oliver Twist did, is 'Please sir, I want some more.'[7]

Data Privacy: Orwell or Huxley, Who Got It Right?

IN ORWELL'S (RATHER GLOOMY) DYSTOPIAN *1984*, we first meet Big Brother, who watches over you and enjoys a cult following.

Omnipresent surveillance by the government and propaganda—what Big Brother says is the truth—are the recurring themes. The Thought Police keep an eye on what you are up to and the Ministry of Truth rewrites history to create a state-sponsored truth. In short, you are under surveillance and you are doomed—you do not even have the freedom of independent, unbiased thought.

In Aldous Huxley's *Brave New World*, however, the totalitarian rulers ensure that their citizens get exactly what they want. His citizens are bloated with amusement and live a life of stress-free consensus, reminiscent of Edward Gibbon's[1] Romans who kept demanding more gladiators and more tightrope-walking elephants. In short, you are under surveillance but you couldn't care less—you are getting the amusement you need.

After the Trump inauguration, when Kellyanne Conway uttered the words 'alternative facts', sales of *1984* shot up (as we have discussed elsewhere in this book). But we should also be reading *Brave New World*, for I really think that this is the world we live in. While both books diss the omnipresent state, I am inclined to think that it is Huxley's parody (he wrote it as a parody of H.G. Wells's *Utopia*, an idea of goodness he detested) that I live in today.

Orwell worried that we may become a culture held in bondage by the state; Huxley laughed that we might become a trivial culture, easily entertained and seeking endless entertainment. Orwell worried about truth and that books might be banned; Huxley laughed that no one might want to read a book. Orwell worried that we might be deprived of information; Huxley laughed that we might have access to so much information that we might just use it irresponsibly and irrelevantly.

At the root of both is a state that knows all. Every thought, every desire, every action and every event is tracked. What we think, what we feel, what we eat and drink, our likes and dislikes, our purchases, our bank, phone and health records, places we visit and people we meet—everything is recorded and analysed. Everything. That's the world we live in today.

The question is, where will this lead us? Are we heading for a gloomy Orwellian or a euphoric Huxleyan nightmare? Or do we have hope?

There Are Cameras All Around Us

For those of us who grew up in the '70s and '80s, the image of the wall-mounted camera as a detestable representation of surveillance is still too fresh. Even today, surveillance is a loaded term—both emotionally and politically. But when we look around, that is all we see.

We live in homes that have surveillance cameras, we work in offices that have surveillance cameras, we head there in lifts that have surveillance cameras, we travel in cabs that have surveillance cameras, we shop in malls and stores that have surveillance cameras, we drink in bars that have surveillance cameras. For all you know, there is a camera watching you read this, right now.

Everybody is watching everybody else.

The US military defines surveillance as 'systematic observation'.[2] And that's what we are subject to. We are open books; governments' ability to peer into our lives is greater than it has ever been before.

And most of it is data we surrender when we transact online, telling the world where we are going, with whom, where we are eating, what we are eating, where we are staying and for how long. In this connected world, we are all naked.

Our fear of surveillance also comes from what we grew up with—stories of the authoritarian governments of Russia, China and Eastern Europe. East Germany (very 'truthfully' called the German 'Democratic' Republic) at one point had a 1,02,000-strong Stasi (their secret police) keeping an eye on a population of 17 million.

Which is one spy for every 166 citizens! Not including civilian informers, of course. I have also found the Catholic confessional an extremely effective surveillance tool, until the Industrial Revolution changed life.

The current situation we are in is one we have put ourselves in willingly, but unwittingly. It is often amusing to see the totally unrelated consequences of world events. The Cold War meant that the US and the USSR competed at every level—which led, happily to space programmes desperate to be the first to put a man in space. This led to the invention of much that makes life so convenient today.

Similarly, 9/11 led to mass fear, which led to the National Security Agency in the US getting extraordinary powers for mass surveillance. So we willingly surrendered our privacy (data) in lieu of freedom from fear. Faustian, but a consoling bargain nevertheless.

The same intelligence platform that the US government uses to tackle insurgents (designed by Palantir[3] while working with the Pentagon in Afghanistan and Iraq) is the one it uses to keep tabs on air travellers, immigrants and ordinary Americans at home.

All of us carry smartphones, don't we? This also means that we are walking around with trackers. Phone location data is what police in Michigan used to find who went to a planned labour union protest. The government in Ukraine used it to see who had attended an anti-government demonstration. And it is not in Michigan and Ukraine alone that the government uses phone location data to find who is where.

It makes for an awkward conversation when you say that tracking phone data is legitimate when it is used to track Osama but an invasion of privacy when it comes to you.

In 1999, Scott McNealy, CEO of Sun Microsystems, made light of it when he said that:

You have zero privacy anyway. Get over it.[4]

That indeed was Huxleyan but the fact is that the world has changed much between 1999 and 2019.

We live in a time and day when all that was previously unmeasurable is being recorded, tracked and analysed. There are billions of Internet-enabled devices embedding themselves into our daily life. This gives governments robust capabilities for mass surveillance.

And mass surveillance, as we know, is dangerous. In the wrong hands it can discriminate based on almost any criteria—race, religion, class, political beliefs. It can be used to control what we see, what we can do, and, ultimately, what we say. And the wrong hands are never far away.

We live in the golden age of surveillance. It is becoming tougher and tougher to get off the surveillance grid, to maintain absolute privacy. Every day, in our digitized, virtual life, we churn out data that is being used without our knowledge. And often without our intentional consent.

The good news though, is that no one entity, including governments (at least democratic ones), has all the data in one place where they can be cross-referenced and analysed. Most of these streams are silos, not integrated and correlated. And the reason they remain unintegrated is that in many cases privacy laws restrict integration and government machinery, generally, tends to be slow in implementing technologies.

But here's the bad news, governments have access to all your data. And it is easy and incredibly worrying to imagine the power of any one agency that integrates all these streams. That this is so technically easy to stitch together is to me the fear of Big Brother.

Here's another fact that worries me: governments, to cover up their inefficiencies and inabilities (and sometimes to bypass legal constraints), often work with private surrogates that become proxy data gatherers for them.

But is this picture all Orwellian and gloomy? Not all of the time.

Can Data in the Right Hands Create a Truly Welfare State?

In 1989, Fair, Isaac and Company introduced the FICO score in the United States.[5] This was a credit score that determined the creditworthiness of a person that lenders could use to evaluate potential risk. It is believed that it was credit scores that led to credit becoming more widely available and less expensive for customers across the world—as it reduced the risk that lenders had to account for.

The FICO score can be thought of as a kind of surveillance. But contrast that with a majority of Chinese, who until recently had no credit scores and hence, no credit. Since citizens did not own houses, cars or credit cards (score a Pyrrhic victory to capitalism here), there is no information to measure. According to the Chinese Ministry of Commerce, the annual economic loss caused by lack of credit information is more than $75 billion.[6]

It is to deal with this that the Chinese government has launched the Social Credit System, to rate its 1.4 billion citizens.[7] The aim is to collect all information available online about China's citizens and companies and have it correlated and analysed. Based on this, citizens will be scored on their political, commercial, social and legal 'credit'. So, everyone has a score that determines their every action in a score-led world.

This is optional now but will be compulsory by 2020. To most of us, this is the Big, Bad, Brother Wolf, the ultimate totalitarian surveillance state. But the Chinese government sees here a desirable way to measure and enhance 'trust' nationwide and to build a culture of 'sincerity'. As the policy states:

> It will forge a public opinion environment where keeping trust is glorious. It will strengthen sincerity in government affairs, commercial sincerity, social sincerity and the construction of judicial credibility.[8]

I get a little worried when people use 'sincerity' and 'honesty' too often. But at the heart of the system is an attempt to control China's vast, anarchic and poorly regulated market economy, to punish counterfeiters, to expose corrupt government officials.

In a country where 700 million people live a large part of their life online, the Social Credit System will also access court, police, banking, tax and employment records. Doctors, teachers, local governments and businesses can now easily be scored by citizens for their professionalism and probity.

It is surveillance, yes, but it does bring the citizen easier access to credit and other benefits, it reduces corruption and it does 'reward' the 'good citizen'. This can be read both as welfare and authoritarianism. Which, again, is the duality that India's Aadhaar represents.

In 2009, India initiated a unique, twelve-digit identification for citizens, called Aadhaar[9]—which means foundation. The number is linked to the resident's basic demographics (name, date of birth, gender and address, with mobile number and email optional) and biometric information (photograph, ten fingerprints and two iris scans). All of this is stored in a central registry and becomes a single-source for online identity verification across the country.

The programme created much furore with multiple public interest litigations being filed on security and surveillance concerns. Eventually the Supreme Court struck down some sections like the one that enabled private entities like telecom companies and banks to use Aadhaar data. But it remained mandatory for filing taxes and such so that Aadhaar remains a convenience and not surveillance. One cannot deny that technology brings convenience. A unique proof of identity that can be authenticated online anytime and anywhere brings mobility to millions of Indians who migrate from one part of the country to another. They can establish their identity electronically, eliminating the pain of paperwork and officialese—of repeatedly providing supporting identity documents each time to access services.

In a greater cause, it helps the Indian government reach millions with various subsidies, benefits and services—an opportunity for the government to streamline its welfare delivery mechanism and thereby ensure transparency and good governance.

With Aadhaar, the government has accurate data on beneficiaries and thus can now enable direct benefit programmes. And its effects are already showing on a country riddled with corruption that has no dearth of welfare schemes but has a serious dearth of transparent systems that can effectively reach the economically handicapped segment of society.

In the late '80s, an Indian prime minister had famously remarked that of every rupee marked for welfare, only 17 paise reached the beneficiary.[10] Eighty-three paise showed a remarkable ability to evaporate along the way. Hopefully with Aadhaar, currency might stop its tendency to vaporize.

But Orwellian Fears Will Persist

In 2016, the Australian government decided to address its budget deficit in a unique manner. It decided to track social security overspending data and retrieve excess payments from beneficiaries. Australia's social security system has unemployment or sickness beneficiaries filing fortnightly statements with the system that administers the payments. More than two-thirds of recipients go off welfare within less than a year. Besides, the system frequently gets identities wrong as people sometimes use different names (as simple as expanding their initials) with employers and could have their wages double-counted.[11]

Despite knowing this, authorities went ahead with retrieval and the system flagged thousands of former claimants as debtors to the government.

While it was passed off as a data-mismatch, this exposes the inherent flaws of such an exercise. A government, if it chooses to, can use the data against a citizen.

Now imagine what China could possibly do. If Xi Jinping can decide to become president for life, he can also take other capricious decisions. He could decide to rate all behaviour positive or negative according to rules set by the government. Then your rating would be ranked against that of the rest of the population and then that would decide everything for you—your chances of getting a date, whether you marry, whether you can get a marriage loan, whether you can have a child ('children' in the plural comes with stipulations), whether that child can go to school or goes to work in an iPhone factory.

In this dystopian world, anything from defaulting on a loan to criticizing the ruling party, to jumping a red light to failing to care for your parents properly, could cause you to lose points. In this dystopian world, you are just a score. This, as Johan Lagerkvist, a Chinese Internet expert at the Swedish Institute of International Affairs, said:

It's Amazon's consumer tracking with an Orwellian political twist.[12]

While data can be put to beneficial use by a welfare state, the fact remains that unregulated and whimsical use of data, especially personal data, impacts the privacy and autonomy of an individual.

Which is why many democratic governments are defining rules and laws for data protection. A good legal framework requires a careful and sensitive balance between the autonomy and privacy of the individual and the legitimate concerns of the state.

In May 2018, the European Union rolled out GDPR (General Data Protection Rules).[13] This is an ambitious data protection reform aimed at protecting individuals' personal data, including right to privacy.

The GDPR includes a number of obligations aimed at protecting an individual's right on personal data. There is an obligation on the part of the companies who have access to that data to provide transparent information. It brings to individuals a number of data protection rights like the right to affirmative consent, right to access, right of correction, right to be forgotten, right to restrict the usage of personal data, right to object against any algorithmic assumption, right of data portability and much else.

On Aadhaar in India, as we saw earlier, the Supreme Court has attempted to safeguard individual rights within a governmental framework that uses data for welfare. Aadhaar could also be regulated by the Data Protection Authority.[14]

The Data Protection Authority is a body that is envisaged as part of India's Personal Data Protection Bill. This bill, drafted in 2018, provides for the establishment of the Data Protection Authority of India that will protect citizens' data and privacy. The proposed bill makes individual consent the centrepiece for data sharing, awards rights to users and imposes obligations on data fiduciaries (this includes all entities, including the state, which determine purpose and means of data processing). It also called for corresponding amendments to other laws, including the Right to Information.

This represents a shift in the definition, treatment and enforcement of the law surrounding personal data and its processing, as it upholds the right to privacy as paramount. These laws leave it to the individual to decide how his/her data is processed and used, and puts fiduciary responsibilities on the data controller.

This draft bill also has provisions for data storage where it makes it mandatory that a copy of a resident's personal data be stored in India. Now, why would the bill mandate that? That is a whole new chapter!

Data Nationalization

While we keep talking about globalization and openness and imagining 'there're no countries' and 'a brotherhood of man',[15] the truth is that protectionism will never leave us. We will always create barriers to restrict free flow of data to protect, favour and promote the domestic over the foreign.

This will be one of the consequences of new laws that will come in place to regulate the digital economy. Nations around the world have already implemented or are taking steps to control data and the flow of data beyond their borders. These 'data localization' efforts foil the very purpose of the web, designed to share information freely across borders. Driven by worries about security, surveillance and law enforcement, and by the realization that data is the new oil, government after government is putting up barriers in what can only be called the death knell of a new kind of international trade that the web has made possible.

China, instead of being part of the rest of the world, chose to develop a Chinese web universe of its own, creating its own Amazon, Google and Facebook. This exceptionalism has inspired Iran to create a 'halal' Internet, free of Western influences (and decadence, one supposes) where it can also control domestic dissent.

Many countries now insist that foreign Internet giants have servers in their countries, making it easier for their governments to monitor traffic. Russia requires all personal information to be stored domestically, Vietnam insists on a local copy of all Vietnamese data and Australia has restrictions on health data leaving the country.

The European Union (EU) is also planning a single digital market (an EU cloud) that will offer some degree of economic protectionism.

Remember the trade barriers of the last century? They have just reappeared as firewalls for data localization.

To be of value, data has to flow across borders—geographic, ideological and economic. In his article, 'Data Nationalism',[16] Anupam Chander, professor of law at Georgetown University, imagines an Internet where data stops at national borders and is examined to see whether it must be allowed to leave the country and, if so, whether it must be taxed. While this may sound funny, this is precisely the consequence of measures nations are taking on keeping data within their borders. Lennon can rock and roll in his grave.

While we strive to protect data within our selfish borders, we forget that it is data that will drive everything tomorrow. Businesses depend on data for R&D, develop new products and services, improve marketing and, in every which way, improve our lives. For them to do this, to be innovative and competitive, they need to be able to share goods, capital, people and data across borders.

A better and less acquisitive understanding of data that fosters cross-border data will foster research, technology and economic growth. The converse will make our world smaller, driving us into smaller and smaller pens as data becomes further and further localized.

Defining data by man-made boundaries in an effort to 'nationalize' it could pose a huge threat to the open, global nature of the Internet. Data nationalism is a fallacious attempt that violates every principle of free trade and will significantly hamper trade in digital goods and services.

Data nationalism is a man-made hindrance for the man-made laissez-faire nature of the cyber world. Understanding this and working around it is critical to the future of international trade and development. It has repercussions on the ongoing struggle between democracy and totalitarianism, and on isolationist tendencies.

The Balance

In Yevgeny Zamyatin's *We* (which many believe was the inspiration for Orwell's *1984* and Huxley's *Brave New World*), citizens live in an urban nation called the One State, constructed entirely of glass where everyone can observe and be observed. And while it might seem like a simplistic metaphor for lack of privacy, with the IoT, we will all be living in glass houses.

Our lives revolve around information and the World Wide Web. It is very unlikely that we can be convinced to get off the grid or soon, even survive off the grid. The current generation has not known a life without the Internet; their only source of information is the Internet, their only way to navigate is Google maps and without a WhatsApp pin, nobody's calling on them. Notice, that each of these is a data trail.

Very soon, once the IoT is up full steam, every heartbeat will be recorded. The net will know what's in your refrigerator, the condition of your liver, your last 6000 purchases and what joke made you laugh the most (because your phone can read the vibrations of your hand).

So, our only hope is to strike a right balance between the bounty the online world has to offer and the protection of our autonomy. As Zamyatin says in *We*:

> Those two, in paradise, were given a choice: happiness without freedom, or freedom without happiness. There was no third alternative.[17]

Let us hope, however, that we will have both freedom and happiness in the days ahead. And that we have the wisdom to understand and differentiate between the two.

In the Huxleyan world everyone partakes of soma, the soothing, happiness-producing drink, and lives a pain-free life of endless amusement. This is a world where nothing matters—and that matters to me.

Jobs and AI: What Will the Human Do?

THERE HAVE ONLY BEEN THREE true economic revolutions in the history of mankind. The first was about 20,000 years ago, the Neolithic Revolution—when small communities became increasingly less nomadic and settled down to a life of animal husbandry and agriculture. This resulted in the first boost in economic productivity.

The second was the Industrial Revolution. It sparked an increase in production and wealth, extended life spans and demolished the class structure in Europe—at the same time, it also reorganized the economic and philosophical views of the Western world.

Both brought with them the pain of social change. Hunting and gathering was easier than spending 365 days ploughing, planting and toiling under the sun—fighting against the vagaries of nature. Equally painful was the farmer to labourer transition—abandoning the farm to go and toil in the new factories. Generations had to reskill themselves to stay productive.

What we are now walking through is the third revolution. I don't know what posterity will call it—The Digital Revolution, The Fourth Industrial Revolution, The Second Machine Age, The AI Age . . . Whatever they call it, our time will go down in history as the third major revolution when man and society, and economic, political and philosophical thought go through what could well be their greatest change ever.

Spearheading the pain of that change will be a complete disruption, not just of employment but even the idea of employment.

Will Humans Go the Way of Horses?

During and after the Industrial Revolution, the horse had the most to complain. It got replaced by the motor. Once the internal combustion engine came in, the poor horse became unemployable! Millions of horses never got their jobs back.

Like Gregory Clark said in *A Farewell to Alms*:

> There was always a wage at which all these horses could have remained employed. But that wage was so low that it did not pay for their feed . . .[1]

But the key difference between horse and man is that men have a vote. And the voice to complain. So it is extremely unlikely that man goes the way of the horse.

Man's relationship with technology is complex. We always invent technology, but then technology comes back and reinvents us.

Going back to the horse example, the shift from the horse-driven carriages to motor-driven vehicles must have impacted the rhythm of life—it would have closed down entire businesses dependent on it.

But then, motorization reinvented us, becoming the engine of our economic progress and prosperity.

We changed, we prospered, we advanced.

Now again, we face a revolution. And again, at the very centre of it, is the car. This time, the car is not replacing beast, but man. With the autonomous car, the man behind the wheel is being substituted by AI.

Much like the last time, impending transformation brings to the fore the dread of change. For, in the short term, change brings with it pain and the ugly spectre of lost jobs and livelihoods. Of course, in the long term what we are looking at is a great future, but as British economist John Maynard Keynes said:

In the long run we are all dead.[2]

Uncertainties loom large above our bewildered heads, as there is a storm brewing.

Technology Is Always a Creative Force Seeking the Right Job

The good news is that AI is secular and blind to the colour of the collar. The bad news is that this means all kinds of jobs will be impacted.

It does not matter whether you are a doctor, lawyer, architect, reporter or programmer, this new wave of automation will impact all professions.

It is estimated that in the next ten to fifteen years, 65 per cent of current jobs, will not exist (according to Kevin Kelly, in *The Inevitable*).[3] But, what will also happen is that millions of new opportunities will be created. Technology always creates more jobs than it destroys—automation always increases the demand for people in roles machines cannot fulfil.

Looking at the past might not be the most efficient way to envision the future but our experience of the nineteenth century tells us that jobs will be redefined rather than destroyed—new industries, new needs and new jobs will emerge. Remember that it was the farmer who redefined himself into a factory worker to manufacture all that we use today.

Luddites protested textile machinery taking over the seamstresses' jobs, but they could not prevent the inexorable march of technology. Seamstresses and other workers in the older textile economy acquired new skills and therefore, new jobs—in building, operating and maintaining the new factories.

And what happened eventually? The cost of production of fabric and garments came down and quality of life improved.

What technology does is create more choice, expand the size of economies and enhances our potential for self-realization. Eventually, everyone benefits. According to Milton Friedman:

> Most economic fallacies derive from the tendency to assume that there is a fixed pie that one party can gain only at the expense of another.[4]

The Era We Are In

The invention of the steam engine triggered the first Industrial Revolution, transforming the world from a predominantly agrarian and rural society to an industrial and urban one.

Electricity and the telephone triggered the second Industrial Revolution—putting the manufacturing process on steroids and creating systems of mass production.

After this came the development of the transistor, which enabled information and computing technology—including development of personal computers and Internet. This triggered the third Industrial Revolution (also called the Digital Revolution). This wave transformed everything mechanical and analog into digital and created a digital economy. Most economists perceive the emergence of new technologies—AI, bio-engineering, IoT, 3D printing, quantum computing, and nanotechnology—as the beginning of the Fourth Industrial Revolution (or Second Machine age). These technologies are fusing the physical, digital and biological worlds, and impacting all disciplines, economies and industries.

AI Is the New Electricity

Who would have imagined that we would be booking accommodation on a platform that does not own a single bed? Or using a worldwide cab service that does not own a single car? Who would have imagined that the whole of the world would be relying on one bookstore which still doesn't have a store?

The beginning of the Internet was not too far in the past. Yet, we already have an Airbnb, an Uber, an Amazon, a Facebook . . .

AI and other associated technologies will disrupt and hence revitalize every industry and create new and hitherto unheard of industries.

AI is the new electricity—a horizontal enabling layer, which will support many intelligent applications. In the age of electricity, we took everything manual and added electricity to it. The fan, for example, or the water pump.

What we will do in the age of AI is the same. We will take everything we have and add AI to it. With sensors and the IoT, everything—refrigerators, air-conditioners, washing machines, cars, weapons, wallets—will get cognified. Everything can do with a little intelligence, even my shoes and socks. And some people. I can see the next 10,000 business plans already—just take 'x' and add AI to it! Possibilities abound everywhere. In fact, it is tough to imagine one sphere of activity which will not be impacted by these emerging technologies.

Soon we will see societies transform as we learn to live alongside robots (of course, one of science fiction's favourite tropes has been a future where man is unable to distinguish between reality and virtual-reality, and human and android).

Today we might be able to see robots only as job-takers but that is because we are not able to envision the new industries and the new jobs that will emerge.

Would you, for example, have imagined a decade ago that video logging for YouTube would be a full-time job? Or that social media would be employing so many people?

The Next Wave of Growth

For a few years now, global economies have been sluggish; globalization, the defining economic model of our times, seems to have run its course. What we see now is artificial growth, created by governments and central banks through aggressive monetary policies—quantitative easing, heavy government spending, etc.

What the world needs now is the next model, the next wave.

But what is the nature of this age we are heading into? Erik Brynjolfsson and Andrew McAfee use the Kodak and Instagram example to illustrate two points about this age in their book, *The Second Machine Age*. The first point that Brynjolfsson and McAfee make is of the bounty this age promises. Kodak was one of the greatest brands of its time. Yet, in a day and age where people take more photographs every day than ever before, Kodak went bankrupt. Just a few months before that, Facebook had acquired Instagram—a simple app that allows millions of people to share their billions of pictures—for $1 billion.

So get this—in a very short time Instagram created seven billionaires, each with a net worth way higher than George Eastman of Kodak, and both Instagram and Facebook are valued many times that Kodak was at its peak.

And the second point they raise is this—while the bounty is there for all of us to see, is the distribution equitable?

Will This Be Jobless Growth, Creating Discontent?

When Instagram was sold, it had a dozen employees. As opposed to Kodak at its peak, when it employed 1,45,000 people. Kodak sustained many lives.

In the First Machine Age—the age of Kodak—productivity, employment and median income all rose in tandem. But in the second, the growth in productivity seems to have been decoupled from jobs and income. And this divergence has its roots in the very nature of the digital economy.

In the digital economy, a set of goods and services can be provided to an infinite number of additional customers, all at the same time, at a cost that is often close to zero. When Facebook acquired WhatsApp for $19 billion, it had 400 million users. And fifty-five employees. They can easily add many millions more, without having to add a single employee.

Today's high-tech industry is less labour-intensive than it was in the past. Data demonstrates that growth has been jobless and polarized since 2000. According to studies, only 0.5 per cent of American workers are employed in industries that have emerged since 2000.

Martin Ford, the author of two bestsellers on the dangers of automation, worries that middle-class jobs will vanish, economic mobility will cease and a wealthy plutocracy could:

> . . . shut itself away in gated communities or in elite cities, perhaps guarded by autonomous military robots and drones.[5]

Keynes coined the term 'technological unemployment' back in the 1930s when he predicted that the displacement of workers by machines would usher in an era of shorter workweeks and increased leisure. In the 1990s, economists Sherwin Rosen and Robert Frank argued that globalization and technology could conspire to create 'superstar' or 'winner take all' labour markets.[6]

Will the Second Machine Age end up proving them and Plutarch right? For it was Plutarch who said:

> An imbalance between the rich and the poor is the oldest and
> most fatal ailment of all republics.[7]

Until now, the consensus among economists was that these developments would have only a minor or temporary impact on the economy. Now they are not so sure.

New Economic Ideologies Will Emerge

Every age and every revolution demands its own ideologies. Much like how the Industrial Revolution created socio-economic ideologies like communism and capitalism.

Land was the raw material for the agri-economy, power for the electric-economy and data and algorithms are the raw material for the digital economy. While old economies were based on the reality of scarcity, what we now witness (and many are not able to come to terms with it) is a new reality of abundance.

People are already debating the idea of an unconditional universal wage to deal with unemployment. A recent referendum on this failed in Switzerland, getting only 23 per cent of the vote.[8] But that might not be the case in other countries (or even in Switzerland again, in the near future).

The greatest challenge for economists is to imagine an unseen future where there could be more Instagrams and WhatsApps and then, to imagine new theories and models around them—theories and models that will create prosperity for all and not just for some.

Politics, Policy and Education in the AI Age

While our economic models sail into uncharted waters, we are also witnessing the beginnings of increased life spans thanks to regenerative medicine and nanotechnology. In this scenario, how will our pension funds and social security handle eighty being the new fifty? More critically, what will be the political impact of a vast new class of 'economically useless people'?

Today more manufacturing jobs can be automated and skilled design jobs account for a larger share in the value of trade. Today's governments cannot count on a growing industrial sector to absorb unskilled labour from the rural areas.

In both developed and developing economies, technology is creating opportunities for those who were previously shackled by multiple constraints. But the numbers of jobs are just not what earlier technological revolutions created.

This is leading to 'premature de-industrialization' and destroying established models in poorer economies. In the US of February 2018, there were 6.7 million people without jobs.[9]

But does 'economically-useless' mean without value? As Yuval Noah Harari puts it:

> I choose this very upsetting term, 'useless' to highlight the fact that we are talking about uselessness from the viewpoint of the economic and political system, not from a moral viewpoint.[10]

Harari stresses that our old political structures were built on humans that were useful to the state, both as warriors and as workers. With those jobs now being taken over by machines, the system stops attaching value to humans.

If our governments are able to put their wisest heads together to look at the demands posed by the new economy, we might be able to benefit from technology. But if they get it wrong, we stare at chaos.

We stare at a bitter, confrontational world, where everyone cries of inequality—both the unemployed poor and the overtaxed rich.

Man, at the very apogee of his evolution, could hit a wall. Information technology and globalization have truly taken our world forward, but it has also had unintended consequences. It has created a considerable population of the disconnected-disgruntled—people who feel that they are not part of this connected, fast-progressing world. Events like the subprime mortgage crisis, for example, have only precipitated the matter.

Brexit and Trumpism (and maybe even ISIS) are all manifestations of this growing malaise. A modern-day Luddite cannot break down or burn an algorithm responsible for his losing his job. But he finds others to blame for his state—foreigners, the establishment, globalization. And the fact is that politicians—and by extension governments—will react to these.

Governments have never been able to change ahead of the demands of technology. And this, always, leads to retroactive legislation and regulation. To come out of this vicious cycle, politicians need to consider not just the fiscal consequences of technological progress but its human, social and ethical costs as well. Only then can we ensure that the 'economically useless' have a productive role in tomorrow's world.

Only then will they be able to look at moving from labour taxes to consumption and capital gains taxes to support a bigger (and growing) unemployable population. Only then will they look at regulating ownership, utilization and distribution of data.

Only then will they look at enhancing the educational system—to help people develop broader skill sets rather than focus on specialization, as we do today. Remember that in most of the world, the educational system is still designed for the factories of the First Industrial Revolution. While technology takes all of us forward at a faster pace, it does look like we are dependent on governments and politicians to fashion the rest of the world around it.

Will AI Be Our Deliverance?

However much we argue against it, the fact is that our existence is fairly Sisyphean. One of the primary reasons is the way we insist on looking at work—both as a way of making money and as a way of finding meaning. It is a beautiful idea to combine both, but it holds an inherent conflict.

The blame lies with God, of course, who cursed Adam and Eve for having eaten the forbidden fruit:

> From the sweat of your brow you will eat your fruit till you return to ground.[11]

And ever since, life has been more the toil of Adam than the life-enhancing creativity of Michelangelo. And rarely have the twain met.

The work practices that followed the industrial revolutions tried to increase productivity by specialization. Specialized workers managing their task with greater skill leads to more productivity than the same number of workers approaching the broader task without specialization. Specializations make modern economies efficient.

This division of labour is to a great degree responsible for worker disgruntlement today. There is a disconnect between what you do all day and who you think you are. And this lack of fulfilment is one of the most critical crises of our times. Imagine the number of people heading out to work with a disconnect. Karl Marx called this 'alienation', a capitalist issue in which workers don't feel fulfilled as they don't see themselves in the object that they have created. (He was right, although 'alienation' isn't a capitalist issue alone.)

These repetitive jobs are the ones that will first lose out to AI. For the simple reason that machines are way more efficient than humans. I agree with Kevin Kelly, founding editor of Wired, when he says that we humans are not designed for efficiency.[12] We are designed for wasting time. Our work is not efficient. Our relationships are not efficient. Our art is not efficient.

Which then makes it sensible for robots to take the jobs, while we dream up new work for them to do. Making whatever it is that we do more enjoyable, more fun and more creative has to be our goal.

Many of us cannot conceive of a world where humans do nothing. We find that a very disturbing proposition. But I remember listening to an interview with Marvin Minsky[13] where he said that he was not too bothered by how people would stay engaged without work. He said that if you can get 50,000 people into a stadium to watch a ball get kicked from one side to the other, man would always find ways to stay engaged and occupied.

So how do we look at jobs in our immediate future? Maybe we should, like Keynes suggested, look at automation as a chance to escape from the drudgery of tedious chores. Maybe Keynes's quote of the charwoman's epitaph should be our inspiration:

Don't mourn for me, friends, don't weep for me never, for I am going to do nothing for ever and ever.[14]

Love, Sex and AI: Is Sex at the Forefront of Progress, Again?

EVERY NEW TECHNOLOGY EXPECTS SOME degree of behavioural change from adopters and, hence, meets resistance. To overcome this resistance, we need a compelling reason. And I can't think of a more compelling reason than sex.

The history of technology is like a textbook on the evolution of sex. According to the futurist Ray Kurzweil, every new technology adopts a sexual theme. Maybe because, like author Nicholson Baker says:

> We want to humanise the products we invent . . .[1]

Gutenberg printed his first Bible in the 1450s. Folks were quick to figure that the press could print more than Bibles—by the 1520s, we had the first printed porn (that too by the Vatican!).[2] After vulcanized rubber was invented, guess what one of the first mass-produced rubber products was—the condom. (Debatable, but according to George Bernard Shaw, condoms were the best thing to come out of the Industrial Revolution.)[3]

One of the first films Edison shot with the Kinetograph camera was a twenty-three-second clip called 'The Kiss'.[4] Very obviously, the man was a genius in more ways than one. In the early '80s, when less than 1 per cent of American homes had VCRs, 75 per cent of video cassettes sold were pornographic.

Technology has progressed on the back of sex. Take the Internet for example. Remember how chatting became popular? Guess who video streaming was first created for? Not BBC, for sure. Do you think Google could have afforded to make YouTube what it is without ads from sex sites? And guess why our e-commerce payment systems are so robust.

When mobile phones started delivering images, guess what images were the most sought-after? And the same was the case with video. When our phone companies promise greater bandwidth and more data, what is it that they really are promising?

So will AI and robotics follow this established, tried-and-tested pattern and largely cater to the sex industry? I think it is definitely worth a peep.

Man's Fascination for the Inanimate

In Ovid's 'Metamorphoses',[5] Pygmalion the sculptor falls in love with a statue he carves and names it Galatea. He is obsessed with her but scared to speak of his affection for a marble being. So he prays to Aphrodite that he may find a bride who resembles his statue.

Aphrodite makes things a lot simpler and ensures that the next time he kisses her, Galatea responds . . . and comes alive.

Today we refer to Pygmalianism as a 'psychosexual abnormality' in which individuals direct erotic fantasies on to objects they create.

But what I am not sure any more is whether we will see this as an 'abnormality' for long. Or whether we will soon just see this as anthropomorphism—our tendency to attribute human traits, emotions and intentions to non-human entities. For very soon, many of us will have to overcome our resistance to interacting with non-humans the way we interact with humans—like we said before, where behavioural change is required, sex is always a driving force. In Japan, inflated sex dolls known as Dutch Wives[6] (from the life-sized bolsters the Dutch used to sleep with; why the Dutch slept with life-sized bolsters, I don't want to guess), have been around since the '60s. The stature society has accorded them is evident from the fact that discarded dolls are often provided funeral rites.

Hollywood has always explored futurism and disconcerting topics way before most of us are ready for them. I see that spirit of inquiry in series like *Westworld* and *Humans* and movies like *Ex Machina* and *HER*.

In *HER*, Theodore (a brilliant performance by Joaquin Phoenix) installs a new software that claims to be 'the first artificially intelligent operating system (OS), an intuitive entity that listens to you, understands you, and knows you' and is not just an OS but a consciousness.

The OS chooses the name Samantha and explains to Theodore:

. . . the DNA of who I am is based on a million personalities of all the programmers who wrote me, but what makes me me, is my ability to grow to my experiences. So, basically, in every moment I am evolving, just like you.[7]

And Theodore responds:

That's really weird, you seem like a person but you're just a voice in a computer.

Samantha replies:

I can understand how the limited perspective of a non-artificial mind would perceive it that way. You'll get used to it.

And she's only half joking.

So will we soon be faced with a day when our robots, much like ourselves, have a consciousness?

When Will Robots Become Sentient?

This brings us back to Alan Turing's famous question:

Can machines think?

It also makes us ask this, 'Can machines feel?'

Turing developed the Turing test, an experiment to determine how a machine could be considered intelligent. In the test, a human conducts typed conversations with two entities and then decides which of the two is human and which a machine. If the interrogator is unable to identify which the machine is, then the machine should be regarded as intelligent.

Therefore, if a machine gives the appearance of being intelligent, we should assume that it is indeed intelligent. Having said that, what if we were to apply the same argument to other aspects of being human—to emotions, to personality, to moods and to behaviour?

In his book *Love and Sex with Robots*, David Levy (founder of the Computer Olympiad) writes that:

If a robot behaves in a way that we would consider uncouth in a human, then by Turing's standard we should describe that robot's behaviour as uncouth.[8]

According to Levy, a machine need not have emotions, it just needs to behave as though it does.

For robots to interact with us in ways that we appreciate, they too must be endowed with emotions, or at the very least they must be made to behave as though they have emotions.

Which puts the human in a very weird daisy-plucking situation: Does the robot love me? Or is it just pretending to love me?

Much like a computer's programmed intelligence, a robot's programmed emotions might be very different from the human version. In many cases, they might even evolve their own emotions. As we begin to recognize the emotions and experiences that lie behind a robot's behaviour, we might learn to find them less artificial. At this point, we might start seeing them as beings.

But how far are we from these sentient beings? How far are we from what the Japanese beautifully call *sonzai-kan*, the feeling of one's presence?

The fact is that we are far from a *Blade Runner* kind of android that looks, moves and speaks like a human. But someday soon, with the incredible pace at which machine learning is developing (developing itself?), we may soon create artificial intelligence that can intuitively perform any task we can and might be able to beat the Voigt-Kampff test—the fictional test in *Blade Runner* designed to distinguish androids from humans based on their emotional response to questions.

Hiroshi Ishiguro, director at the Intelligent Robotics Lab in Osaka believes that humans are designed to interact with and place their faith in other humans.[9] So the more human-like our robots become, the more acceptable will they become and the more open will we become to sharing our life with them.

Ishiguro and his team are at the forefront of a young science called HRI, human-robot interaction. This combines AI, engineering, cognitive sciences and social psychology to understand our relationship with robots better—and then, create better robots.

HRI tries to analyse why we might want to interact with robots and why we might even begin to feel affection for them.

Do Some of Us Prefer Machines to Our Own?

One of the things that make us human is our readiness to attribute human traits to non-human objects of our affection. The Greek philosopher Xenophanes[10] was the first to use the term 'anthropomorphism' to describe this tendency.

He noticed that Greek gods were blue-eyed and fair-skinned and African gods were brown-eyed and dark-skinned—a striking similarity between the worshipper and the worshipped. We are only too quick to transfer human qualities to non-human objects if it suits our purpose.

Being able to see human attributes in a non-human might be a boon for those among us who are not great fans of human interaction. In *HER*, Theodore, who is unsuccessful in initiating and sustaining relationships with women, predictably starts falling in love with Samantha.

Their friendship becomes more intimate and inevitably leads to sex (unfortunately only the voice variety). But this is incomparably better than the phone sex that Theodore has had with anonymous partners before.

The fact is that the world over, people are beginning to develop a preference to interaction with computers than with humans. This might explain why computers are having a huge impact on education, guidance counselling and psychotherapy. As long back as 1980, it was found that clients felt more at ease communicating with computers than with human counsellors.

What explains this preference? An interaction with a computer brings people a sense of privacy and safety and makes them more willing to disclose information. This is a perfect antidote to the difficulties many of us face in forming satisfactory human relationships.

Sherry Turkle, professor of social studies of science and technology at MIT, describes this preference as an infatuation with simulated worlds.[11] Much like Narcissus and his reflection, people who work with computers can easily fall in love with the worlds they create, or with their performances in worlds created for them by others.

While much of this is true for a significant proportion of people in today's connected world, there also are many who just enjoy being with computers because they are fun and because they empower us.

Sherry Turkle has found that children deem simple toys to be alive if they believe that the toy loves them and if they love the toy. I am sure you are reminded of Calvin and Hobbes. The emotional attitude of the human is to a great extent responsible for the perception of life in a toy, or a humanoid robot.

If users believe that their robot loves them and that they love their robot, they are more likely to see the robot as alive. And if they perceive the robot as alive, chances are the owner will develop increased feelings of love for the robot, thereby creating an emotional snowball.

Note that we are still referring to the robot and its 'owner'. After David Levy's book *Love And Sex With Robots*, Kathleen Richardson[12] of the *Campaign Against Sex Robots* (yes, this exists) wrote a position paper that Levy was drawing on prostitution as a model for human-robot relations and that as a consequence we might be faced with a dangerous existence where humans would lose the ability, in relations with other humans, to recognize them as human subjects. Yes, she said this.

This was in 2007, after Levy predicted in his book that humans would be in sexual relationships with robots by 2050. But then, it looks like humans have proven both Levy and Richardson wrong.

The Sex Doll Is Now Almost the Real Thing

It honestly is unfair to refer to the latest AI-powered robot partner as a sex doll. I know it is anthropomorphic, but it does feel like we are demeaning her. For she is not a plastic blow-up doll any more.

Today's robotic sex doll is an excellent example of convergent technologies. Voice and facial recognition software, motion-sensing technology and animatronic engineering combine to create dolls that can give you a warm, smiling welcome when you come home and entertain you with snappy conversations. And never, ever, frown.

Abyss Creations calls their life-size (and lifelike) doll 'the world's finest love doll'. Called RealDoll, these are constructed of platinum silicone and are designed to match the appearance, texture and weight of the human form.

Abyss also made news with the launch of Harmony,[13] the world's first talking sex doll. According to the CEO of Abyss, Harmony helps people find a level of companionship that they may not be able to achieve otherwise. With AI, the doll will have a persistent memory and will remember everything about the user, his hopes, fears, favourite food . . . the works. If you tell her you are hungry, she's likely to say, 'Well you told me pizza is your favourite food, maybe you should have that.'

Harmony has over eighteen modes, smiles, blinks and frowns. She can hold a conversation on music, movies and books, share jokes and quote Shakespeare. She remembers everything about you, remembers your birthday and your mother's. She can be docile or submissive, whatever you want her to be. And, has a figure that could give a porn star a complex. The only drawback is her Scottish accent.

Harmony and other such AI-enhanced robots are designed to be as much a partner as a sex toy. Recently Zheng Jiajia, an AI expert and engineer, made himself a robot after tiring of seeking a human partner.

He named the robot Yingying[14] and married her. Yingying can speak a few words (I can bet 'headache' is not one of them) and identify Chinese characters. He intends to keep creating upgrades until she has all the features he expects from his dream spouse.

For more and more people, this is making sense. It is also freeing them from the emotional strain of human relationships.

Humans, Robots and the Midway

When we start discussing AI, most of us tend to imagine the machine to human journey. As this entire article has been all about. We talk about pygmalianism, we talk of anthropomorphism—we consider ourselves the most significant entity and consider the rest of the world from the context of our values and experiences (that's anthropocentrism). What we are not accounting for is that it is not just the machine that will evolve. We ourselves are very likely to change, as well. As we learn to live with machines, we will change socially, emotionally and even culturally.

In the past ten to fifteen years, much of our behaviour has changed. Teenage couples, instead of hanging out with each other and building relationships, are 'texting out' with each other. Even adult dating is seeing a considerable dip.

Ideas we have held sacrosanct, like marrying to have kids and having kids being a natural sequel to marriage, don't hold any more. Japan, in 2016, only registered 1 million births; the lowest since it started keeping count. There are multiple reasons attributed to this; women putting careers ahead of childbirth, men unwilling to have children without the security of a regular job, people's inability to form relationships and a general disinclination towards sex.

And this is not a passing phenomenon. When we correlate this with the impact AI will have on jobs, this acquires a worrying hue. And if this is the case in a developed Japan with just 3 per cent unemployment, you can well imagine what the future holds for other nations.

How we think and how we behave is undergoing drastic change and it is this changed human that is walking towards the evolving android. In the course of this change we will be faced with a whole lot of questions we don't have answers to, yet. For what confronts us is something we haven't been able to define in its entirety.

Sophia: The Saudi Citizen[15]

Sophia made her official debut at Saudi Arabia's Future Investment Initiative as the world's first robot with citizenship rights. Somehow this does not fascinate me, even though people have been discussing this for a while now.

What fascinates me is that she made her appearance without the abaya or the hijab that all Saudi women are supposed to wear. She also arrived alone, without the customary male companion.

So what's happening here? Is it that female robots already have more freedom than female humans? Or is it that we have not accorded robots gender yet? Now that they are getting so lifelike and so smart, we are forced to revisit that increasingly thinning line between machine and human. There are a lot of issues that await definition (much of that has been covered in our essay, 'Ethics and AI').

Sophia—created by Hanson Robotics—also went to the Cayman Islands on a date with Will Smith. It was clear though that the entire interaction was awkward for Will Smith. We are still to get used to the idea of interacting with a non-human object as if it were human. We are fine with Alexa and Siri, but with Sophia, we are in uncharted terrain.

An Integrated Future?

That awkwardness brings me to an article in the *Daily Mail* about Erica, created by Hiroshi Ishiguro, which will soon be replacing a news anchor on a Japanese TV channel. Ishiguro believes she might soon develop an 'independent consciousness'.[16] But what I found interesting was the *Daily Mail*'s headline—'Erica, the creepy robot that is so life-like she appears to "have a soul"'. Note the word 'creepy'—we still are not fully used to the idea of a robot that could possibly have a degree of 'humanness'.

They called it 'creepy' because of what roboticist Masahiro Mori calls the Uncanny Valley theory.[17] This is defined as the level of realism in robots that we, as humans, can handle. The less realistic it is, the more empathy we feel (like what we feel for R2D2). But as the robot moves closer in appearance to humans, our ability to distinguish the real from the artificial gets affected, resulting in a pushback. The Uncanny Valley happens because we are encountering something very familiar and, at the same time, unknown.

But this is still the infancy of our life with robots. We have many valleys to overcome. In our effort to perfect the machine and create ideal humanoids, we will end up learning more about human affections, emotions, love and sex simply because we will have to define these for the machine. In much the same way that our advances in AI will force us to learn more about our consciousness.

In this journey, we would have expanded our senses, our minds and our options into an androgynous future where our sexuality would be both human and robotic. Figuratively, a better human.

Ethics and AI: Ethics, Now Not for Man Alone

SOPHIA, AS WE SAW IN the last chapter, is the hottest lady in town. Sophia is a social humanoid robot and in October 2017, she became a Saudi Arabian citizen—the first robot in the world to receive citizenship.[1]

Now, if I were to run away with Sophia, who would the Saudi cops be looking for? A thief, a kidnapper or an eloper? For Hanson Robotics, who developed Sophia, could claim that I had stolen their property. The Saudi Arabians could claim that I had kidnapped their citizen. And a few romantic engineers could claim that the feelings could possibly have been mutual and that we eloped.

The fact is that technology has evolved much, much faster than our laws. And unless we actually put our noses to the grindstone, we will soon be in a fix. In fact, we already are.

Cars: The New Outlaws

On 7 May 2016, the owner of a Tesla Model S in Florida put his car on autopilot. The car failed to detect an eighteen-wheel truck and trailer on the highway and tried to drive under it. The owner died and that went down as the first death attributed to an autonomous car.[2]

On 18 March 2018, an autonomous Uber hit a woman who was walking outside the crosswalk in Arizona—she went down as the first pedestrian to be killed by an autonomous car.[3]

Thousands of accidents have happened across the world between these two dates. The difference is that we understand these thousands of accidents and we have mechanisms in place to address the consequences but we have not evolved rules and regulations to address accidents with autonomous cars.

The Oxford definition of law is that it is:

the system of rules which a particular country or community recognises as regulating the actions of its members and which it may enforce by the imposition of penalties.[4]

Who exactly are the 'members' in the Florida and Arizona accidents and who will be 'penalized'?

Is the owner to blame, for owning the car? Is the manufacturer to blame, for having created a car with an autopilot? Is the company that made the software to blame, for not accounting for human inconsistencies and inefficiencies like stepping carelessly off the sidewalk? Or do we go after the Internet service provider?

A few naughty boys with black insulation tape can convince an autonomous car that a stop sign is actually a U-turn. This would not have worked with a human, but it could cause grief with an autonomous car. Again here, who is liable?

Mr Musk launched his Tesla Model S into space and, as we speak, it is driving across our galaxy and is unlikely to run down any hitch-hikers (but it would help if Arthur Dent and Ford Prefect watch out). You and I, though, are not in space and we are going to see autonomous cars on the road very soon. What laws will govern them?

Machines: Sapient Now, Sentient Soon

Our previous experience with robots is restricted to fiction. We have had super-helpful robots like the cutely named Irona, Richie

Rich's maid-cum-bodyguard and KITT (Knight Industries Two Thousand), the talking car that is David Hasselhoff's sidekick in *Knight Rider*.

At the other end, we have seen rogues like HAL, from *2001: A Space Odyssey* who starts malfunctioning and refuses to shut down. HAL starts taking on and killing humans in his effort to achieve his programmed directives.

These, of course, depict our own hopes and fears, as all fiction does. These extremes are just a reflection of the fact that we have always looked at robots as plastic, as only capable of obeying commands who, at worst, can malfunction.

It is only rarely, in movies like *Ex Machina*, that we touch upon the point that what we create might be more than just chips and plastic, that the creator's ego and his biases might play a part in the creation as well.

As robots evolve and machine intelligence starts putting together information much like people do, they might also inherit our biases, our superstitions and worse, our hates. We just might end up with more than what we bargained for.

This could be the reason why in recent years, many folks have been sharing their apprehensions about robots and the future, and these apprehensions should be taken seriously considering the stature of the folks sharing their worries. Stephen Hawking, Bill Gates and Elon Musk have all shared their worries about AI running amok, of the possibility of super-intelligent machines establishing a new world in which humans have no relevance.

These fears led to the signing of the Future of Life Petition[5] to ban AI weapons, following a UN meeting in 2017 on 'killer robots'. Not surprisingly, the meeting ended inconclusively. As a robot might have commented, 'humans are inefficient'.

We also have examples like Arnie's *Terminator* to worry about—scenarios in which robots develop an ability to interact with the world and then desire to conquer it. This could happen, as we read in sci-fi, due to machine hubris. It could also just be a result of the machine's quest for efficiency (like in the case of HAL).

Sir Martin Rees, physicist and astronomer royal, also warned about:

> dumb robots going rogue or a network that develops a mind of its own.[6]

Sir Rees and his colleague Huw Price have created the Centre for Study of Existential Risk at Cambridge to study and help avoid such catastrophic events.

Let me remind you that we are just getting into a new relationship, with machines. A relationship that we honestly do not know much about: a relationship where we are entrusting vital tasks to machines. Tasks like driving, surgery and replacing us in the combat zone.

This means that for the first time, machines that are not directly controlled by us (programmed by us, but not controlled), are going to be taking life and death decisions in complicated, unstructured environments.

Should Machines Be Entrusted with Decisions That Require Moral Judgement?

When we create thinking machines, we are also opening up a whole host of moral and ethical issues.

1. Machine rights: What are the rights of robots and what is the moral obligation of society towards them? We need to look at it much like we look at human and animal rights. Does Sophia have the same rights as other citizens of Saudi Arabia? Sophia is female, in which case does she enjoy rights due to a

female in Saudi Arabia? Or is she a machine, in which case we will have to define machine citizenship rights.

2. How do we code morality into machines? If yes, whose morality? Like we spoke earlier, how will we ensure that the coder's biases do not come into play? In *Alice In Wonderland*, the cat tells Alice:

> We're all mad here. I'm mad. You're mad.[7]

How do we ensure that our lunacy does not creep into our machines?

3. How do we ensure that our machines do not turn rogue on us and in the process, harm us? Remember Frankenstein's monster, who is not as dumb as most think him to be—he teaches himself to read and completes 'Paradise Lost'. Then, he goes rogue and kills Dr Frankenstein's brother and his wife.

4. How do we secure these autonomous agents from being hacked and misused? Security consultants IOActive showed how easy this is.[8] They hacked Alpha 2, an otherwise adorable humanoid personal assistant that is capable of picking up and handing you things that you need, like a screwdriver. IOActive hacked that helpful hand and made Alpha 2 repeatedly stab a tomato with a screwdriver. Remember that it might not be a tomato tomorrow!

The fact is that we have not, at least this far, arrived at conclusions on 1 and 2 and ways and means to prevent 3 and 4. What happens when machines commit acts that are bad, from a human perspective? For humans, we have penal codes and courts, what about robots? The fact is that all of us know that there is a whole Pandora's box out there. And everyone is waiting for someone else to open it.

Do the Answers Lie in Science Fiction?

Considering that science fiction was able to think up most of what we are creating today, maybe that's where our answers lie, as well.

In his 1942 story 'Runaround', Isaac Asimov introduced the Three Laws of Robotics:

1. A robot may not injure a human being or, through inaction, allow a human being to come to harm.
2. A robot must obey the orders given to it by human beings except where such orders would conflict with the first law.
3. A robot must protect its own existence as long as such protection does not conflict with the first or second laws.

These laws were the organizing principles and unifying theme for Asimov's robotics-based fiction. He spent much time testing the boundaries of his three laws to see where they would break down, and to see if they would create paradoxical or unanticipated behaviour.

Asimov himself accepted that no set of fixed laws can sufficiently anticipate all possible circumstances. They do not take into consideration the current evolutionary curve of cognitive machines. It assumes that robots are slaves. It does not take our anthropomorphic tendencies into account and the fact that we might want to see machines as more than slaves. It assumes that a robot follows human instruction, not taking into account today's machine's ability to take a better, more informed, data-led decision. What if the machine knows better?

But then, this might be a great place to start as we have no other benchmark or guideline. Our idea of what is right and wrong, what is acceptable and not is about to undergo some drastic changes.

Indeed, our idea of what is human and what is machine, might change.

We will soon see a time when individuals fight for the right to legally and socially declare their love for an artificially intelligent being. Much like before, we will be a little hesitant to accept a different form of relationship but then, eventually, we may have to find a way to accept it.

Machines will also raise the issue of acceptability. Much as Arthur C. Clarke writes in *Odyssey Two*:

> Whether we are based on carbon or on silicon makes no fundamental difference; we should each be treated with appropriate respect.[9]

As We Engage with Robots, What Are the Rules?

To begin with, we have not identified what the rules that govern these sapient machines are. What is human? What is machine? What lies in between?

Remember the controversy on whether Oscar Pistorius could contest in the Olympics? The International Association of Athletics Federation (IAAF) allowed him in 2012 and Pistorius came in sixth in the 100-metre final. In 2014, however, the IAAF ruled out the participation of Markus Rehm, a long-jumper with a prosthetic leg in Olympics 2016.[10] The fact is, we don't have a policy.

Once we define these, we can move on to the problem of coding morals into machines to ready them for engaging with humans. This is a tough task, considering philosophers and theologians have been debating human morals for ages and we are still debating.

Applying human morals to autonomous machines comes with its own set of problems. Let us consider the classic trolley problem,[11] evolved by Philippa Foot and Judith Thomson.

A runaway train is about to kill five people standing on track 1. Next to it is track 2 where there is only one person. You are watching the entire scene, standing next to a lever that can shunt the train from 1 to 2. Should you make that deliberate switch, saving five people and in the process killing that one person who would have survived if you had not intervened?

Simple math tells you that five persons dying is worse than one person dying. But then, is it just math? Isn't there a moral distinction between actively killing and passively letting die? When you move that lever, are you a saviour who takes responsibility for saving five people or a murderer taking responsibility for killing one person?

Let's take it a step further. What if that one person is a baby? Or what if that one person is your son? With the power of the lever in your hand, would you sacrifice your son to save five people? Or would you passively sacrifice five people to save your son?

Replace the human next to the lever with a machine and we run into a whole host of new problems. The choice won't just be a question of killing one or five, according to Rob Reich, director of Stanford's Center for Ethics in Society. He has many more questions.

> Will these cars optimize for overall human welfare, or will the algorithms prioritize passenger safety or those on the road? Or imagine if automakers decide to put this decision into the consumers' hands, and have them choose whose safety to prioritize. Things get a lot trickier.[12]

Again, the owner of a robot car might reasonably expect that his car (or slave) owes allegiance to him and should value his safety above that of other drivers and pedestrians. What happens if the car is publicly owned? Like a city bus? The publicly owned car has no obligations, so what does this do to the moral calculations?

The fact is that our own ideas of morality and ethics are subjective and, hence, not clearly defined. If we cannot get to one definition of ethics or morality, how do we align AI's ethics and morality with our existing value system? How do we programme 'harm' or 'justice'?

We See Humans As Capable of Moral Decisions, Can AI Replace This Human Ability?

There is no denying that AI is capable of a speed and capacity for processing that is far beyond human capabilities. But can we trust AI to be fair and neutral, always?

We are an extremely biased species. We have a tendency to seek, interpret, favour and recall information in a way that confirms our preexisting beliefs. The more emotionally charged the issue, the stronger and more persuasive our confirmation biases get.

Look at issues where we have been unable to agree on a common, moral stand. What is the moral status of the human embryo? Is the treatment of animals such as guinea pigs in the food industry ethical (even if it is for research that leads to human betterment)? Again, in the same lab, do we see the monkey as different from the lab rat?

What are our obligations towards humans with severe dementia? Where do we stand on euthanasia?

We are biased about all of these. How do we ensure they do not creep into AI? How do we ensure that in Google Photos—where AI is used to identify people, objects and scenes—racial biases do not come in? Or that an algorithm used to predict criminality does not show a racial bias towards specific ethnicities and communities?

One of the biggest questions facing us today is whether Facebook's team of 'content reviewers' had their biases when it came to what showed up on its news feed during the 2016 US electoral battle. Worse, whether the machines that replaced them continued with those biases.

Used right, AI can become a catalyst for positive change. However, the sheer complexity of human value systems makes it very difficult to make AI's motivations human-friendly. Unless we are able to create a flawless theory of ethics (and regulate that well) AI's utility could lead to many potentially harmful scenarios.

What is also unfortunate is that this might lead to AI's true potential never being realized—if we do not get the legalities right, we are not going to see autonomous cars on the roads, are we?

Before We Reach the Brave, New World, We Will Make Mistakes

German philosopher Friedrich Nietzsche's idea of the Übermensch[13]—the 'superior man' or 'overman'—who can rise above conventional Christian morality and values to create and impose his own values is what we need today. From that ethically flawless human should flow the ethically flawless machine.

I sincerely believe that many mistakes lie ahead. And we have to face the fact that people will die. Still, I really think that where we will go will be a better world. Remember that the routes Columbus, Magellan and da Gama discovered were paved with the watery graves of thousands who ventured before them.

The challenges that lie ahead of us span technical, regulatory, philosophical and even theological realms. Over and above the technicalities posed, we will find ourselves in multiple moral quandaries. It might even force us to ask questions of ourselves and tweak our idea of who we are.

There's a whole, unimagined world that lies ahead of us. I like to think of us as people catching glimpses of the future, awaiting eagerly for what is to follow. As John Lennon said:

We were all on this ship in the sixties, our generation, a ship going to discover the New World. And the Beatles were in the crow's nest of that ship.[14]

We are sailing full steam ahead. But as we go, I have a word of advice—be kind to every machine you meet on the way, never thump your fridge, never kick your wheel. It might pay to be in their good books.

THE MAGIC OF MATH

Math is all around us.
And math's ability to find patterns and sequences
where man cannot, is in many ways what is
driving us forward today.
Here are a few joys
that math has brought us.

The Periodic Table: A Matter
of Counting

THE CHEMIST IS A FAIRLY recent character in our history. Until say, about the seventeenth century, we had no chemists, we only had alchemists.

The ancient alchemists dealt primarily with the purification and transformation of metals and, sometimes, delved into spiritual purification as well.

What the alchemists worked towards was what all of us wanted—eternal life and eternal riches. Hence the efforts to discover the elixir of youth and the attempts to transform other metals into gold. All of this gave alchemy a slightly mysterious (and hocus-pocus) air, with images of bearded, secretive, solitary alchemists at work besides bubbling beakers and cauldrons.

When we think about it, things haven't changed much. Our image of the chemist is still that of a man in a lab coat working in isolation.

Frowned upon by the Church and therefore feared by the common man, this art (or pseudoscience) needed a desperate image change and that arrived with the publication of Robert Boyle's *The Sceptical Chymist* in 1661.[1] In it, Boyle argued that all matter consisted of atoms and clusters of atoms in motion. That every phenomenon we observed was the result of particles in motion colliding with each other.

What was also significant about Boyle's pronouncements was that with them, he rejected the prevalent theories of the day.

Including the (then) still popular ancient Greek theory of the four classical elements with which the Greeks explained the nature and complexity of all matter—earth, air, water and fire (Aristotle added a fifth, ether).[2] Boyle migrated us from a philosophical classification of material to a scientific classification and, hence, is rightfully the founder of modern chemistry.

Accidents, Discoveries and the Lack of Structure

One of the reasons chemistry stumbled along for a while before it adopted the rigour of other sciences is that it had to battle the powerful forces of Christian orthodoxy, alchemy and classical Pythagorean belief. The Pythagorean philosophy of numbers is best exemplified by Philolaus of Tarentum who wrote:

> All things, at least those we know, contain Number; for it is evident that nothing whatever can either be thought or known, without Number.[3]

Western chemists combined Christian scripture with classical learning, began seeing trinities everywhere and delved deeper into mystic triadic numerology. Often their scientific purpose became a quest for trinities and wherever they discovered or squeezed in one, it became sacred.

Not surprisingly, much like his older cousin the alchemist, from whom he derived his name, the early chemist was also a bundle of contradictions, as his 'science' was in many cases a science of assumptions. And accidents. These were not men following a structured, scientific approach but gentlemen stumblers stumbling into discoveries.

Nothing can explain this better than the discovery of phosphorous by Henning Brand in 1675.[4] Brand was very sure that he had found the perfect ticket to unlimited wealth, the one that had eluded alchemists all this while—the philosopher's stone, the legendary substance that could turn other base metals into gold. His secret: human urine.

Through various processes, he had managed to convert urine into a translucent, waxy substance (not stone enough, though). Although it did not glitter, the substance did glow and often, on exposure to air, combusted spontaneously. That was phosphorous . . . which fortunately found its use in the manufacture of matches.

This wasn't the case always. There were many discoveries and inventions that found no immediate use. A humorous example is the discovery of nitrous oxide or laughing gas in the early 1800s.[5] For many years, it had no purpose except that it was the drug of choice for English youth until, in 1846, the discovery of the anaesthetic properties of nitrous oxide eased much pain.

The science desperately needed a structure and it was Antoine-Laurent de Lavoisier[6] who pushed chemistry into the modern age. Born in 1743 into minor French nobility, Lavoisier co-authored the *Méthode de Nomenclature Chimique*. Published in 1787 in Paris, this was the first-ever attempt at a methodical classification of all available elements.

In an age in which everyone with a beaker and some urine to spare was discovering something or the other, Lavoisier never discovered an element. (Though he did name oxygen and hydrogen and recognized the role of oxygen in combustion.) But what Lavoisier did do was take the discoveries of others and try to make sense of them.

Soon after the Revolution, Lavoisier was accused by the 'citizens' of selling watered-down tobacco and other crimes. He was summarily guillotined.[7]

By then, he had already laid the foundations for Dmitri Mendeleev.

The Need for Order in Chemistry

After Lavoisier's execution, his wife Marie-Anne Paulze Lavoisier—herself a chemist and contributor to Lavoisier's work—married Count von Rumford,[8] the famous British physicist. He founded the Royal Institution of Great Britain in 1799 and, at that point in time, it was the only institution that actively promoted the youthful science of chemistry.

Chemists were still not united in a common cause and continued to work in isolation with the result that in those times, H_2O_2 meant water to one chemist but hydrogen peroxide to another. C_2H_4 was ethylene to some and marsh gas to others. This lack of a common convention was a dangerous situation.

Into this situation walked in the proverbial mad scientist—Dmitri Ivanovich Mendeleev. With a dream.

> I saw in a dream a table where all elements fell into place as required. Awakening, I immediately wrote it down on a piece of paper, only in one place did a correction later seem necessary.[9]

There is also a story that Mendeleev was inspired by solitaire, the card game which has cards arranged by number vertically and by suit, horizontally. Whether by game or by dream, Mendeleev had created a periodic table of the elements that collated the properties of the elements discovered that far. What it also did—and this is what makes him a genius—is that it predicted the properties of elements yet to be discovered.[10]

The periodic table was based on Mendeleev's Periodic Law which stated that elements, when listed in order of their atomic numbers, fell into recurring groups, so that elements with similar properties occurred at regular intervals.

Mendeleev and Patterns

American science writer Michael Shermer says that humans are pattern-seeking, story-telling animals who are quite adept at creating stories about patterns (that exist or don't).[11]

The story of Mendeleev's periodic table is one of the pattern-seeking human. At that point in the history of chemistry, there were many who were trying to organize and classify all the known elements under one system but had always ended up with two massive obstacles. The first was that they knew that there were elements yet to be discovered that would have to find a place on the table they created. The second was that not all the published information on the known elements was correct.

Around the same time that Mendeleev was dreaming of or playing cards (depending on which version you want to follow), many others, like the German chemist Julius Lothar Meyer,[12] were trying to arrive at the same conclusion but were stumped by the two obstacles mentioned above.

Mendeleev's genius was in spotting a pattern—that when arranged a certain way, certain characteristics of elements were periodically repeated—and finding a way to codify and communicate that pattern. He arranged the elements in horizontal rows called periods and vertical rows called groups. This instantly showed one set of relationships when read vertically and another when read horizontally. This system enabled him to address the two obstacles that others faced: prediction and correction.

In Mendeleev's periodic table, hydrogen came first on the chart because it has one proton and hence the atomic number 1. Uranium has ninety-two protons and, hence, came towards the end. Wherever there were no elements, there could be a prediction. Using this capability of the table, Mendeleeev had predicted the properties of gallium, germanium and scandium way before they were discovered. With this, chemistry became just a matter of counting, as the British science writer Philip Ball[13] pointed out.

In 1913, British physicist Henry Moseley[14] built on Mendeleev's table and created the modern periodic table which addressed the few inconsistencies that the old table had. It also has a lot more elements that fill the beautiful gaps Mendeleev left for them in his table.

Descriptive science observes, records, classifies and describes phenomena. Inferential sciences make inferences based on available data. When he predicted the properties of substances yet to be discovered, Mendeleev's work crossed the imaginary line between inferential and descriptive sciences. He could predict, based on the description that he made regarding the chemical elements.

The Genius of the Table

For chemists, the table brought an orderliness and clarity that led to significant momentum for the science. But for me, the beauty of the table lies in the mathematical pattern that no one else saw. Except Mendeleev. It is mathematics and its ability to identify sequences that actually brought us the periodic table, one of chemistry's single greatest advances.

In Mendeleev's day, there were just sixty-three elements but his ability to see the pattern helped him complete an imaginary picture. He could see—with an accuracy that will please every mathematician—where new elements should slot in, perfectly. Before the table, chemistry was confusing and refused to be classified. But math made chemistry as easy as counting.

Today, there are 118 elements of which element number 117 has a temporary name, Uus. After the death of British fantasy writer Terry Pratchett, his fans have petitioned that 117 be named Octarine (Oc) as a tribute to him.[15]

That would be poetic tribute to math and Mendeleev as well. For Octarine, in Pratchett's Discworld books, is the colour of magic.

Math and Art: The Numbers That Underlie Beauty

I LOVE MATH AND I love art. So, I am not very sure what I was poking through when I came across Hamid Naderi Yeganeh.[1] Hamid is an artist and has created some stunning work. Only, where the name of the piece should be, you are more likely to find something like this:

> This image shows 40,000 circles. For k=1, 2, 3 . . . 40000, the centre of the k-th circle is (X(k), Y(k)) and the radius of the k-th circle is R(k), where . . .[2]

. . . and it goes on into more formulae. Because this is what Hamid's art is, a visual representation of mathematical formulae.

Hamid calls himself a mathematical artist and his work really is stunning. As is the work of a whole lot of artists who are using math to create intricate pattern-based art. In fact, fractal art is now a category of its own.

While this is pretty cool and contemporary, mathematical artists have been around for ages. In fact, I have plenty of mathematical artists for neighbours. Go for a morning stroll in any south Indian town and you will find an intricate mathematical pattern freshly drawn with rice powder in the front of every Hindu home—the kolam.[3]

What is amazing is that as we travel deeper into the villages, these patterns get more intricate and more complex. So here are

women, in many cases illiterate, creating complex patterns and
perfect mathematical presentations in an ethnomathematical effort
that is stunning and intriguing at the same time. While I have no
authoritative source to date this practice, one can safely say that
it has been around for several centuries. Hamid and the kolam
aunties are not exceptions. Everywhere we recognize a pattern and
everywhere we visually convert that into art, is mathematics. As
British theoretical physicist Paul Dirac said:

> God used beautiful mathematics in creating the world.[4]

Patterns are all around us on the planet, in space and time and in
the workings of the human mind. The mathematician spots and
examines these patterns—in numbers, in shapes and in motion.
This is what the artist does as well—she identifies and gives
expression to patterns real and imagined, visual and mental, static
and dynamic.

Mathematics and Art: The Conjugal History

Math and art have been in a relationship for a long, long time
and this relationship exists, in representation, across all cultures.
While kolams (and rangoli) in India might be the only survivors,
pattern-drawing has served its magical and religious purposes
across the world.

The first to put this relationship down on papyrus are, as
is often the case, the Greeks. Aristotle speaks about Pythagoras
and his followers that they were the first to take up mathematics
and advance the subject. But they got so carried away with it,
according to Aristotle, that:

> . . . they fancied that the principles of mathematics were the
> principles of all things.[5]

In the fifth century BC, the Greek sculptor, Polykleitos[6] presented his aesthetic theory, the Kanon, which laid mathematical bases for artistic perfection. According to him, perfection could only be achieved little by little, through many numbers.

What this meant was that each statue should comprise of clearly definable parts, each related to the other by ideal mathematical proportions and balances. For example, Polykleitos treated the last phalange of the little finger as one side of a square. Rotating that square's diagonal gives us a $1:\sqrt{2}$ rectangle, which is the size of the next phalange. This is repeated for the next phalange, then repeating it with the whole little finger provides the palm. The palm provides the forearm, the forearm the elbow, and so on. So a ratio becomes a system capable of describing the human form through continuous geometric progression.

Much later, Leonardo da Vinci would illustrate what is now called the *Vitruvian Man*,[7] based on the notes of the Roman architect Vitruvius. The *Vitruvian Man*, again an attempt to define the proportions of the human body, shows us that Renaissance artists had a clear idea of the blend of mathematics and art. In fact, this sketch best exemplifies da Vinci's attempt to relate man to nature and to the patterns he observed around him.

It is this quest that also led to da Vinci's illustration of Luca Pacioli's *De Divina Proportione* (on the *Divine Proportion*).[8] The subject was mathematical proportions and their application to geometry, architecture and visual arts (perspective). Pacioli famously said:

Without mathematics, there is no art.[9]

It was da Vinci's brilliant illustrations of Pacioli's concepts that helped make popular the idea of geometry.

The title of Pacioli's book derives from the golden ratio.[10] Two quantities are in a golden ratio if their ratio is the same as the ratio of their sum to the larger of the two quantities. The golden ratio (raised to the status of a divine ratio by Pacioli) has been a subject of much interest (and debate) for some of the world's greatest minds. While it does appear in patterns in nature and appears regularly in geometry, there is no evidence to substantiate the golden ratio across nature. Nevertheless, everyone, from mathematicians to artists, biologists, historians, psychologists and architects have debated it. Endlessly.

The acropolis (including the Parthenon) bears in mind the golden ratio. The cathedral at Chartres and even the one at Notre Dame have elements that subscribe to it. Many instances of the golden ratio appear in the Sistine Chapel, the most prominent being in the Creation of Adam. According to a 2015 study,[11] the fingers of God and Adam touch at the golden ratio of the width of the painting. The famous Great Mosque at Kairouan in Tunisia and the Buddhist stupa of Borobudur both subscribe to the golden ratio. While it might not be divine, the ratio does appear secular.

Ratios aside, we also find a lot of math in Renaissance art. Both da Vinci's *Last Supper* and Raphael's *The School of Athens* subscribe to a ratio of 12:6:4:3. Even before that, curvilinear perspective was already showing itself in painting. In 1523, Parmigianino[12] (the little one from Parma) had painted his self-portrait in a convex mirror with his face undistorted at the centre, with the background curving around it and his hand appearing large at the edge. A century before this, Dutch painter Jan van Eyck had painted the *Arnolfini Portrait* which had a convex mirror with reflections of people.

Artists have also used the cavalier perspective to represent three-dimensional space. Imported into Europe from the Chinese who had been using it from almost the second century BC, the cavalier perspective does not attempt to give an illusion of what can be seen, but gives an idea of depth. The Chinese acquired this from the Indians who in turn supposedly got it from ancient Romans.

In this context, the early twentieth century was a time of frenzied activity, both for science and art. Scientists and mathematicians were venturing into hitherto unknown (and in many cases, subatomic) areas. As has always been the case, the scientific zeitgeist of the era was playing a leading role in defining the art of the era.

Science and Hypothesis,[13] the seminal work by French mathematician Henri Poincaré was widely read by the artists of the early twentieth century. Poincaré opined that Euclidean geometry could well be just one of the many possible geometric configurations. This suggested the possible existence of a fourth dimension. His influence can be seen in the work of cubists like Pablo Picasso and Jean Metzinger. They were convinced that painting could be expressed mathematically, in colour and form.

The cubists were also inspired by the advances being made in crystallography[14] (in 1912, Max von Laue had just discovered that crystals could diffract X-rays). While the scientists were going from macro to micro, so were the artists—their interest had also shifted from human features to the underlying geometry as can be seen in Picasso's *Portrait of Daniel-Henry Kahnweiler*. They were also able to now see the crystalline nature of landscapes, as can be seen in Georges Braque's *Houses at l'Estaque*.

Mathematical models also inspired the Dadaists[15] and the inspiration has been transmitted, with greater intensity, to mathematical artists like Hamid.

Geometric Algorithms and Perspective in Art

You look at the Italian painters, especially the Renaissance artists, and you see considerable knowledge and the use of the geometric algorithm. Paolo Uccello incorporates linear perspective in the

Battle of San Romano. The *Last Supper* and *Mona Lisa* also use linear perspective with a vanishing point for depth.

Uccello's *Perspective Study of a Chalice* is an even better illustration of the geometric algorithm that went into Renaissance painting. Take a look at it and you will be surprised at the resemblance it bears to contemporary wireframe design.[16]

When you think about it, this is not so surprising. Both Uccello and today's computer artist are trying to answer the same question—how does one represent volumetric shapes? And how do these basic shapes come together to create the reality that we see?

While today's computer artist shares a bond with the Renaissance painter when it comes to an ability to represent volume, the resemblance ends there. Most of these artists were not just painters or sculptors but were multifaceted men—they were scientists, architects and mathematicians.

Da Vinci invented the anemometer, multi-barrel cannons, the parachute, a self-propelled cart and much else. He left behind sketches for a flying machine, a helicopter, an armoured car and others. Michelangelo, while not a great inventor, was great at giving shape on paper to the ideas of others. Piero della Francesca authored books on math like *Short Book on the Five Regular Solids*, *Abacus Treatise* and *On Perspective in Painting*.

So, what was it about Italian artists and math? Why did they have this fascination for math and geometry?

Michael Baxandall has an extremely interesting answer for that in his book *Painting and Experience in Fifteenth-Century Italy*.[17] The Italian artists, according to him, were skilled in math thanks to the lack of standardized containers in Italy!

The Italian artist was a member of the merchant class and, as merchants, they needed to be skilled in volumetric gauging to look at containers of all shapes and sizes and arrive at their respective volumes! To do this, your algebra and geometry needed to be perfect.

This would shake up most of our artists today, but the fact is that to be a Renaissance artist in Italy, you needed a sound mathematical education.

Geometry and Religious Art

Geometry, art and God have been fellow travellers for a while now, the first recorded instance coming (as usual) from the ancient Greeks. According to Plutarch, it was Plato who said that:

God geometrizes continually.[18]

The mandala[19] is the perfect coming together of math, art and religion. From the Sanskrit for 'circle', the term 'mandala' refers to the sense of wholeness and harmony created by the circular form. Mandalas are way more complex than the kolam and combine geometry, religious symbolism and meaning.

In a mandala, the symmetries increase as we move outwards. The centre has only bilateral symmetry, but the outermost circle has infinite symmetry. Therefore the centre, in its perfection, represents the order of the gods and heaven while the outer circle represents the chaos of mankind and the material world.

Alongside his Buddhist and Jain counterparts with their mandalas, the ancient Hindu priest had to get his math right as well. Much like the Italian merchant/artist, knowledge of math and geometry was critical to the Hindu priest's function.

In fact, it is possible that the need to determine the right time for Vedic ceremonies and the accurate construction of altars was what led to the development of astronomy and geometry in Vedic India. The Taittiriya Samhita and the Rig Veda (1700–1100 BC), some of the oldest Hindu texts, contain rules for the construction of fire altars.

It is probably the math required for the construction of altars that led to the development of geometry, especially the rules for geometric shapes like triangles, rectangles, squares, circles and trapezia, equivalence through numbers and leading from there on to squaring the circle, estimations for pi and early forms of the Pythagoras theorem.[20]

The ancient Indians, Greeks and Egyptians knew how to double the sizes of relatively complex geometric figures.[21] They probably developed these calculations to alter the sizes of their altars during calamities. It was believed that the plague could be alleviated by doubling the size of the altar (doubling a cube is also referred to as the Delian problem).

Many scientists, as well, believed in the divine geometer which is why they also keep spotting math in religion. The math, the patterns and the role of the divine geometer that we keep seeing in religious practices is sometimes a human construction laid atop nature and often religious art has brought a cultural context to the underlying pattern.

Art Takes from and Art Gives to Math

Filippo Brunelleschi[22] is considered one of the founding fathers of the Renaissance. How a goldsmith managed to transcend the lifelessness of pre-Renaissance art to develop a technique for linear perspective and realism in art is lost in medieval mists. But the linear perspective he formulated dictated the pictorial depiction of space until the late nineteenth century.

For Brunelleschi—who was also an engineer, architect, sculptor, mathematician and ship designer (and hence, of a scientific temperament like other Renaissance geniuses to follow)—the two famous panels in which he first explored the linear perspective were more an expression of his ideas on Euclidean geometry than an artistic expression. This had a profound influence not just on the art of the era but also on modern science.

While Euclidean geometry has to do with our mental conception of the world around us, projective geometry captures some of the patterns that enable us to visualize the world— because our visual input is two flat two-dimensional images falling on our retina that our brain is then able to convert into a three-dimensional image with depth perception.

Brunelleschi's theory of perspective led to French mathematician Girard Desargues's research on projective geometry in a classic case of art stimulating mathematics. Desargues's work led to further work on geometric projections by Brook Taylor, Johann Heinrich Lambert and Jean-Victor Poncelet.

Galileo once said:

> The universe is written in the language of mathematics, and its characters are triangles, circles, and other geometric figures.[23]

Therefore, in his opinion, artists who needed to understand the world around them needed to first understand mathematics and mathematicians needed to be able to appreciate art with the application of geometry and rationality.

Desargues looked at Brunelleschi's work critically and was able to bring centuries of work in optics from Alhazen to Kepler to a fitting conclusion.

Origami has also been much used for a better understanding and explanation of Euclidean geometry and mathematics. We have the American mathematician John Montroll and physicist Robert J. Lang who are proficient in origami and use it to explore the relationship between aesthetics and its underlying mathematics.

Closer home in India, in 1893, T. Sundara Row demonstrated geometric proofs with paper-folding in his work *Geometric Exercises in Paper Folding*.[24] Paper-folding has also been explored in Maekawa's and Kawasaki's theorems and the Huzita-Hatori axioms.

So, art does not just imitate life, it imitates math as well and as we have just seen, very often math imitates art too.

The Truly Mathematical Artist

The 1940s could well be among the most turbulent years ever in world history and this had its repercussions, naturally, on art as well. Very soon we would see surrealism, abstract expressionism and the emergence of Latin American art. Many would see this as an escape from a life that had become quite horrible for nearly everyone. (At the other end, we also had socialist realism in Russia.) While all this chaos was happening around him, Maurits Cornelis Escher[25] was finding inspiration in symmetry.

Earlier in his career, Escher focused on studies of plants, insects and landscapes. Then he happened to travel through Spain and Italy, concentrating on architectural drawings and townscapes.

Moorish architecture interested him and he became increasingly interested in the mathematical structure of the tiling of the Alhambra and the Mezquita Cathedral. These intricate decorative designs based on geometric symmetries featuring interlocking repetitive patterns triggered his interest in the math of tessellation.[26] The rest is history.

Escher was not mathematically trained but yet, his work is easily the best example of an artist whose work explores multiple connections between art and math. He figured out the math he needed to bring his ideas to life.

He explored polyhedra, stars, living structures, mobius strips, knots and spatial grids in his work. He explored multiple geometries—Euclidean, projective, hyperbolic and spherical— and sometimes fused them. He explored topological distortions and transformations, multiple perspectives and visual recursions.

He explored combinatorial geometries and abstract mathematical concepts.

He explored symmetry and tessellation in the plane, on the sphere and in the Poincaré disk. He also developed his own theory of the classification of planar tilings and their symmetric colouring, anticipating the studies of later mathematicians and crystallographers.

From Escher's early work, we see a preference for repetition and clean shapes. By the mid-'30s, his work was beginning to show the style he is known for today. Distortions, optical illusions and recursions were very visible.

Escher might not have understood mathematical recursion but recursion is what most of us know Escher's work for. Recursion is a simple concept that most of us have seen at the barber's shop. When a barber has a mirror in front of you and one behind you, the reflected mirror reflects itself and does so indefinitely.

In many of his pieces, Escher combines pattern repetition and recursion in unique ways; exhibiting complex mathematical and physical ideas. In *Swans* (1956), the swans are tiled very precisely with the same distance between adjacent swans and swans in the next row. They also are in a closed loop, a concept made possible by recursion.

Escher's interest in mathematics, geometry and topology led to his fascination for concepts like the mobius strip—paradoxical concepts that are common in math but take the layman a little effort to comprehend, as they visually defy physics as we know it. Much of his later work focused on these optical illusions, teasing our vision and our idea of perspectives.

His most famous work, of course, is *Relativity* (1953) and this could well be the best example of his experiments with illusions, patterns and recursion. In *Relativity*, we see three different planes and people on all three planes, all bound by the laws of gravity. Our idea of perspectives tells us that at some point, two people on two different planes should cross each other, but they never do. Each plane is brilliantly extended beyond our field of vision.

If you wish to see an apt example of a fractal, take a look at *Circle Limit III* (1959).[27] At the centre are fish perfectly aligned to each other. But as we go further out, we hit the chaos of the mandala, with the pattern becoming more complex and more and more fish fitting into the same area until the border of the image becomes an infinite repetition of the same design. This is a brilliant example of recursion and fractals, a good two decades before Benoit Mandelbrot began to study fractals.

Fractals: Going beyond Euclidean Geometry

It was the French-American mathematician Benoit Mandelbrot who coined the term 'fractals' and 'fractal geometry' in 1975. He poetically described fractal geometry as 'the forms that Euclid leaves aside' and stated that things considered 'rough' or 'chaotic', like clouds and the jagged coastline, actually had a degree of order.[28]

He was able to see a mathematical structure in objects like trees, clouds, snowflakes and mountains where we (or Euclid) cannot spot a pattern or structure (hence rough).

He was also able to see that these shapes have something aesthetic and intuitive in common. Think about a small sand dune and you'll see that it has the same shape as a large sand dune, a small cloud is similar to a large cloud. This similarity at different scales explains fractals (to a layman).

Mandelbrot believed that fractals were more natural than the artificially smooth objects of Euclidean geometry. In the introduction to the *Fractal Nature of Geometry*, he wrote:

> Clouds are not spheres, mountains are not cones, coastlines are not circles, and bark is not smooth, nor does lightning travel in a straight line.

The man did write well.

Since the universe is fractal in nature (and not Euclidean), Mandelbrot's fractal mathematics captured the infinite complexity of nature. This inspired scientists across the board—in medicine, engineering, cosmology, genetics. It also inspired artists.

Fractal art first became popular in the late '80s with colourful, computer-generated patterns. Today it is a genre of digital art where generative art, computer art and fractals combine to produce abstract art. Hamid Yeganeh, Carlo Ginzburg and the musician Bruno Degazio are leading fractal artists. With computer graphics, today's mathematicians can also express their mind with a 'performance', much like how a musician does music.

Kerry Mitchell, who wrote the *Fractal Art Manifesto,* dispels the notion that fractal art is computerized art, unpredictable and lacking in rules, something that anyone with a computer can do. Fractal art, he claims:

. . . is expressive, creative, and requires input, effort and intelligence.[29]

Mandelbrot's simple yet profound insight helped us see order in this fractal universe we live in; order where we formerly saw only chaos.

Now AI Creates (or Makes) Art

In 2015, Google shared DeepDream, a computer vision programme created by Alexander Mordvintsev. DeepDream, as the name suggests, creates dream-like hallucinogenic effects by over-processing images.

The programme detects known patterns (like a face or a tree) in images and then uses that as a pattern to algorithmically generate psychedelic or surreal images. (The images bear considerable resemblance to LSD-induced hallucinations because of a functional resemblance between the artificial neural networks and certain layers of the visual cortex.)

Is DeepDream a work of art? Or is it just an algorithm? Or a mathematical formula expressed visually? Will a Hamid Yeganeh be mentioned in the same breath as a Warhol, a Picasso or a da Vinci a few generations later? Will an AI system that 'creates' art tomorrow be considered an artist or a programme?

According to Mike Tyka, one of the brains behind DeepDream, artists are artists even if it is AI and not a brush helping them create art:

Ultimately, they're making all the aesthetic choices.[30]

From seeing math in art to having math create art, we have come a long way indeed. We question the mathematical and fractal artist much like the people of the day have always questioned the art movement of their day. We wonder, can what mathematics creates be considered art? Can mathematics create beauty? To that I can only say that G.H. Hardy has the last word:

Beauty is the first test; there is no permanent place in the world for ugly mathematics.[31]

Let us just add a corollary to Hardy's thought and say that if it is not beautiful art, it will not stand the test of time.

The Idea of Math: Where Did
It Come from?

MOST OF US WOULD STILL be able to state the Pythagoras theorem from memory. Pythagoras is credited with providing the first proof for the theorem, sometime in the fifth century BC.

But the world has existed for 4.5 billion years. And all that while, the square of the hypotenuse has been the sum of the squares of the other two sides. So how old does that make the Pythagoras theorem? As old as 4.5 billion years or twenty-five odd centuries?

There are two roads that diverge into the mathematical woods right now—the Platonist path and the non-Platonist path.[1]

You can take the road that claims that as long as this world has existed, the Pythagoras theorem has too. For, what it proves did not come into existence in the fifth century. If you do that, you would be a mathematical Platonist and believe that mathematics is a discovery.

As I heard Sir Roger Penrose once say in an interview:

> I like to think of mathematics a bit like geology or archeology, where you're really exploring beautiful things out there in the world, which have been out there, in fact, for ages and ages, and you're revealing them for the first time.[2]

Not to be left behind is Srinivasa Ramanujan, the Indian mathematician who famously said:

An equation for me has no meaning unless it expresses a thought of god.[3]

Mathematical Platonism is the metaphysical view that numbers exist independent of us; that just as we did not bring planets or atoms into being, neither did we bring mathematics into being. It exists as a collection of abstract mathematical objects independent of man, his thought, his language and his practices.[4] It has a reality independent of the ordinary reality of physical objects and such.

A mathematical truth, therefore, can only be discovered because it exists a priori and not as a consequence of human experience. Even if the world were to end tomorrow, mathematics would still exist.

All mathematical Platonists would claim, like Paul Dirac, that:

God is a mathematician of a very high order and He used advanced mathematics in constructing the universe.[5]

Now, if you were to take the other road and say that this was indeed a Pythagorean invention and not a discovery that would make you a non-Platonist.

And while less romantic, the non-Platonist has a point as well. That we find math so ubiquitous to the physical world around us is because we invented math to do precisely that! It is our invention and we keep making more up as we go along, to explain how the universe works. If the world ends tomorrow, math disappears alongside us and so does the *Complete Works of Shakespeare* and the square on the hypotenuse.

When we argue a cause, we do tend to cherry-pick problems for which we have found a solution. All we are looking at is problems to which we have applied math and succeeded. We ignore the many where math was not applied, or math wasn't successful at proving. Transistors are a lovely example. We had beautiful formulae that could describe transistor behaviour until we went sub-micrometre and discovered that all our elegant math did not hold at all in a quantum world. If math indeed existed a priori, then our equations should have held true.

There is no guarantee then that the mathematical descriptions we create will always be universally applicable, which makes math nothing but a human construct.

Let's soothe this rather loud and philosophical mathematical argument with some music. Music is a rather interesting lens through which to view this debate.

Music and mathematics have always sailed together. From the time of Plato, harmony was considered a fundamental part of physics.

Not just the Greeks, the Chinese and the Indians also took a mathematical approach to music, attempting to prove that harmonics and rhythms were bound by mathematical laws and that understanding these was essential for a better understanding of our world and of the music of the spheres.

As the German mathematician Gottfried von Leibniz said:

> Music is the pleasure the human soul experiences from counting without being aware that it is counting.[6]

The Pythagoreans, Frequency and Patterns

> Let no man ignorant of geometry enter here.[7]

This is what tradition says was inscribed on the doorway of Plato's academy. Plato's philosophy and therefore that of Aristotle and later the Western civilization was influenced by Pythagoras. When Plato said:

> . . . god ever geometrises

it was Pythagoras and his thoughts that Plato was echoing. Pythagoras believed in the cosmic mathematician, which is why he could hear mathematics in the music of the cosmos:

> There is geometry in the humming of the strings, there is music in the spacing of the spheres.[8]

There is math in music. But did the math always exist in the music of the cosmos or is it just a layer of symmetry that we invented and then applied on to music? Here is another Pythagorean story that deepens the dilemma. (I'm 99 per cent sure that this story is cooked up, but I steadfastly hold on to that 1 per cent possibility that it is true. For it is anecdotes like these that make mathematics poetry.)

So here is Pythagoras strolling through the market (at Samos or Kroton) when he passes the smithy. Imagine in the background, a blacksmith hammering away. Something about this strikes Pythagoras as odd.

Some of the hammer sounds were harmonious while the others were not. Pythagoras rushes back to the smithy to investigate (as they always do in stories). He finds a mathematical relation between the weight of the hammers and the sound they produce.

If the weight of two hammers forms a whole-number ratio (say 2:1), the strike is musical. Because when we use two hammers, one half the weight of the other, what we produce is the simplest musical interval—the perfect octave. The perfect octave is the interval between one musical pitch and another with half (or double) its frequency. Pythagoras took this understanding forward and figured that the pitch of a vibrating string is proportional to, and can be controlled by, its length. Thus a string would be one octave higher than another that was twice its length. As we know from school, the shorter the string, the higher the pitch.

While this story is apocryphal, it has a beautiful note to it. It makes the Pythagoreans the first to look into the expression of musical scales in terms of mathematical ratios (although Indians would debate this). Or, to put it into a Platonist perspective, they were the first to spot the patterns that unite numbers and music.

Musical pieces often have repeating choruses or bars. In mathematics, we look at patterns to explain the known and predict the unknown. Similarly, musicians look for notes they recognize to find notes that are less familiar. These patterns are fundamental to both mathematics and music.

A Mathematical Harmony

Music and mathematics inhabit a different, more beautiful world. As Bertrand Russell stated in one of his radio lectures:

> Mathematics must live, with music and poetry, in the region of man-made beauty, not amid the dust and grime of the world.[9]

Music and math always overlap—from the complexity of a Bach fugue to the melody of a Nusrat Fateh Ali Khan to the rhythm of an Ustad Zakir Hussain. All of these have math to it; it is just that sometimes we don't notice it. What is it that makes us fall in love with certain pieces of music? Why do some pieces become excessively popular and some pieces fall through the cracks?

German composer Johann Pachelbel's 'Canon' in D major, for example, is an eternal favourite because of its repetitive structure. For this very same reason hip-hop is popular with its rhythmic beats and looping breaks. Is it the preexisting mathematical structure that made us fall in love with these, then?

Or is it just a function of the fact that once we know how a pattern works, we tend to keep repeating it? Most of the time without knowing the math behind it? Remember the foot-tapping opening chords of the Beatles' song 'A Hard Day's Night'? Jason Brown, a professor of mathematics, used a mathematical tool (a Fourier Transform) to analyse the instruments used to make up these opening chords.[10] He is now using the results as inspiration for new songs.

It remains to be seen whether Jason Brown can become James Brown. But if he does create music that you want to dance to, remember that these beats, rhythms, harmonies and melodies are *created* with mathematics. These are not compositions to which we later ascribe a pattern.

Music Theory and Pattern Recognition

The basic units of Sanskrit poetry are two types of syllables—the short syllable (one beat) and the long syllable (two beats). If you are writing a poem and have 'n' number of beats left to complete a stanza, how many combinations of longs and shorts would you have? Around 1100 CE, Hemachandra, the Jain scholar, was considering this and he came up with the sequence 1, 2, 3, 5, 8, 13, 21, 34 . . . Here if 'n' is 1 the answer is 1, if 'n' is 2 the answer is 2, if 'n' is 3 the answer is 3, if 'n' is 4 the answer is 5, and so on. These are called the Hemachandra numbers.[11]

Recognize this recurrence relation? Yes, this indeed is the Fibonacci series.[12] Only, Hemachandra, and before him ancient Indian mathematicians Virahanka and Gopala, was discussing the Fibonacci sequence centuries before Fibonacci. Even Pingala's work, in the third or second century BC contains this sequence, called *mātrāmeru*. (By the way, Hemachandra was also called *Kali-Kāla-Sarvajña*—meaning 'he of the Kali Yuga who knows all'.)

But here of course the debate is not Hemachandra versus Fibonacci. The debate is which comes first, the sequence or Fibonnaci. Can we argue that the math of the sequence was always there, waiting for centuries to be discovered?

Much like the golden ratio, the Fibonacci sequence is one of the fundamental sequences omnipresent across the cosmos in various structures and patterns. In the structure of spiral galaxies, in how seeds are placed in a sunflower, in the pine cone, in petals of flowers, in hurricanes. It is practically everywhere.

Many would claim that the sequence is an integral part of the universe and all Fibonacci did was come along later and discover it.

Going back to music, is modern mathematics the foundation of all music? No. But can music be described mathematically? Most definitely yes. Basic elements of music such as form, rhythm, metre, pitch and tempo exhibit mathematical properties and have analogies in geometry. Hemachandra and other Indian poets, musicians and prosodists used these mathematical and geometric patterns in their studies of metre and music.

Music theory and its relationship with patterns is also a great aid to the musician—composer and performer. A Carnatic classical singer, for example, will sing hundreds of variations of an alap (the opening sequence in a classical concert). Does he or she memorize each and every one of these notes? That would be impossible.

What the singer does is recognize and understand a pattern. With this ability for pattern recognition, a singer builds a musical memory. This very same ability also helps the aficionado remember and appreciate a piece as a whole, rather than the isolated, dissociated syllables.

Music and mathematics might not be bonded axiomatically, but the relationship they share is what makes the world a happier place. As Ralph Waldo Emerson wrote:

. . . for we do not listen with the best regard to the verses of a man who is only a poet, nor to his problems if he is only an algebraist; but if a man is at once acquainted with the geometric foundation of things and with their festal splendour, his poetry is exact and his arithmetic musical.[13]

Music Came First, Pattern Later

John G. Cramer, a physicist at the University of Washington, decided to recreate the sound of the Big Bang.[14] He used data collected by satellites inspecting electromagnetic radiation remnants from the Big Bang. A computer programme converted this data into sound. For some, it sounded like an old computer game powering down. For many, it sounded like a long, drawn-out fart.

But from this cosmic hum onwards, we have to accept that music is as much a storehouse of our history, culture and heritage as anything else. It has been there all along. It has been part of us since the time man lived in Africa, closely connected with nature—when there was a direct and explicit connection between forest sounds and music.

In fact, tribes like the Bayaka of the Central African Republic still dance to the natural music around them, like the music of rain. For them, their music is the music of nature.

Music is old and intrinsic to man. Didn't we just see the math later? Isn't the pattern we recognize just an artificial layer of symmetry that we are laying atop music? Isn't that artificial layer—mathematics—just an artificial human construct where none maybe, exists?

This Is a Question That Boggled Even Einstein

How can it be that mathematics, being after all a product of human thought which is independent of experience, is so admirably appropriate to the objects of reality?[15]

I found this quite amusing: replying on Twitter to someone who wished he had better English skills to understand what Neil deGrasse Tyson tweeted about. Tyson said:

> Learn Math first. That is the language of the Universe. Later, you can worry about understanding my English.[16]

Everywhere you turn, you find a Platonist.

Discovered or Invented?

If it boggled Einstein, it cannot be easy; which is what makes the question even more tantalizing. Philosophers and mathematicians down the ages have argued it out, without consensus, which I think there never will be and which, to me, is the eternal beauty—almost akin to peering into God's mind. (If He indeed is a mathematician.)

Think about it. As invention or as discovery, we as a species have something that can describe *most* of the physical world as we know it. With a great degree of precision! Newton's theory had an accuracy of 10^7 and by the time Einstein's theory came along, it had gone up to 10^{14}.[17]

Dr Richard Feynman had to put it more interestingly.[18] Speaking of mathematical accuracy in the mid-'80s, he said that it was the equivalent of measuring the distance from LA to NY (over 4800 km) to within the width of a human hair. A truly astonishing science, the boundaries of which we are yet to discover.

We might also, with the power of deduction that math itself has put in our hands with AI, discover more and more profound truths about the universe that show math to be independent and unbound, a fundamental cosmic truth.

I believe it is the beauty of math that poses to us such beguiling and intriguing questions. I also believe that the beauty is that it is a combination of discoveries and inventions. Hear me out.

Hemachandra and maybe many Indian mathematicians before him knew of the existence of the sequence, but it was Fibonacci who defined it. And having defined it, made possible the many discoveries that followed. Once a mathematician 'invents' a concept, all manner of discoveries become possible.

Imaginary numbers (complex numbers) are another example. Although it was first proposed by Hero of Alexandria in the first century AD, it started gaining acceptance only in the eighteenth century with the work of Swiss mathematician Leonhard Euler, and later in the early nineteenth century with the work of the German genius, Gauss.[19] Once it was defined and packaged, it spawned a whole lot of discoveries and inventions, including applications in quantum mechanics. While imaginary numbers did not change the essential nature of mechanics, it gave us a way to comprehend it.

The discovery of fractals set off a flurry among Platonists, who held that mathematicians had discovered and not invented them. But the fact also is that fractals are analytical mathematical expressions that have been invented by the human mind to explain a curve or a geometric figure. It is we who have invented them and put them to use to model structures in which patterns recur.

It is good that we have this argument. And have been having this for centuries. Because if we accept a Platonist approach and agree that math is discovered, will we be motivated to dive deeper? Will we be motivated to challenge the last mathematician who presented his version as the proof to a theorem? It would be akin to agreeing to creationism. For once we accept that the planet is only 6000 years old (as Bible scholars still hold), what motivates us to seek the truth behind man and the cosmos?

I believe that the triumph of the human spirit is the belief that we have a lot more to invent and challenge. And that is driving math to places we honestly have no idea about. We invented it and we make up more of it as we go along when we need to explain more and more of the new world that we see.

Let's keep asking the questions. For as Roger Bacon said:

Mathematics is the door and key to sciences.[20]

And may I add, to music as well.

The Prediction of Neptune: Calculated into Existence

THERE ARE NO CLAIMANTS TO the discovery of Mercury, Venus, Mars, Jupiter and Saturn. All man had to do was look up and there they were, right there, in the night-time sky. Uranus and Pluto (demoted a little later) needed telescopes. And Neptune needed a pen.

That's right. Neptune is not a planet visible to the naked eye, nor was it one that an astronomer observed first. It was a planet that a French mathematician, Urbain Jean Joseph le Verrier,[1] calculated must exist. And here's the story of how a planet appeared where a mathematician calculated it should.

In Various Ways, Math Has Always Explained the Universe

Since the time of the ancient Indians and Babylonians, mathematics has been at the very centre of astronomy and cosmology. Much of the use for math in astronomy then was to forecast planetary positions in alignment with each civilization's scriptures.

In the sixteenth century, our idea of the cosmos changed—with the announcement in 1543 by the Polish astronomer and mathematician Nicolaus Copernicus that the Earth and all the other planets revolved around the sun. This led Johannes Kepler, the German mathematics teacher, to evolve the laws of planetary motion,[2] which in turn led to Sir Isaac Newton's deduction of how forces between the planets interacted—specifically, gravitational forces.

Note: this again was a mathematical deduction. Newton said:

> I deduced that the forces which keep the Planets in their Orbs must be reciprocally as the squares of their distances from the centres about which they revolve; and thereby compared the force requisite to keep the Moon in her Orb with the force of gravity at the surface of the earth and found them to answer pretty nearly.[3]

Newton's reservations about his own calculations and the observation of tiny irregularities in the motion of Mars led Albert Einstein to devise his theory of general relativity—in which he explains the fundamentals of gravity, space-time, relativity and quantum theories.

It was mathematics that led the way. Observation followed.

What math is—whether it is an invention or a discovery—remains an eternal debate, but what we know for certain is that it has an uncanny, magical ability to see patterns in nature to discover and explain the realities of life.

As Ian Stewart says in his book *Calculating the Cosmos*:

> . . . there are mathematical patterns in the motions and structure of both celestial and terrestrial bodies, from the smallest dust particle to the universe as a whole. Understanding those patterns allows us not just to explain the cosmos, but also to explore it, exploit it, and protect ourselves against it.[4]

What Led to the Calculation of Neptune?

In 1781, astronomer Sir William Herschel discovered Uranus.[5] (He was also the first astronomer to describe the structure of the Milky Way as spiral.) After Uranus was classified a planet, astronomers were a little perplexed by its strange orbit. There was a series of irregularities in its orbit that could not be explained by Newton's laws of gravitation. They could be explained, however, if the gravity of a farther, unknown planet were disturbing its orbit.

Le Verrier addressed these discrepancies with Uranus's orbit and the laws of Kepler and Newton with mathematics. He calculated the location of a planet impacting Uranus's orbit and sent it to his friend, astronomer Johann Gottfried Galle at the Berlin Observatory.

Galle spotted and confirmed the existence of Neptune on the very night that he received le Verrier's letter. And that too within 1° of the predicted position![6]

Math, Patterns and the Ability to See Beyond

This is the magical story of the first planet that was calculated into existence. As the French astronomer, François Arago, put it beautifully, le Verrier discovered a planet:

. . . with the point of his pen.[7]

Here was a man who calculated the existence of a planet that is 4.4 billion kilometres from Earth, shrouded in blue methane clouds that whip around the planet at 1600 kmph and cannot be seen from the Earth except through a telescope.

But nothing can hide from math.

SECTION IV

THE END OF MYSTERY

The data-crunching abilities that AI comes with,
together with math's ability to spot patterns, can
help end some of our greatest mysteries.
But do not mourn the end of mystery;
we will always find more.

Astrology: Will Data Science Change Astrology's Fortunes?

14 BILLION YEARS AGO WAS heard the first note.
A BIG BANG.
And it's been playing ever since—the wise say, in B flat.
Around seventy million years ago came an opposable thumb.
And Neanderthal walked just 2,50,000 years ago.
Man, erect and proud, took a little longer.
We became hunter-gatherers.
We had only the forces of nature around us,
We were in awe.
The sun, the moon, the stars
Hummed a silent song as they twinkled along.

The ages kept rolling by.
Stone, iron and bronze.
(Heavy metal came later.)

And faintly, we began hearing the song.
We started keeping the beat of time.
The nature, the pattern, the pass of days.
The sun, the moon and the heavens have a rhythm, the listeners said,
And that's winter, summer, monsoon, spring.

We started wondering,
Are we alone? Are we created?

Is someone up there in the sky? The one with intelligent design?
Otherwise, this wonderland, this hugely curious place,
Couldn't have been; imagined, designed, engineered, crafted.

And we started worshipping.
The celestial, the wrath of nature, drought, flood, tsunami, fire.
Animism sated us awhile.

While much didn't make sense, much did.
We figured.
The dance in the sky, the changes on the Earth are correlated.
We figured.
This is the language of the creators, their twinkly, sign language.

In Babylon.
In China.
Along the Nile and about the Indus.
The Greeks.
The Mayans.
Each made meaning of his own sky.
And its changing, repeating patterns.
The same story, with different gods.

Each culture developed its own methodology for making meaning
    of the sky.
Started keeping account of the stars.
And juxtaposing the pattern in the sky
    to foretell the script to which we were born.

We extrapolated these patterns to our human lives.
We cleverly divided the sky into twelve parts.
Into familiar forms—bull and sheep and lion.

And now that we had the zodiac,
The rest of the narrative was easily told.

The pattern and the animal foretold our tale.
We were born to a script,
And fatalistically, lived this script tight.

3800 years ago, or so goes the tale,
Abraham wrote the Book of Formation.
Astrology, cosmology, all the secrets of life.

The Jews kept account.
An account of stars, of things, of everyday life.
They noticed eclipses, conjunctions, exaltation
. . . celestial harmonies and synchronies.
They noted Jupiter and Saturn, line up thrice in Pisces.
A once in a millennium occurrence.

Soon, they were able to see more.
A Star, they said, will herald the Son of God.
'I see him, but not now;
I behold him, but not near;
A Star shall come out of Jacob;
A Sceptre shall rise out of Israel.'¹

Sometimes, events did follow the pattern told.
Sometimes, most times, not.
Sceptics called this superstition.
And people's ability to ignore the inconsistency of prediction,
    as conformation bias.

Believers couldn't care less.

For him who believed, patterns worked.
The inconsistency with scientific logic became the shortcomings
    of science.

The believers identified.
With the characterization in the zodiac.
The believers identified.
With the said descriptions of their personality.
Their likes and dislikes.
Their mating preferences.
Therein lies a good case of collaborative filtering.[2]

Too generalized, psychologists will say.
Too broad-based, this zodiac and our natures.
We all have some cockroach,
Some frog, some scorpion,
Some goat, some sheep, some fish in us.
But somewhere the data provided by time, by stars,
By formations,
The astrology of things had been appropriated by religion.
And that put it beyond the pale,
Beyond the rigour of questioning.
The answers of astrology could never be subject to the questions
    of science!

There have been honest attempts, and here and there.
But with sincere and due respect to all of them,
They were all on a meek scale.
With modest ambition and objectives.

But at no other time in the history of man,
Have we been able to see farther,
Look deeper, hear clearer.

We see more stars than Abraham.
More constellations than Ptolemy.
Make better models than Copernicus.

Mathematics, statistics, data sciences, astro and quantum physics.
    We know all the particles.
This is the age that Kepler and Galileo fantasized about on
    Sundays.

Isn't it time then for the search?
For the 'God's particle' of the astrological kind?
Compute the patterns, scientifically?
The stars and their mysteries,
Astrology deserves a large Hadron Collider of its own.
I think so.

With our ability to map every movement in the sky.
With our ability to gather all data of events,
And shape of human life.
With our ability to big data all these inputs.
With our ability to see the causal relationships.
With our ability to detect the absence of them.
With our ability to bring enormous computational power.
With our ability to comprehend patterns.

We have a need to know.
That is what makes us erect and proud.
To know if there is a correlation,
Between the great bear and the bear market,
To know if stars are dumb or smart.

I am no Yuri Milner,
I can't spare no millions.

For aliens.
Enthusiasm and energy, yes I have.
Curiosity and passion, yes.
(And maybe, some money)
Let's look at a data science-led, scientific inquiry into this mystery.

Let me know, let me know for once.
Is that just a diamond in the sky?

The Happiness Pill: Science or Fiction?

I REMEMBER THE POSTERS WE had to create in school. These would then be put up on the walls to add to the visual disaster that our classrooms usually were.

Many of these had to do with happiness. Like 'Happiness is love' (this would be peppered with hearts), 'Happiness is a pure mind' (this would have clouds), 'Happiness is helping the poor' (bags of gold). But we never had 'Happiness is an ice cream' or 'Happiness is no homework'.

From our formative years we have been taught to associate happiness with noble thoughts and deeds. Pleasure derived from any other act is a cheap thrill. Why is that?

Remember the story of the king, who had everything (cue wealth), but wasn't happy? The cure, says the ubiquitous sage, is a happy man's shirt.[1] So, the king climbs mountains, crosses seas and does whatever else it is that kings on quests do, but he fails to find a happy man.

At the very end of his journey, he finds a happy farmer. But to his dismay (and enlightenment), the man has no shirt. Insidiously, a connection is made between wealth and sorrow and poverty and happiness.

My father would often hold forth on why we should not associate happiness with 'things'. But my mother, if she found any of us siblings grumpy, would quickly whip up some dessert. Our father's lectures did make us feel nobler. But it was mother's dessert that made us happy.

German philosopher Friedrich Nietzsche held that making happiness one's ultimate goal makes one 'contemptible'.[2] For him, anything of true worth in life had to be earned through struggle, pain and suffering.

What is happiness then? Does the happy man necessarily have to be shirtless? And most importantly, can we create happiness?

What Is Happiness?

This brain of ours is a truly magical piece. It weighs about three pounds and has about 100 billion neurons—each neuron connected to hundreds of others around it. Everything we do and feel is a function of electrical signals relayed along the right neuron paths.

The brain is also a chemical marvel. It has, among others, the four primary happiness chemicals—dopamine, oxytocin, serotonin and endorphins. Each has a different role.

Dopamine (often called the happiness drug) gives us the pleasure of anticipation. Oxytocin makes us feel empathy and keeps us bonded (critical for the social creature). Serotonin is the regulator, deciding whether you should be sad or happy. Finally, the endorphins mask pain or discomfort, helping us push harder at things we love.

These unbelievably complex electrical and chemical processes help us feel emotion—any emotion, be it unadulterated joy or devastating sorrow.

When my mother announces that she is making dessert, my brain becomes a pyrotechnic display—with neurons firing pleasurable signals all over and dopamine levels shooting up as I revel in anticipation. Oxytocin makes me feel all warm and fuzzy about my mother. When I take a blissful spoonful, serotonin confirms that I have every right to be happy (about 80 per cent of serotonin is in the digestive tract). And finally, endorphins push me beyond the two bowls I should have stopped myself at. I am bloated, but happy.

To me this is happiness, what the dictionary defines as a state of feeling pleasure or contentment. But we can never get folks to agree that happiness is something as simple as this.

Most religions teach us to shun to be happy. (Except Buddhism which recognizes more vanilla forms of happiness like wealth and friendships as happiness goals for the common folks.) Socialism tells us to share and be happy but for a capitalist, that definitely isn't happiness.

The Epicureans held that pleasure was life's sole, intrinsic goal—which they defined as an absence of pain and fear, and advocated a simple life (very different from the 'eat, drink and be merry' hedonism they are usually associated with).

For Aristotle, happiness wasn't even a state. It was an activity.[3] According to him, every living thing had a unique function— man's function being to reason, since only man can reason. The activity of performing one's function well was happiness.

I do not deny that these definitions of happiness have had their use and their day. And in many ways, our different ways to define happiness may be responsible for the semblance of order we see in the world we live in. The fact is, however, that there cannot be a one-size-fits-all happiness model; for happiness is intensely personal, subjective, evolving, contextual and most often a function of what I do not have.

For a blind man, one would assume that there could be no greater happiness than vision. But once his vision is restored, his idea of happiness becomes different.

No Two Happiness-es Are Alike

Happiness is a function of each individual's temperamental construct, phase in life and context. To me, the pattern of happiness for each of us is as unique as our fingerprint.

For the single, happiness could be about meeting someone new. For the hitched, it could also be about meeting someone new. Both are different happiness-es. While a business goal achieved might make me happy today, tomorrow it might be my child's achievements that I eagerly anticipate rather than my own.

Imagine a family of four. Dad, mum, sixteen-ish daughter and fourteen-ish son. The father wants to chill with a beer when the mother wants to hit the spa while the son wants to go skiing and the daughter wants to go shopping. Even in this closely-knit small sample, each individual's source of happiness is different and no two sources need be alike; which is why family holidays often look better when they are over (and in the pictures).

Each of us needs a personal happiness formula that matches our temperament, life-stage and context. Is it possible to create a model for happiness? If we can get that right, we could raise the happiness levels of individuals, communities and nations which would go a long way towards making a better world, I should think. I know that I am making happiness sound extremely prosaic and algorithm-y, but yes, I do think technology is a solution.

We Are Not Just Biology Any More

We are not just bio-organisms any more. Not mere multi-celled organisms that have evolved from fish to bipedal to explorers of neighbouring moons. Be it in our DNA or our brain, we are now data-driven organisms.

The average human body processes 3×10^{24} bits of information in a day. Compare this to 10^{18} bits, which is the total of all human information shared through our libraries.[4] Man is a complex information processing system.

Accepting this, that we are embodied information and not just a biological entity, is the first step to entrusting technology with the delivery of happiness. For, the happiness pill can only be created for a culture that is premised on an algorithmic model of the self.

The human individual is a bundle of inputs (data collection), algorithmic processes (data analysis) and outputs (data use). If we are to look at it objectively, the algorithmic self is nothing but the data it consumes and the content it creates. Subjectively, it converts input resources into outputs of emotion.

It is this info-organism for which technology needs to create happiness.

A Personalized Pill for Happiness

I believe technology can create not just a formula for happiness but one for unbroken happiness. And when I say 'unbroken happiness', I refer to a state of perpetual happiness, where the crests of pleasure are not interrupted by troughs of relative sorrow.

I believe that is possible because of the confluence of technologies we witness today—neurosciences, IoT, statistical sciences, social media, big data and biotechnology. And of course, AI.

In neurosciences, we are witnessing a coupling of neuroscience with cognitive science, computer science, mathematics, genetics and humanities. With IoT, we have surveillance technology that can assess our needs and moods on a real-time basis. With developments in statistical sciences, we have the ability to see patterns we otherwise never would have. With social media, we can read, predict and then influence behaviour. With big data we have the ability to process and store all our data and insights. And with developments in biotechnology we can eliminate (inherited or otherwise) predispositions to potential sources of sorrow, like diseases.

The way all these disconnected and interconnected pieces are coming together and falling into place, it looks like the universe is conspiring for tech-driven happiness.

Let's look at what I have on you. I already have all the information I need about you as an individual. I also have the technology to bucket preferences and contexts. AI and IoT bring me the ability to understand you and gauge your needs around the clock. I can make a fair assessment of what will make you happy at a given point in time.

Mathematicians and statisticians (and now every marketer) can predict and influence your behaviour and preferences based on the content you create online and on social media's likes, dislikes and opinions. These can easily be converted into customized recommendations for your delight.

Now if I marry a little pop psychology and a little philosophy to your need context, I can evolve a formula for your personalized happiness. This I could deliver to you in multiple ways, either individually or in combinations.

I could deliver it to you as a pill—a combination of the right chemicals that your brain needs for your personalized happiness. A combination of pills that use your body's biotechnology to keep you happy. I could also deliver it to you on social media.

With social media, we can address two critical happiness factors—the hunger for positive feedback and the thirst for instant gratification. For many people in advanced economies, their happiness is a function of what their peer group thinks of the airbrushed version of their reality that they keep putting up on social media—Photoshopped DPs and fantastical, happy holiday pictures. This is what my social group imagines my life to be and, in many cases, this is what I come to believe it to be as well.

So, I use social media both to understand your needs better and as a delivery mechanism. Every time I deliver you happiness via social media, you will also reveal how you could be made happier. And I keep getting better and better at keeping you continually happy. (Amazon shows you what to read next, I show you what would make you happy next.)

This goes beyond the individual as well, because we know now that social networks can impact moods. Studies have shown that emotions can spread online to generate large-scale simultaneous clusters of happy and unhappy individuals.[5]

One of the primary reasons I see all of this coming true very soon is because we are witnessing our biology integrating with our technology.

This combination of genetics and AI could keep our hormones, neurotransmitters and the neural network in perfect harmony. The dopamine, endorphin, serotonin and oxytocin would be melodiously orchestrated.

Is this then the holy grail for the happiness industry?

The Happiness Industry

Whatever name we call it by, the happiness industry has always been around.

For the ancients, happiness was what their scriptures prescribed it to be. Subscribing to them brought them happiness. Religion, as a premier happiness industry, continues to be in business.

Rationalists need to find ways to be happy as well and they choose philosophy, and sometimes socio-economic ideologies as their happiness industries. As for the humanist, there are a whole lot of industries out there delivering (or promising to deliver) happiness. (Ironically, all of these happiness industries violently spread sorrow to defend their happiness formulae and beliefs.)

J.D. Salinger once said:

I am a paranoid in reverse. I suspect people of plotting to make me happy.[6]

It was not said in this context of course, but I really love Salinger's quote, for someone or the other is always trying to sell us happiness.

The truth is that all of us subscribe to one industry or another—to religion, to philosophy, to ideology or at the very least, to the indulgence industry re-emphasizing the fact that as humans, we need the happiness industry.

None have succeeded completely. But technology's ability to deliver happiness could finally succeed to an extent that the others have only dreamt about.

Technology Takes You Where None Have Been Before

Technology offers you happiness, right here, right now. All you need to do is to accept that you are an info-organism and your happiness pill is ready—tailored to your needs.

To me creating happiness—with curated, personalized recommendations to connect with each individual's contexts of mood and time—seems to be the idea of our times. What man has been seeking all along is now at a store near you—brought to you by bio-engineering and AI. No mountains to climb, no deities to appease, no grind. And no bias—the rich, the poor, the man, the woman, everyone can have happiness delivered, all day.

This would be the perfect drug, as Aldous Huxley might have said, for the brave new world.[7] To keep you euphoric, blissful and positive, all the time. It would bring you all the advantages of religion, every -ism and alcohol. Without the side effects.

On Extraterrestrial Life: Is It Still Possible to Believe We Are Alone?

TWO THOUSAND YEARS AGO, WE sincerely believed that we were the sole reason for the existence of this universe. Six centuries ago, we believed that the sun revolved around our planet, for our benefit. Only five centuries ago, we believed that the Earth was flat (some still do). What will we learn tomorrow? Everything is a possibility.

There are an estimated 200 to 400 billion stars in the Milky Way.[1] That's $2-4\times10^{11}$, if you can wrap your head around it. If we were to bring the entire observable universe into the picture, that number goes up to 7×10^{22}, that's seven sextillion stars.

Now, there is nothing special about the evolution of our solar system, or Earth's history or biological evolution. We just are typical, much like our planet is. Scientists apply the mediocrity principle to put this a little more politely.

The mediocrity principle states:

> . . . if an item is drawn at random from one of several categories, it's likelier to come from the most numerous category than from any one of the less numerous categories.[2]

Which means that (much as we would not like it) in this unimaginably huge universe, our planet is neither special nor privileged.

If that be the case, would it not be safe to assume that life could also have evolved elsewhere, considering the categories we are drawing from has about seven sextillion stars, each with its own exoplanets? This is what prompted physicist Enrico Fermi, out for a leisurely lunch with his colleagues, to jump up and wonder:

Where are they?[3]

'Where Are They?'

Seemingly simple, this lunchtime question went on to become the famous Fermi paradox—for there seems to be a significant contradiction in what we know and what must be.[4] Arguments of scale and probability favour intelligent life in the universe (in abundance), but there is an absolute lack of evidence of intelligent life having ever arisen anywhere other than on the Earth.

This contradiction is beautifully captured by Thomas Carlyle:

Thinking about stars, if they be inhabited then what a scope for misery and folly, and if they were not inhabited, then what a waste of space![5]

If alien life does indeed exist, why is it that they have not contacted us? And even, why is it that we have been unable to see them?

There are enough and more theories that have come forth to explain this lack of contact. Primary among these, and among the most appealing, is the zoo hypothesis put forward by astronomer John A. Ball in 1973.

The zoo hypothesis begins with the assumption that a large number of alien cultures exist and are observing us from afar.[6] It also says that they are intelligent enough to respect an independent natural evolution and sociocultural development.

And avoid interplanetary contamination of all kind. It is necessary to understand that other civilizations, if they developed, could well be ahead of us—the time between the emergence of the first civilizations within the Milky Way and subsequent civilizations could be vast.

Remember that our civilization is in its infancy in cosmological terms. Our planet was born 4.54 billion years ago, which is just a third of the age of the universe. What could a civilization with a half-billion years' head start be capable of? The zoo hypothesis explains the apparent absence despite the plausibility.

This also is how a more evolved man has attempted to treat his siblings who have had lesser exposure to the developed world.

With the Jarawas in India's Andaman Islands, what we attempt to do now is minimize contact so that they are free to evolve at their own pace. In spite of our best efforts, the tourist menace is wreaking havoc with the Jarawa population, changing their habits and spreading disease. John Ball must be right; aliens must be a lot smarter than us.

The zoo hypothesis also assumes that intelligence is a physical process that acts to maximize the diversity of a system's accessible futures. A fundamental motivation for the hypothesis then becomes that premature contact would 'unintelligently' reduce the overall diversity of paths the universe itself could take.

There are, of course, possibilities within this. Alien civilizations might await benchmarks in advancement by the human civilization before they initiate contact; standards that we might need to pass to understand them. They might also avoid contact to reduce risks of contamination or just because contact brings them no added advantage—technologically advanced civilizations could well have come to the realization that contact without benefit is just avoidable risk.

Edward Snowden of WikiLeaks has a completely different take on what he believes is a solution to Fermi's paradox. In conversation with Neil deGrasse Tyson, he came up with the theory of alien encryption.[7]

According to him, all sentient societies naturally evolve to encrypt their communication, which means that all evidence that is out there could most probably be indistinguishable from cosmic microwave background radiation. They might be talking to us; we might just not know how to hear them.

Many also believe that this interest in aliens and our constant quest to prove their existence is a natural human impulse, in many ways not too different from our quest for God. And in this context, many quote Shermer's last law. Michael Shermer, science historian and founder of the Skeptics Society, modified the last of Arthur C. Clarke's three laws to say:

Any sufficiently advanced extraterrestrial intelligence is indistinguishable from God.[8]

In *Plurality of Worlds*, science historian Steven Dick speaks about how Newton's mechanical universe erased the spiritual universe that existed until then. That lifeless void is what we try to fill with our search for extraterrestrial intelligence. Evidence of aliens (much like our belief in God) would help us validate our conviction that we are part of a larger and infinitely more meaningful cosmic drama.

But my favourite theory is Calvin's, when he confides in Hobbes:

Sometimes I think the surest sign that intelligent life exists elsewhere in the universe is that none of it has tried to contact us.[9]

John Ball would also agree. And when we look at the world around us, we would as well.

When We See It, Will We Know It?

Here's a bigger conundrum, now. After all this talk, if we do come across alien life, will we be able to recognize it? What form will it be in?

In science fiction and in imagination, aliens have always been variations on the human theme. Not surprising, considering our anthropomorphic tendencies. Why, we have even given all our gods our own forms and cutely rationalized it by saying that the gods created us in their form.

According to Snowden, we are not capable of deciphering their communication. Will we, then, be able to recognize them? Most probably not. For two simple reasons.

The first reason is that we do not know how life would have evolved (assuming it has) on a different planet. It would be foolish to look for other carbon-based life forms. Life would possibly have evolved in a radically different manner under radically different conditions and could well be nowhere near our understanding of organic life.

The second reason is that life on different planets might have transcended the H++ era (beyond transhumanism). They might just be information, for all we know. They would possibly have achieved super intelligence long ago and their biology (whatever it is like) might have merged with their technology—Alien Intelligence would have merged with Artificial Intelligence.

I sincerely believe that if and when we do connect with an extraterrestrial intelligence, it will be a case of their technology meeting ours. Rather than a cute being stepping out of a starship and asking to be taken to our leader.

Somewhere, radio waves could meet and the future of the human race could get charted. For, I believe that if we do make contact, it will definitely change the future of the human race, for better or for worse.

Will Technology Resolve the Mystery?

There have been all kinds of alien watchers around. The tragic kind include the infamous cult in California called Heaven's Gate.[10] Led by Marshall Applewhite and Bonnie Nettles, they believed that the Earth was about to be recycled and the only chance of survival was to leave (not very different from the Noah myth, when you think about it).

In 1997, Applewhite convinced his disciples that there was an alien spacecraft accompanying the Hale-Bopp comet and thirty-nine of them committed mass suicide in an effort to leave the planet and reach the spacecraft. Of course, they didn't call it suicide, they called it 'graduation from a human evolutionary level'.

The USAF (United States Air Force) and others get calls, regularly, on thousands of sightings of UFOs (Unidentified Flying Objects). Polls have shown that almost 50 per cent of Western cultures believe that aliens exist. If that comes as a surprise, what comes next will blow your mind.

A poll[11] conducted by the Roper Centre for Public Opinion Research in the early '90s concluded that around 3.7 million Americans believed that they had been abducted by aliens at some point. Of course, I would think that most of these are hoaxes and folks looking for some easy popularity. But there is no reason to assume that all are frauds though, and psychologists may be able to explain quite a few of these.

Believing in them are several insurance companies offering alien abduction insurance. The UFO Abduction Insurance Company, from Florida, claims to have sold 5000 of these.[12] All it takes is a one-time payment of $9.99 for a $10 million-coverage. You have to provide evidence of abduction though.

While this might be one way to watch out for aliens, there are a whole lot of others who appear to be a little more serious about this quest. For many years, NASA has been working on multiple projects to find Earth-like planets in space that one can assume would be capable of fostering life.

For long, scientists believed we were in a Goldilocks Zone,[13] where life could proliferate. (After Goldilocks finding the porridge: too hot in the first bowl, too cold in the second bowl and just right in the third bowl.) They believed that the Goldilocks Zone was small—not colder than Antarctica (penguins can survive here), not hotter than scalding water (desert lizards), not higher than the clouds (eagles) and not lower than a few, deep mines (deep mine microbes).

But then, in the last thirty years, our idea of life has changed. We have seen microbes survive in nuclear reactors, we have seen microbes that love acid (and some men, too) and microbes that dwell in boiling water. This means that our idea of where life can exist has evolved and expanded.

It also expanded NASA's Goldilocks Zone of what could be considered hospitable, what might suit life 'out there'. NASA's Kepler space telescope found, in 2009, several planets orbiting their stars that could be termed to be in the Goldilocks Zone. Planets that could, possibly, host life.

It was machine learning that helped us arrive at this stunning possibility by analysing Kepler's data.[14] And that's the reason we are discussing extraterrestrials in the first place. Man would never have been able to analyse that data and come up with the possibilities with which we are now confronted. But technology can.

I really think that technology will make all our discoveries in the days to come, not man. It will be technology that will help us resolve the many mysteries that we still grapple with. Technology will be Alexander's sword for every Gordian knot that exists today and will come up tomorrow.

Technology will show us more of the universe and, in the process, of ourselves. As Carl Sagan put it:

In the deepest sense the search for extra-terrestrial intelligence is a search for ourselves.[15]

The Signs Are Here

In 2016, Yuri Milner funded Breakthrough Listen at the Berkeley SETI Research Center. Breakthrough Listen is a programme that seeks to search for signs of extraterrestrial communication in the universe.

On 30 August 2017, the project picked up a series of fifteen radio bursts that came from a dwarf galaxy about three billion light years away. These came from a known source from which bursts had first been picked up in 2015.[16] At first, scientists thought these Fast Radio Bursts (FRBs) were the result of some catastrophic event like a supernova. But when it got repeated in 2016 and was vastly different in 2017, things got interesting. Because it meant that whatever object or intelligence produced the FRBs, was still there.

Explanations for these signals range from rotating neutron stars with extremely powerful magnetic fields to even energy sources used by extraterrestrial intelligences to power spacecrafts. But whatever these signals are, they left their source three billion light years ago—when life on Earth had just evolved and was still single-celled.

Here again, I would like to remind you that all of these learnings are made possible only with our new-found ability for intensive data analysis. The data recorder at The Green Bank Telescope,[17] which recorded these bursts, records 6GHz of bandwidth at 24GB/second—making it the highest data rate recording system in radio astronomy (and they will soon be doubling this). And once we have the data, astronomers will use a computing cluster with 64 GTX 1080 GPUs to analyse it.

Are We Ready?

Most of us would think we are ready. But not Stephen Hawking (wonder if he knew more).

Hawking warned us that we should be wary of communicating with alien civilizations as they could turn out to be marauders who would be keen on plundering resources from fertile galaxies across the universe.

In a documentary titled 'Stephen Hawking's Favourite Places', he spoke about Gliese 832c, a potentially habitable exoplanet, sixteen light years away, that is our fifth-closest known potentially habitable exoplanet. Hawking said:

> One day, we might receive a signal from a planet like this, but we should be wary of answering back. Meeting an advanced civilisation could be like Native Americans encountering Columbus. That didn't turn out so well.[18]

If a man of Hawking's ability was worried, so should we. It might be a little too late, though, as we have been sending out radio and TV signals for more than a century now.

Now all we can do is wait . . . and hope that data can solve the mystery for us . . . and that the resolution is peaceful.

Simulation: Are You and I Evolved Marios in Someone's Game?

INSCRIBED IN THE TEMPLE OF Apollo at Delphi are the words: 'Gnōthi Sauton' (know thyself).

Who am I? This is a theme that has enamoured philosophers across civilizations, that science-fiction writers have fantasized about, that religions have conveniently appropriated and manipulated.

Eventually, as is almost always the case these days with ideas that have plagued us since man started thinking, it is AI that is coming up with possible explanations.

What, exactly, is our existence?

In *Advaita Vedanta* is Adi Sankara's 'Dakshinamoorthy Stotra', in which he states:

> . . . the world is only as real as the image that is seen in a mirror—*visvam darpana drusyama nagari, thulyam nijantargatham*.[1]

This is similar to Plato's allegory of the cave in which there are people chained and immobilized and can only see shadows projected from behind them on to the wall in front of them.[2] Having known no other reality, they perceive the shadows that they see to be the reality of the world.

The Chinese have the story of Zhuang Zhou.[3] Once, Zhuang Zhou dreamt he was a butterfly, flitting and fluttering about, happy with himself and doing as he pleased. He didn't know that he was Zhuang Zhou. Suddenly he woke up and there he was—Zhuang Zhou—solid and unmistakable. He now didn't know if he was Zhuang Zhou who had dreamt he was a butterfly, or a butterfly dreaming that he was Zhuang Zhou.

Closer to the modern day, we have *Meditations on First Philosophy* (1641) where René Descartes speaks of the Evil Genius, a malicious demon who deceives us, making us believe that we are living our lives when the reality is very different. Some Cartesian philosophers also opined that the Evil Genius was capable of great deceit—even altering the fundamentals of math and logic in its effort to deceive us convincingly.

In his book *Reason, Truth and History*, Hilary Putnam took Cartesian thinking further with his brain-in-a-vat hypothesis. That our brains are sitting in a vat of nutrients in a lab. And that the nerve endings are connected to a supercomputer that provides all the sensations of everyday life—thus deceiving us into believing we are living a life.

Imagine! You are just a brain sitting in a vat somewhere and that brain is constantly being fed sensations and experiences. Right now, you (the brain) are told that you're reading and that is exactly what you are experiencing. All that we think is just something that someone wants us to see and think. All our history and all that we believe and know is just data that we have been fed. Is this our reality?

If you have watched the *Matrix*, it combines the Evil Genius idea of Descartes and Putnam's brain-in-a-vat experiment. In the movie, humans have been enslaved as an energy source by advanced machines. Instead of realizing their plight though, humans implicitly believe the false reality that they are being fed through a giant simulation created by the machines.

In the movie, Morpheus, who knows the real nature of the simulated world, coaches the protagonist, Neo:

How do you define 'real'? If you are talking about what you can feel, what you can smell, what you can taste and see, then 'real' is simply electrical signals interpreted by your brain.[4]

'Everything That We Call Real, Is Made of Things That Cannot Be Regarded As Real': Niels Bohr[5]

The nature of our reality has been a favourite trope with sci-fi writers as well. This is worrying because if you notice a recurrent theme in this book, much of what we have covered are themes that began with philosophers, were picked up by sci-fi writers and then have been proved or implemented by our current scientific, quantitative and algorithmic abilities.

Growing up in India, I was exposed to ideas like *drishti-shrishti-vada* from *Advaita Vedanta*, which talks about the doctrine of creation through perception. This doctrine holds that the world comes into existence only as a process of man's observation; that this world of ours is an imaginary construct. But then, more recently, I was rather amused to come across the same idea in particle physics—that the universe doesn't exist if we are not looking at it.

For that is what quantum physicists have to say about quantum reality. From the '20s onwards, sophisticated experiments like the double slit[6] demonstration have shown that subatomic particles can act like waves as well as particles (unlike what was previously believed). They do not have clearly defined positions or sizes *until* we make the physical act of observing them.

Only when we try to observe them (for purposes of measurement), do particles take a definite position. In other words, our observation is what compels particles to exist in the manner they do.

If this is true (and I am not one to argue with empirical science), then it is we who create our reality by observation. We perceive our reality into existence, particle by particle.

If you are confused, you are in good company. This phenomenon puzzled Einstein as well. He once asked Niels Bohr, the proponent of the quantum theory, if the moon would not exist if nobody looked at it. Bohr asked in response (smartly, I would think) how Einstein could tell that the moon was there if he was not looking.[7]

What Is Our Reality, Then?

The debate is essentially between idealism and materialism, and it has been something philosophers have been contending with since ancient times.

Materialists believe that matter preexisted the mind on Earth and hence can exist independently, while the converse—mind existing independent of matter—is not a possibility. Idealists, however, maintain that the basic element of reality is the mind (or the spirit). That the spirit exists before and apart from matter and that matter is no more than a passing phase, or illusion.

So, is matter driving our existence? Or is there a spirit that is driving all that we know as our universe? Is all that we see—space, matter and our sense of volume—just an illusion? Is what Bohr said true, that all we regard as real, isn't?

Is all that we perceive, physically and otherwise, just something that someone wants us to see and think? In the digital age, science is indeed beginning to see a similarity between our reality (as we perceive it) and virtual reality. This assumption would have been ridiculed until recently, but in the times of data and AI, we have to (and can) consider these possibilities.

Let us then, examine a few of the arguments in favour of the hypothesis that we might be living in a simulation. But, bear in mind what Carl Sagan said:

. . . extraordinary claims require extraordinary evidences.[8]

The Big Bang Simulation Theory

As all of us know, the leading explanation for the origin of the universe is the Big Bang Theory. In essence, it states this universe was originally a tiny singularity which exploded and over the course of the next 13.8 billion years, has inflated to become what it is today. Of course, no one was around to observe it; what we know comes from mathematical models and formulae.

But wait, this cannot make sense to a materialist, that in the beginning there was nothing and then, something came out of that nothing. It is impossible to explain to a materialist.

If you look at the world as a virtual construct then the Big Bang model works perfectly. Because virtual worlds always begin with information influx from a zero state—because they always need to boot up.

Think about a computer game. Every time you start the game, a big bang occurs from the perspective of the game. One moment there is nothing and in the next, the characters in the game are in position, ready to continue where you left off last night.

From the perspective of the characters in the game, creation always comes from nothing because before it boots up, there is no space or time, as defined by the rules of the virtual world.

The Non-locality Simulation Theory

Quantum particles, from what we understand now, are up to all kinds of mischief. Apart from wave–particle duality, there's a lot more roguery that's on, like non-locality and entanglement.

In 1982, physicist Alain Aspect demonstrated that subatomic particles are able to communicate instantaneously with each other, regardless of the distances separating them.[9] The only problem was that it violated Einstein's contention that nothing can travel faster than the speed of light.

This requires a little explanation. Particles that share an origin have an entangled twin which is entangled not in the sense that they are together spatially but because their physical properties—spin, momentum, position, polarization—are correlated. So, for all you know, the pair could be separated by light years.

Now, if you were to measure one particle for spin, and you find it to be clockwise, the other particle would be seen to have an anti-clockwise spin. (Do remember, as we discussed earlier, it is only when you measure that a quantum particle assumes a value [in this case, for spin]). How is it then that the other particle in the pair knows instantly of the experiment that was performed and assumes the opposite value? To the best of our knowledge, information can only travel at the speed of light, at best. But this is instantaneous and thus defies the laws of classical physics. This phenomenon was called non-locality by physicist John Bell.[10] Even Einstein called it 'spooky action at a distance'.

So, are particles free from the constraints of this physical world? Because in a physical world that follows the rules of space and time, two particles that are separated by infinite distances cannot respond to each other instantaneously . . . but they *can* respond, if the world is a virtual construct.

If the world is a virtual construct, as it is in a simulation hypothesis, non-locality is easily solved. For if space is an illusion, then the question of time required to travel an illusory distance does not exist.

In a virtual world distance doesn't limit correspondence, since all the points on the screen in a simulation are equidistant from the source of the simulation. For example, in a computer game all points on the screen are at an equal distance with respect to the processor; on your screen you could have two different locations, say Eiffel Tower and Buckingham Palace (separated by 428 km and a channel), but both are equidistant from your processor.

Therefore, if our universe was indeed a simulation projected on to a three-dimensional screen, then the processor would be equidistant to all points on the universe. Non-locality of quantum particles is, then, easily answered.

The Quantum Bits Simulation Theory

If non-locality could imply that space is an illusion, what quantum physics tells us about matter is even more overwhelming.

Imagine a character in a computer game and how he interacts with physical objects in the game, like a chair or a gun or a car. While what he interacts with is ostensibly physical, the fact is that it is mathematics—just a few lines of programming that define those physical objects.

In a digital world, everything is built of bits or pixels. If we keep breaking down what we see, we eventually end with the smallest particle—the pixel.

The virtual world looks like the world we live in and also behaves in a similar manner. In the past century, physics has discovered that matter is quantized, composed of fundamental indivisible particles, billions of times smaller than an atom.

Space is quantized, time is quantized, energy is quantized, light is quantized as photons and electricity as electrons, and on and on. Everything is made of individual bits, which means the universe is computable.

This would make eminent sense if we were in a simulation. Just as in a virtual construct every computer-generated image can be broken down into its component pixels, in nature everything that we see can be broken down into quantum bits.

The Pattern Simulation Theory

In a virtual world, every digital object created by the same code is identical. In computing terms, objects are just instances of a general class.

This seems to hold true for our real world as well—all quantum objects are identical in each class, like every photon is identical to the next one, as are electrons. Therefore, while every object we see in our world has its own character, the foundation is made of identical building blocks.

This could well be the reason that everything we see around us has such neat symmetries and such repeatable patterns. Are we then just a programme?

The Holographic Principle Simulation Theory

The holographic principle[11] comes to us from string theory and a property of quantum gravity that states that all the information contained within a region of space can be determined by the information on the surface of it. Hence, the three-dimensional volume of space can be represented as a hologram of the surface.

Let us try and use a simple example to understand this better. Think about the usher at the door of the theatre. By counting the number of people going in or coming out, he has a precise idea of the number within. Therefore, information represented at the surface (the door) tells him of the volume inside (the theatre).

Does this imply that our idea of the volume of space is an illusion, again? Are we just a holographic rendering in a three-dimensional construct?

In fact, a whole lot of issues in physics, including quantum physics and Einstein's theory of general relativity, could be reconciled if we actually were in a two-dimensional universe.

This is in a way similar to Plato's cave, which we touched upon a few pages ago, where what the observers see are just shadows, but for the prisoners, that is their reality. We, as humans, are bound to the impressions that are received through our senses. And for all we know, our idea of volume might just be an illusion.

Alain Aspect conducted a most remarkable experiment demonstrating that the web of subatomic particles that comprise our physical universe—the so-called 'fabric of reality itself'—possesses what appears to be an undeniable 'holographic property'.

Are We All Marios, Then?

So then, are we just characters in someone's video game? Are we just playing out our parts in a 3D projected universe?

If I were a character in a computer game, and it was programmed for complexities, consciousness et al, then I would live with the illusion that I am real.

In a computer game programmed for high complexity, you and I would actually believe that we have free will and that we are the masters of our life—that we govern our activities.

Although the latest studies show that free will is just another illusion and that the experience of willing an action is just a post-event causal interference that our thoughts actually caused some behaviour. This is what leads us to think that we make choices when actually we don't. But that is a different subject that requires an entire chapter.

If space, matter, volume and now free will are all illusions, are we truly simulations? To make matters even more complicated, is our subconscious connected to the original consciousness that created this simulation? For, not just our conscious self, but our subconscious self also seems to be able to create physical experiences when we dream in our sleep. (Perhaps Christopher Nolan's *Inception* was not fiction after all.)

Who Then, Is the Creator?

From all that we have seen, evidence seems to support the concept of an imaginary world more than a materialistic world.

Which is why I am surprised that religions are not up and about supporting the simulation hypotheses because, if you ask me, this makes for a great theological argument on creation. (Our idea of God might have to be refashioned a bit, but hey, that is affordable collateral damage.)

In any case, regardless of who stakes a claim, who is the creator? Is there someone who has programmed us and are we a mere string of code?

The human brain has over 100 billion neurons and well over 100 trillion synapses. It is estimated that every second of time that the brain experiences can be simulated with somewhere between 100 trillion to 100 quadrillion binary operations.[12]

For our level of technology that would be an impossibility. But with increasing computing power, with quantum computing, it would be possible at some stage to create sensory input to the brain with enough fidelity to convince the simulation that it is a real person.

Therefore, you could be just a brain sitting in a vat on a table, but you think you are out fishing and can feel the sun on your skin and the tug on your line.

In 2003, Swedish philosopher Nick Bostrom authored the paper 'Are We Living in a Computer Simulation?' In this he argued that if technological progress continues unabated, then we would overcome our current software and hardware shortcomings and reach an advanced stage. This civilization would be able to convert planets and other astronomical resources into enormously powerful computers.

He also believes that the human civilization is likely to go extinct before this stage and that the post-human civilizations that follow are likely to run simulations to trace their evolutionary history, which he refers to as an 'ancestor simulation'.

Ancestor simulation sounds decidedly exciting and, if we can perform it, eminently educational. Imagine being able to run ancestor simulations of the time man developed speech, to see how over thousands of years we would perfect what eventually went on to become our greatest tool.

Bostrom believes that if we take this assumption to be true, then chances are that we already are living in a simulation.

If the simulations are fine-grained enough (and if we are to accept functionalism as a philosophy of the mind) then it is possible that these simulations could be conscious. Then it could mean that a vast majority of minds like ours do not belong to the original biological race but to people simulated by advanced descendants of the original race.

Ancestor simulation aside, there also are enough theories of simulation by advanced alien civilizations. The same Alain Aspect experiment we discussed before also demonstrated that the web of subatomic particles that comprises our physical (hopefully) universe possesses holographic properties. Based on this, physicist David Bohm argued that an objective reality does not exist.[13] That despite its apparent solidity, the universe is just a phantasm, an illusion.

Of course, there are scientists out to prove that we are as real as, well, we think. They believe the universe is too complicated to simulate.

Some argue that as simulated systems get more complex, the computational resources needed to run them also increase. Now this could be linear, meaning that every time the number of particles in the simulation is doubled, the computational power also needs to be doubled. It could also be exponential, which means your resources double every time a new particle is added.

Our universe is made up of 10^{80} particles. To simulate that, we would need a memory that is made up of more atoms than the universe contains.

But none of these arguments or hypotheses bring us the answer to our original question.

What Are We?

Are we then holograms? Or brains in a vat? Or are we just characters in a game a kid is playing in some advanced civilization?

Do we exist? Maybe we do, if we are to go by the argument put forward by René Descartes. Descartes pointed out that the very idea of doubting one's existence was proof of existence:

> At least we can be sure we ourselves exist, because every time we doubt that, there must exist an 'I' that is doing the doubting.[14]

Soon I believe we will know more about this world of ours. I think our technologies will soon find out if you and I exist in a real world or in a make-believe illusion.

But then again, I pause in doubt. For any evidence that we discover to prove or disprove simulation could itself be simulated.

SECTION V

THE NEW MAN

Who is this new Adam we are inventing?
What will he be?
How will he define himself?
What will he believe in?

Transhumanism: Will We Be Immortal or Extinct in 2100?

RAY KURZWEIL IS SEVENTY YEARS old. He takes about 200 vitamin and mineral supplement pills a day. So many, that he has hired someone to manage his pills for him. He also has scheduled one day a week for longevity treatments.[1]

All of this is for a simple reason. Kurzweil believes that humans will become immortal by the middle of this century. And he wants to be around when that happens.

When Kurzweil does that you do not laugh, you head for the nearest pharmacy. For, while many have spoken about the coming explosion of intelligence and its consequences on the human race, the one man responsible for putting this debate out in the open is Kurzweil: inventor, researcher and futurist.

Many futurists have predicted an explosion of intelligence, an expected outcome of the development of AI. We will, at some point soon, come to a stage where AI will become capable of recursive self-improvement. Once this occurs, the possibilities and ramifications are unlimited and unknown.

Once machines start improving themselves and designing their own progress, will they decide that humans are an unnecessary drain on the planet's resources and end human life as we know it? Or will we be able to take advantage of technology and gift ourselves immortality? The truth is that we can only make assumptions of what will follow this explosion of intelligence.

Scientists have a term for this explosion—singularity.

Singularity: The Certainty We Know Nothing About

As a term, singularity is borrowed from the original singularity of creation. All we know (or think we know) about the original singularity is that it was one of infinite density which contained all mass and space-time before quantum fluctuations caused it to expand. This was the Big Bang, 13.772 billion years ago.[2] We know what came after, but we can only make assumptions about what went before.

In the case of technological singularity, we know what comes before (we are living through it, right now) but we can only make assumptions about what will come after because as soon as AI becomes capable of improving itself, we can only make assumptions about the path it will take.

But what we know for sure is that the singularity will soon be upon us.

Professor Vernor Vinge was the first to use the term in his 1993 essay, 'The Coming Technological Singularity':

> The evolution of human intelligence took millions of years. We will devise an equivalent advance in a fraction of that time. We will soon create intelligences greater than our own. When this happens, human history will have reached a kind of singularity . . .[3]

But the man who made the debate popular is the man with the pills—Ray Kurzweil. In his book *The Singularity Is Near*, Kurzweil proposed his Law of Accelerating Returns wherein he stated that the rate of change in a wide variety of evolutionary systems tends to increase exponentially.[4]

Kurzweil's views were an extension of Moore's Law. This was an observation by Gordon Moore that the number of transistors in a dense integrated circuit doubles every two years.[5] Moore's observation of this historical trend can easily be applied to social change, productivity and economic growth, not just to technology.

When you think about it, Kurzweil's law does explain the exponential progress of technologies like computer memory, transistors, genetics, nanotechnology, robotics, internet traffic, magnetic storage, decrease in device size, robotics and artificial intelligence. In the last four years, we probably have seen more change than we saw in the previous forty.

Our Biology Is Already Merging with Our Technology

Observe man today and you will see that our technology is already merging with our biology. From the smartphone that brings each one of us all the intelligence of the cloud, to technology that is helping us edit the genome to make us disease-free, to intelligent prosthetics, our technology is already playing a role in our biology—these are all enhancing our abilities, not compensating like last-gen prosthetics used to.

To add to this, we are also developing a new generation of capabilities that—with neural interfaces, adaptive signal processing and complex systems modelling—can integrate the power of technology with that ability which characterizes us as Homo sapiens, our ability to experience insights and apply intuition.

According to Arati Prabhakar,[6] former director of Defense Advanced Research Projects Agency (DARPA):[7]

> We and our technological creations are poised to embark on what is sure to be a strange and deeply commingled evolutionary path.

But as soon as singularity has been achieved, we would have created an artificial super-intelligent being which Kurzweil believes will be more powerful that all human intelligence combined. At this point, we would have transcended our biology and would cease to be the species we are, at least theoretically.

But for this to happen, we would have to reach the artificial super intelligence stage (ASI).

Artificial Super Intelligence—How Soon?

AI is now a much-touted term and as is usual with popular terms, everyone has a different understanding of it. AI could range from a computer that is slightly smarter than a human at one specific task, to a machine that is a trillion times smarter than the human and adept at all tasks.

As of now, we are at the artificial narrow intelligence (ANI) stage, as we have discussed at length elsewhere in this book. We have computers that are better than humans at a single, specific (or narrow) task. This is also called weak AI and is far from this super intelligence we are talking about. In fact, between ANI and ASI, we have to cross a stage called artificial general intelligence (AGI).

Leading AI thinker and philosopher Nick Bostrom defines super intelligence as:

> . . . an intellect that is much smarter than the best human brains
> in practically every field, including scientific creativity, general
> wisdom and social skills.[8]

As is obvious by that definition, we are far from it.

There has been enough speculation and debate about what and when the tipping point for ASI is. As is the case with predictions, we can never be sure about any of the suggestions. But a whole lot of really smart folks like sci-fi author Prof. Vinge, AI expert Jeremy Howard, scientist Ben Goertzel and Bill Joy, co-founder of Sun Microsystems, have put a lot of thought into it.

They believe that exponential growth is already at work and though the crawl of AI is currently slow, it will blow right past us in the next few decades.

Many believe that we are nowhere close to super intelligence. And these include people whose opinions you cannot ignore like Microsoft co-founder Paul Allen, research psychologist Gary Marcus, computer scientist Ernest Davis, and tech entrepreneur Mitch Kapor. They believe that futurists like Kurzweil underestimate the challenges that lie ahead.

Elon Musk, one of the greatest entrepreneurs of our time and founder of SpaceX, Neuralink and co-founder of Tesla, is a little apprehensive. In a comment on edge.org, he said:

> The pace of progress in artificial intelligence (I'm not referring to narrow AI) is incredibly fast. Unless you have direct exposure to groups like DeepMind, you have no idea how fast—it is growing at a pace close to exponential. The risk of something seriously dangerous happening is in the five-year timeframe. Ten years at most.[9]

And he said this in 2014.

The popular view among scientists, thinkers and AI experts is that we would arrive at AGI by 2040. And probably arrive at ASI by 2060. Prof. Vinge's 1993 prediction for singularity was 2030. And Ray Kurzweil's is 2045 (so he estimates twenty-five years of pills ahead of him). As is the case with all predictions, the timeline is the issue.

When we talk about ASI is also when immortality and extinction appear in the same sentence.

The H+ Era. Will We Flourish? Will We Flounder?

H+ (humanity+) represents transhumanism, an international movement that seeks to transform humanity by making sophisticated technology available that can greatly enhance human intellect and physiology.

Although the idea existed, the term 'transhumanism' was first made popular by the British biologist Julian Huxley who noted that:

> The human species can, if it wishes, transcend itself—not just sporadically, an individual here in one way, an individual there in another way—but in its entirety, as humanity.[10]

While many have been talking about it for over a century, we are the ones who might be the witnesses to these species-changing moments. When we achieve ASI, Homo sapiens will cease to be human as we know it; it will transcend biology (and physics and chemistry) to enter a transhumanist stage.

So, what awaits us at this stage of human evolution?

> The rise of powerful AI will be either the best, or the worst thing, ever to happen to humanity. We do not yet know which.[11]

This single statement by Stephen Hawking is enough to get the smartest among us worried. ASI for sure, is our deliverance, our Judgement Day. The only problem is we don't know how we are going to fare on Judgement Day.

For 800 million years after it was created, the Earth was a lonely planet. Then it saw the first signs of proteins and nucleic acids that were the foundations of life. For the next 3.8 billion years, life evolved.

Many believe that these 3.8 billion years are nothing but a transitional phase between primordial organic life and the era of the machines—a post-human future.

As the brilliant William Reade prophesied:

We live between two worlds; we soar in the atmosphere; we creep upon the soil; we have the aspirations of creators and the propensities of quadrupeds.

There can be but one explanation of this fact. We are passing from the animal into a higher form, and the drama of this planet is in its second act.[12]

Cosmologists believe that this future, this second act, could extend into billions of years. Machines might not need this planet and its atmosphere to survive and might be able to explore space extensively, as humans never could.

Nanotechnology, genetic engineering, artificial intelligence, there is a lot that is happening. Much of it is interconnected and the development and behaviour of this interconnected network is intrinsically difficult to model, predict or control. It is from here that the worries emanate: whether ASI is a threat to our existence or our key to immortality. Today we stand at that fork where two roads diverge in the yellow wood. And the unadulterated truth is that we are not the ones deciding which road to take.

These two roads lead to two very different ends. Let us try to see both.

First, Let's Consider an AI Takeover a.k.a. Our Extinction

An AI takeover refers to a scenario in which AI becomes the planet's dominant form of intelligence, dethroning man from his seat at the top of the intelligence chain.

Robot rebellions have been a major sci-fi trope for ages, including really popular ones like HAL 9000 from *A Space Odyssey* and Skynet from *Terminator*.

In fact, the term robot comes from a 1921 Czech sci-fi play called *R.U.R* by Karel Čapek. Ironically, it comes from the Czech word 'robota' for slave! In the play, the robots end up annihilating the human race.

The same situation confronts us in Mary Shelley's *Frankenstein*, where the good doctor wonders whether it would be sensible to grant the monster's request for a wife; whether their offspring would destroy humanity.

Stephen Hawking and Elon Musk have also advocated research into precautionary measures to ensure that the super-intelligent machines of tomorrow remain under human control. In fact, Isaac Asimov went a step further and framed the Three Laws of Robotics[13] for his imaginary world. The laws were to ensure that there were constraints on the behaviour of androids and automatons, to ensure the safety of humans. (And in his stories, he ensured his laws were followed.)

But laws like these do not hold for super-intelligent machines. Because these laws assume a master-slave relationship between man and machine and do not take into account a machine with a superior intelligence of its own; that operates in the interests of its own survival and growth.

In his book *The Future of the Mind*, Dr Michio Kaku talks about interviewing Dr Rodney Brooks, former director of MIT Artificial Intelligence Laboratory and co-founder of iRobot:

> First, no one is going to accidentally build a robot that wants to rule the world. He [Dr Brooks]says that creating a robot that can suddenly take over is like someone accidentally building a 747 jetliner. Plus, there will be plenty of time to stop this from happening. Before someone builds a 'super-bad robot', someone has to build a 'mildly bad robot', and before that a 'not-so-bad robot'.[14]

But of course, the good doctors Kaku and Brooks are not accounting for the bad doctors, like Dr No.[15] There always could be a rogue builder or creator who passes on cognitive biases.

One force we know for sure that will drive a super-intelligent machine is the desire for efficiency. It becomes possible then that ASI might see humans as a resource risk, as a species that is rapidly and incessantly consuming the limited resources of the planet—therefore needing elimination. Without malice, without vindictiveness, without vengeance, our race might just get eliminated for the energy needs of the machines.

It is also possible that the machine might see humans as a threat or an impediment to its goal of accelerated progress and hence, eliminate us.

It could also be sheer accident. As Nick Bilton wrote in the *New York Times*:

> Imagine how a medical robot, originally programmed to rid cancer, could conclude that the best way to obliterate cancer is to exterminate humans who are genetically prone to the disease.[16]

In any of these scenarios, we are extinct. If science progresses and we do not survive, then what the good Lord said in the *Genesis* is true:

> For you are dust, And to dust you shall return.

Our corporeal self, our consciousness, our memories, our thoughts, our laughter and our tears, will all be dust. We will pass as a footnote in the evolutionary history of the machines.

The Second Possibility: Immortality

Some of these extinction assumptions are based on the belief that machines are motivated by the same emotional desires that often drives humans, including the desire for power. But then again, machines might just not have that desire, or cultivate it.

There is also the distinct possibility that with ASI, we will completely transcend our biology and go on to become an eternal race (I really shock myself with how we humans are beginning to sound more and more like how we defined our gods). That we will go on to achieve digital or biological immortality. Transhumanists believe that with the singularity, we will also transcend the need for a biological body, that singularity will bring us digital immortality—the ability to upload our minds and copy and port consciousness.

It might sound futuristic, but the reality is that neural engineering is making significant strides towards modelling the brain and developing technologies to restore or replace some of its biological functions.

The only thing holding us back today is that we do not yet know how this physical substrate of cells that makes up this organ becomes our conscious, mental world of thoughts, memories and feelings. Once we cross this bridge, we will enter an era where we will be able to distil our consciousness and save a copy on the cloud.

Stephen Hawking believed that the brain was like a computer and so it was:

> . . . theoretically possible to copy the brain on to a computer and so provide a form of life after death.[17]

The Blue Brain Project[18] in Switzerland attempts to create a digital reconstruction of the brain by reverse-engineering mammalian brain circuitry. They believe the project will help identify the fundamental principles of brain structure and function.

Ray Kurzweil also believes we might soon be able to copy the brain:

> By 2045 . . . we will be able to send billions of nanobots— blood cell-size scanning machines—through every capillary of

the brain to create a complete non-invasive scan of every neural feature. A shot full of nanobots will someday allow the most subtle details of our knowledge, skills and personalities to be copied into a file and stored in a computer.

Now this is even more interesting—Roger Penrose believes that consciousness is a quantum mechanical phenomenon arising from the fabric of the universe.[19] According to him, our ability to sustain seemingly incompatible mental states is a real quantum effect. And that quantum computing might help us upload the brain.

Again, all of this might sound like science-fiction but there already are people actively working on this. Or at least are thinking about it.

We could also achieve a more traditional immortality by achieving biological immortality. We have already discussed at length elsewhere in this book the advances made by medical and other sciences whereby we might be able to make our biological self disease-free and death-free.

We might also soon be able to clone our body and then live eternally by moving from clone to clone. Imagine your body is like a smartphone and your consciousness is on the cloud. When you wear out the current model (or get bored with it), you just pick up the next model and transfer your consciousness into it and head for the party with a new look.

That could be our future. One in which our mind will clone itself and then migrate from platform to platform for all eternity.

Then again, we might decide that we do not need one corporeal self forever. For that would indeed be boring. We might just decide to be an intelligent, immortal consciousness that adopts whatever form it feels like. Much like shape-shifters in mythology and folklore. Much like our gods (again) we might just take whatever form or avatar we wish and live for all time.

In *Altered Carbon*,[20] the physical body is a 'sleeve' which can accommodate any 'stack', which is a disc-shaped device that stores a person's memories and is implanted behind the neck.

If science progresses and we survive, we will manipulate the genome, rearrange the atoms and clone our consciousness. Our descendants will transcend our biological limitations and acquire super-intelligence and, bodied or disembodied, we will live forever.

If Tomorrow Comes

One thing I know for sure is this: we resemble our ancestors that wandered the African plains. But, post-singularity, our descendants won't. They will have as much in common with us as we have with the amino acids that gave us birth. They will debate our intelligence much as we debate the intelligence of our forefather, the single prokaryotic cell. They will be a different race.

Which is why, I believe we will be immortal. Either we achieve true immortality and we are able to keep our consciousness or both our consciousness and our bodies alive. Or our ideas live on forever, as machines.

We might be a transitory phase in the universe's larger scheme of things. But we are not a footnote, we have played a role.

Data Religion: Is Data the Next God?

IN GREEK MYTHOLOGY, THE FIRST ruler of the cosmos is Uranus, the Sky. One would have thought that Uranus and Gaia, the Earth, would make a reasonably compatible couple. But Uranus turns out to be a cruel husband, father and god. So Gaia conspires with their son, Cronos, to depose him. And Cronos does that quite spectacularly (and Oedipally)—by cutting off his father's testicles.[1]

A vengeful Uranus prophesies that the fate of Cronos wouldn't be any different. While he does become king of the cosmos, the curse is never far from Cronos's mind. Eventually, it does come true—Cronos is deposed by his son Zeus in the Battle of the Titans.

This defeat of the old gods led by Cronos by younger gods led by Zeus could well be an allegory for the transition from hunter-gatherer to settled farmer. But whatever it is, it makes a strong point—that gods die.

Every god has to make way—and be replaced by successor gods. This prophecy of Uranus has held true, from the time of the first man roaming the African savannah to now.

When the hunter-gatherer looked up and saw lightning play out its fury in the sky, he had no way to explain it. Every gap in his comprehension became something to appease. Every gap became a god.

As he travelled with his people, he found in natural phenomena more and more gaps that his limited knowledge could not comprehend. His descendants who settled down by fertile riversides understood the magic and capriciousness of nature better. But yet, when they huddled around the fire on cold nights, there was much they could not explain about the dark beyond the light of the flames. And we had more Gods of Gaps.

God is our ignorance. As Robert Ingersoll put it beautifully in *On the Gods and Other Essays*:

> No one infers a god from the simple, from the known, from what is understood—but from the complex, from the unknown, and incomprehensible. Our ignorance, is god; what we know, is science.[2]

Every time science explains a miracle, we demote a god from the scriptures to the textbook—from a divine legitimacy to a gross simplification. Like the creation myths becoming the theory of evolution. Like the gods of lightning being relegated to a science text on static electricity.

In many ways, this also mirrors our evolution as a society. The angry, vengeful god of the Jews evolved into a merciful, benevolent son in Jesus. The many shamanic deities of Arabia were replaced by a more contemporary, monotheistic god that Mohammed brought to the tribes.

I also find it extremely amusing that we refer to the Higgs boson as 'the God particle'. This last unresolved part of the standard model of particle physics, this last gap, we again go and name after God.

We will soon fill that gap. And kill that God.

Gods Are Not Immortal. They Die

In Neil Gaiman's brilliant work *American Gods,* the old gods led by Odin take on the new gods led by Mr World (the new god of globalization) in a fight for relevance. According to Gaiman:

Gods die, and when they truly die, they are unmourned and unremembered.[3]

The day Benjamin Franklin discovered how lightning works, many gods died across the planet. History is replete with dead gods.

And it is not just knowledge and science that kills gods.

Faced with the scientific and cultural transformation that the Industrial Revolution was, we needed new answers that Karl Marx and his angels provided. They understood the technological and economic realities of the day and had relevant answers to the new needs of industrialized society. Also, original ideas about how to make the best of these unprecedented opportunities.

Asked to define communism, Lenin once had this to say:

Communism is power to the Soviet workers plus electrification of the whole country.[4]

Lenin was woke (as they now say) to the need of the hour. But Brezhnev and Castro held on to the ideas of the Industrial Revolution in the era of the Computer Revolution.

Unfortunately, the gods that were contextually relevant for the nineteenth and twentieth centuries were useless in the twenty-first. As Vladimir Putin said recently:

Whoever does not miss the Soviet Union has no heart. Whoever wants it back, has no brain.[5]

A Lenin born today should be looking at how capitalism can be more equitable in the knowledge economy rather than looking at class wars.

Civilization will witness change—religion has to keep pace with our technological and social development. Hindu scriptures, which prohibited Brahmins from crossing the sea—*samudra ullanghana*—had to adapt. Wahhabi Saudi Arabia, which saw cinema as un-Islamic, has just repealed the ban on theatres. The Catholic Church now has the grace to look embarrassed when the question of contraception comes up.

The religions we have today have lost touch with the day's realities. What religions believe in and what their followers believe in seem to be diametrical opposites.

Have Today's Religions Passed Their Use-By Date?

Religion has fought against every single thing that we hold sacred today. Against free speech, democracy, sex education, reproductive technologies, reproductive rights, stem-cell research, women's and civil rights, and the advancement of science.

And who has religion fought for? Over the years, religion has aligned with human sacrifice, inquisitions, war, slavery, intolerance, fascism, genocide, torture, despotism, child abuse.

Look at who religion's friends are—it displays a fondness for the supernatural, the authoritarian, the misogynist, the anti-democratic, the anti-intellectual, the anti-scientific, the anti-progressive.

One could even argue that it is religion that has held back the progress of man. The rise of Christianity in many ways marginalized scientific and mathematical advances made by the Greeks and later adopted by the Romans. If science had continued to build on the achievements of the Greeks into the Middle Ages, we might as well have been living in an unimaginably better world today.

All of us know that in the 1540s, Copernicus proposed a heliocentric model of the universe, putting the sun rather than the Earth at the centre. But what most of us don't know is that the Greek Aristarchus of Samos had formulated a similar model eighteen centuries before that!

If Christianity had not applied the brakes on pagan sciences, we might have been saved from the Dark Ages. The Galileos and even the Newtons might not have had to start from where Aristotle left off, nineteen and twenty centuries before, respectively.

If we had not lost these centuries, who knows how many diseases we would have vanquished. Would we have conquered death? Who knows how advanced our intellectual and moral natures would have been. Would we still be killing and dying in the name of religion?

Without doubt, religions and gods have been our stumbling blocks (bringing us to our knees at times). As a civilization, would we have been better off without them?

With our new-found abilities to manipulate the genome, rearrange the atom and augment the mind—we will soon be able to defeat pain, disease, suffering, and maybe even death. When the cardiologist, the oncologist and the geneticist exist, why do I need God?

Why should I die hoping for eternal life in heaven, when science offers immortality right here on Earth? Without suffering and death (their crutches) the religions of today will lose their raison d'être. Is obsolescence staring Him and His establishment—religion—in the face?

Gods Are Expiring. But Maybe We Still Need Them

This is an argument I hear often, that religion and gods have no place in this techno-world. Every single time I hear that, I am reminded of the Samkhya school of Hinduism[6] which believes that God is a necessary metaphysical assumption demanded by circumstances.

This god could be the Norse Odin or Mr World, the god of globalization, as circumstance demands. But we, as humans, need our gods—for more than gaps in our comprehension.

We require their presence to address some age-old human needs—the need to believe that there is an external source for our sorrows and our joys, that fate can indeed deliver happiness, that our souls transcend this life and much, much else.

For all the damage that it has done, religion has also provided meaning. For many, it is the only consolation—to resolve the challenges of their lives and identity crises. In general, we all just want something to believe in, to make our lives easier and purposeful.

We need our gods as much as they need us. We need them to exist in the heavens we create for them.

We are not bound by the ignorance or fears of the hunter-gatherer and we might not need to appease lightning any more. But that is not to say that the twenty-first century, and the ones that follow, can do without its gods.

Religion is essential to our human self, so if old religions and old gods fail to answer our questions, we will demand new religions and new gods. Our constant need for meaning and the need to fill gaps will lead to the creation of new beliefs. In short, we will always seek a new source for legitimacy.

How should religion reinvent itself then, in an era where technology is integrating with our biology to create a smarter man—to invent a new Adam? What new god can bring us significance and meaning?

What Role Can Religion Play Today?

Yuval Noah Harari attempts to define this new source in *Homo Deus*. According to him, religious mythologies once legitimized divine authority. After that came humanist ideologies that legitimized human authority. Today, in Silicon Valleys across the world, tech gurus are creating the new creed—one that legitimizes the authority of algorithms and AI. Harari calls this 'dataism'.

Coined by the *New York Times* writer, David Brooks, dataism refers to a data-driven ideology—an obsession with data that assumes it is the best overall measure of any given scenario and that it always produces the most valuable result.[7]

Dataism derives from the confluence of two scientific tidal waves. The first is Charles Darwin's publication of *On the Origin of Species*, when the life sciences came to see organisms as biochemical algorithms. The second is Alan Turing's idea of the Turing machine, following which computer scientists have learned to engineer increasingly sophisticated electronic algorithms. Dataism puts the two together. Dataists believe that the entire universe is a flow of data, that organisms are algorithms and that humanity's cosmic vocation is to create an all-encompassing data-processing system—and then, merge into it. At a slightly more practical level, they believe that given enough biometric data and computing power, this all-encompassing system will understand us humans much better than we understand ourselves.

Dataism asserts that the same mathematical laws apply to both biochemical and electronic algorithms. It collapses the barrier between animals and machines and believes that electronic algorithms will eventually decipher and outperform biochemical algorithms.

This 'all-encompassing system' does understand us well, already. Harari quotes this book buyer's example to show us how well it does. How does the humanist choose a book? He wanders into a store and browses until he finds something that attracts his attention and matches his tastes. And the dataist? He just goes to Amazon, which does all of this for him.

In *Homo Deus*, Harari writes:

> We are already becoming tiny chips inside a giant system that nobody really understands. But no one needs to understand. All you need to do, is answer your emails faster.

And speaking of emails, Gmail is doing exactly that. I have been watching Gmail's smart replies with great interest. If you notice, all your mails now have an automated, quick response that you can choose. I have waited, in vain, to see the system come up with a wrong response. Or even one that is not relevant. It hasn't, yet. Those quick responses Gmail provides are exactly what I would have chosen to respond with. The system understands all.

Science is already giving us what we need, without us having to understand it. Sounds a little like religion? There's more, then.

Look at what dataism promises us. Happiness, peace, prosperity, even eternal life—but here on Earth with the help of data-processing technology, rather than after death with the help of bearded men and plump cherubs. (Sounds ambitious? But remember that all religions spread by making promises, not by keeping them.)

Much as socialism took over by promising salvation through social justice and electricity, so, in the coming decades, new techno-religions will take over—promising salvation through algorithms and genetics. We will go on to create more mysteries and more unknowns that will require more gods.

We already see the rumblings around us. Elon Musk's argument that we are living in a simulation (and he is not alone).[8] Enrico Fermi's contention that a few billion galaxies necessarily means there is other life out there.[9] We will build these new gods until science shows us otherwise.

But these new gods do have an advantage. Unlike the old ones who existed just in our imagination, these new guys will be part of us with their access to biotechnology and algorithm. These are not gods that rest in the scriptures and the skies like Odin. These are gods like Mr World in Neil Gaiman's *American Gods*, who are part and parcel of our lives—like social media, like sensors within and without us, like IoT, like nanotechnology in my veins, like brain-computer interfaces. They will not only control our minute-by-minute existence, but will be able to shape our bodies, brains and minds and create entire virtual worlds, complete with its hells and heavens.

Where dataism also has an advantage is in its ability to fill many of the gaps that religions of the past have not been able to. Dataism can take a very algorithmic look at happiness as opposed to the many metaphysical explanations we have been given all along. Algorithms in combination with genetics might be able to eventually eliminate pain and disease from our lives. I also believe that dataism, with its new ability to churn numbers in limitless proportions, will bring us a deeper understanding of the cosmos.

As we take AI to new frontiers, we are also forced to ask a whole lot of questions about ourselves—who we are, what consciousness is, what self-awareness is. These were all questions that we had conveniently left to religion and philosophy as we didn't have concrete answers. But now, we can approach these questions from a scientific, algorithmic, quantitative perspective.

All of which means that dataism is able to fill many of our biggest gaps; by definition then, a new God. All dataism now needs is a St Paul. And we already have him in Yuval Noah Harari.

The New Gods on the Block

Before dataism is able to build its Sistine Chapel and elect a pope, there already are offshoots springing up.

There's Kopism in Sweden, a recognized faith founded a decade ago which already has branches worldwide. The name is derived from the words 'copy me'. It celebrates the DNA's biological drive to copy and be copied. According to their US branch:

Copying is fundamental to life and runs constantly all around us. Shared information provides new perspectives and generates new life. We feel a spiritual connection to the created file.[10]

Besides a spiritual connection to created files, Kopism has no gods or supernatural agents.

There also is Way of the Future, a religious non-profit organization devoted to the worship of AI. Founded by Anthony Levandowski of Google's self-driving car fame, it intends to:

> ... develop and promote the realisation of a Godhead based on artificial intelligence and through understanding and worship of the Godhead, contribute to the betterment of society.[11]

Many in Silicon Valley also find solace in quasi-cultish concepts like the Singularity, the hypothesis that machines will eventually become so smart that they will outperform all human capabilities— leading to a superhuman intelligence so sophisticated it will be incomprehensible to our tiny fleshy, rational brains.

For some transhumanists, religion and science converge conceptually in the Singularity. According to them, God if he exists, is an 'it'. To them, this god is the most powerful of all singularities, and has already become pure, organized intelligence that spans the universe through a subatomic manipulation of physics.

(See how the new lingo of a new religion is replacing the lingo of old religions? All of this makes me wonder if Stephen Hawking and Elon Musk are right to be sceptical about AI.)

But traditional religions are not giving up so easily—Florida's Christian Transhumanist Association's Pastor Christopher Benek, its founding father (pun intended), believes that:

> The church does a terrible job of reaching out to Silicon Valley types.[12]

Benek argues that advanced AI is compatible with Christianity— it's just another technology that humans have created under guidance from God that can be used for good or evil. The pastor thinks religion and AI are compatible, I think it is just his survival instinct speaking.

May You Find the Gods You Want

While gods and humans kill each other, we also have nice folks like the creators of the Church of The Flying Spaghetti Monster—also called Pastafarianism.[13] Their god is a monster made of spaghetti that is flying across space. While they are a good laugh, they also take serious efforts to oppose the teaching of creationism and intelligent design in schools. Unlike the US that refuses to, New Zealand recognizes Pastafarianism as an official religion.

Some of these we might find silly, even hilarious, but then all religions were once new and viewed with scepticism. Religion outlives all this. Like the old joke goes, religion will survive because it is the only endeavour where the customer blames himself for product failure.

Many gods have died and many more have taken birth. For every god that dies, we will create a new one. We will never be without one. It could be dataism, it could be something else.

Whatever the new religion is, I hope it brings you all that you have always wanted—happiness, prosperity, eternal life, etc. After all, that is what all religions promise and I hope at least one will finally deliver.

The Upgrade to God: Is God
Man's Next Avatar?

The midday sun slips behind the mountains,
The Yellow River turns for the sea.
Trying to see for a thousand miles,
I climb one more storey.[1]

THIS SHORT POEM BY WANG Zhi Huan encapsulates our journey thus far. At every point, we have tried to climb higher, see farther.

We were not at the top of the food chain (on a scale of one to five, we rank 2.21, alongside pigs and anchovies),[2] yet we rule this planet. The human's inherent abilities have not changed much since Og was in the cave, yet we are exploring Mars today.

Our ability to develop tools and technology has overcome our physical limitations—the wheel, the steam engine, earthmovers, electricity, the telephone, automobiles, prosthetics have all extended our physical abilities and reach.

So far, technology has augmented only our physical capabilities and our external reach and power. What we are poised to see is the augmentation of the human body and mind.

Advancements and convergences in digital technology, artificial intelligence, genetics and nanotechnology are enhancing and refreshing our biological and mental capabilities. Human ability, which so far has progressed on external tools, will now advance by upgrading the body and mind. Or, interestingly, by merging directly with the tool.

Our biology is getting rewired, right from our genes. And our intelligence has expanded to the intelligence of the cloud. Our biology and technology are increasingly coterminous and we look ready to chart a new evolutionary path.

We have climbed another storey.

Everything Seems to Be Happening Faster

The planet is 4.5 billion years old. The oldest material available on Earth is zircon crystals, 4.3 billion years old. Life began on Earth about 3.8 billion years ago, with single-celled prokaryotic cells.

From there to Homo sapiens took a mighty long time, for man has been on this planet only for about 200,000 years. So, we have been on the planet only for about .004 per cent of the planet's existence, and our recorded history is just about 5000 years!

Our first storey—fire, sharp-edged flint, the wheel—took us tens of thousands of years. For people of that era, even a thousand years brought little technological change. Og in the cave and Og's descendant twenty-five generations later lived exactly the same 'solitary, poor, nasty, brutish and short'[3] life.

But by 1000 AD, one could see paradigm shifts every couple of centuries. In the nineteenth century, we saw more change than in the nine centuries preceding it. And then the first twenty years of the twentieth century saw more change than in all of the nineteenth century. Today, paradigm shifts take just a few years.

Just about a century ago, most of the people on the planet had not seen an electric bulb. But if you were to tell a child today that his grandparents saw an era before light bulbs, he would most probably double-check with Alexa.

All of this only tells us this one thing—the pace of change is accelerating. Biological life and technology have followed a similar evolutionary pattern, they take a while to get going but when they do, they speed up in earnest. What we are stepping into now is the explosive part of the evolutionary curve of technology.

In 1965, Gordon E. Moore, (co-founder of Intel) observed that the number of transistors in a dense integrated circuit doubles every two years. He estimated that by 1975, it would be possible to cram 65,000 components on a quarter-inch semiconductor. But by 2017, AMD's (Advanced Micro Devices) commercially available Epyc had 19.2 billion transistors on a single chip. And it is all of fourteen nanometres.

In his 2001 essay, 'The Law of Accelerating Returns', the futurist Ray Kurzweil proposed extending Moore's Law to describe exponential growth in diverse forms of technological progress. He stated that whenever technology hits a barrier, a new technology is invented which will help us overcome that barrier.

Kurzweil observed that extraordinary change would become increasingly common and it would bring:

. . . technological change so rapid and profound that it represents a rupture in the fabric of human history.

He predicted a technological singularity by around 2045 in his book *The Singularity Is Near: When Humans Transcend Biology.*

During the Singularity, Kurzweil predicted that humans will transcend the limitation of our biological bodies and brain. Non-biological intelligence would alter how humans learn, play, work and wage war. In his book, he talked of nanobots that would allow people to consume whatever they want and yet be as fit as they wish. He spoke of nanobots that will fight diseases, replace organs and augment the brain. Kurzweil claimed that eventually the human would be so augmented that he would be able to alter his physical manifestation at will.

In short, our technology will merge with our biology. This change will not happen at the pace of the past. And this change is almost upon our species.

As Usual, Science-Fiction Has Anticipated Reality

As we have noticed many a time elsewhere in this book, science-fiction's ability to anticipate our reality is uncanny. From H.G. Wells predicting the spacecraft in the 1890s to Jules Verne anticipating the submarine in the 1870, fiction is replete with representations of what the future would bring.

It is not surprising therefore that science-fiction has also anticipated the impending merger of biology with technology. As far back as in Greek mythology, Hephaestus—the Greek god of all mechanical arts—is assisted by two living female statues made of gold who are filled with 'minds and wisdom'.[4]

Closer to our times, in Auguste Villiers de l'Isle-Adam's 1886 book, *The Future Eve*, we have Hadaly, a woman run by electricity. This was the book that popularized the word 'android'.

And how can we ever forget Philip K. Dick's *We Can Build You* and *Do Androids Dream of Electric Sheep*, which eventually became the premise for *Blade Runner*. He visualized a world where androids and humans were indistinguishable—except for the human's ability to empathize.

Blurring the lines between human and machine has been a popular sci-fi idea for a while. In the recent movie *Ghost in the Shell*, Scarlett Johansson is Major Mira Killian, a cyborg super-soldier with superhuman abilities who investigates her past to discover that she was a human anti-augmentation radical who was abducted and turned into a cyborg.

But today, this is not pure science-fiction any more. What fiction imagined, technology will soon engineer.

We are about to climb that storey. And when we do, what we see there could be one of these three possibilities or a fusion:

i.   Machines becoming human—robots/humanoids
ii. Engineered biological beings—through nanotechnology and genetic/stem-cell therapies
iii. Humans becoming machines—cyborg

I think each of them deserves some explanation.

Machines Becoming Human

At this point in our evolution and in the evolution of AI, the prospect of machines evolving the intelligence and consciousness equal to humans is still is in the realm of science-fiction.

Let us look at intelligence first. It will be a while before machines develop the level of intelligence needed to master their own and our destinies. At this point, our greatest achievements are machines that can understand and obey voice commands, not issue them. With each passing day, the intelligence of machines is equalling or excelling that of humans at *specific* (not all) tasks— think GPS, language translation, autonomous cars, emotion sensing. Over the years, we can expect the computational abilities of machines to grow exponentially to pass the Turing test in most scenarios.

It will take another few decades before they exhibit the full range of human intellect, emotions and skills we exhibit today. They will also claim to have feelings (or at least have the ability to convince us that they do).

Which brings us to the consciousness part. A computer today knows more about water, tidal waves and tsunamis than the world's most intelligent scholar on the subject of water. But can the computer 'feel' wet? Not yet.

In the movie *AI*, the robot-boy David loves his human owner. He wishes he were 'a real boy' so that his feelings for his owner would not go unrequited. According to Ray Kurzweil, this is evidence of David's 'humanity':

> But he should be considered a real boy if he can express that deepest, richest emotion we have. He should be considered part of human civilisation.

This 'humanity', what makes us 'human', I believe is consciousness. It is our consciousness that gives meaning to an otherwise (fairly) meaningless, mechanical world. If we are to go by the Copenhagen interpretation,[5] then it is our consciousness that creates the reality around us. Which, in my mind, makes consciousness supersede intelligence. Besides, we can replicate intelligence, but not consciousness which is why, even in the distant future of humanity I do not foresee disembodied intelligence—where the source of intelligence is devoid of a corporeal self but has the ability to learn, understand and deal with new situations, which require great intellect and sentience. Like Brainiac 417, the super-intelligent but intangible member of the Justice League.

There are many reasons we need more intelligence than the human can currently provide. As a growing civilization, we are in greater need of resources for us to thrive and the resources available on the planet are not going to last indefinitely, which means we need to look at resources on other planets.

Science-fiction has of course anticipated this in *Interstellar*, in which a global food crisis forces astronauts to travel through wormholes[6] in the quest of a new home for humanity.

We will need much intelligence for this quest. Much more than natural human intelligence can promise today.

While we need this, we also fear that a superior intelligence will be able to unseat us from our acquired position at the top of the food chain. That a machine turned humanoid would decide whether humans need to be terminated, enslaved or treated as equals. (At the end of *AI*, man's inventions have outlasted him. And the planet is populated by a race of super-intelligent androids.)

Now, what if the future were to be one of engineered biological beings?

Engineered Biological Beings

If you believe in Darwin instead of a bearded man in the sky, you would agree that we got here thanks to natural selection. The theory of natural selection tells us that our genes are a naughty, curious bunch, perpetually interacting with the environment around us and making random changes in their structure.[7]

These changes, if found useful, survive. This is how the opposable thumb evolved. This is how our broader foreheads narrowed. This is how we have become who we are.

Now what if we were to remove the world 'natural' from natural selection? What if these were deliberate changes made by us? What if we take what we need to rise above the challenges placed upon us by our natural environment and splice that into our genes?

If we do this, then the theory of 'natural' selection gives way to 'unnatural' selection and what follows will be a breed of genetically perfect humans.

If you ask me, losing 'natural' from natural selection would be the most stellar step in the evolution of man after the opposable thumb. Would we even be qualified to call ourselves Homo sapiens?

The prospect is staggering. A few tweaks to our DNA, to our hormonal systems, to our brain structures and we would be a superior, engineered race—free from disease and with a longer shelf life. Or even immortality.

This is happening around us as we speak.

This Is Not Science-Fiction Any More

Genetic sciences have seen enormous advances in reading, writing and hacking our own DNA. Today, scientists can splice out a heart condition from a gene sequence.

Thanks to precision gene-editing techniques like CRISPR-Cas9,[8] it won't be long before gene-editing is a regular feature that can be used to prevent most inheritable diseases. Why roll genetic dice when we know that intervention can ensure a healthy child?

If you, like Angeline Jolie, had your genome sequenced and figured that you carry the BRCA1 and BRCA2 mutations, which predict an 87 per cent possibility of breast cancer and a 50 per cent possibility of ovarian cancer, what would you do? Jolie opted for a double mastectomy and later, an ovario-hysterectomy. What she has done is eliminated inherited disease.[9]

Gene-editing can indeed create the engineered human.

Nanotechnology is also allowing us to redesign and rebuild our bodies, our brains and the world we live in, molecule by molecule. Considering nanotechnology allows us to play at the atomic level (and considering everything is made up of atoms), the possibilities are endless.

Nanorobotics allows us to create robots that are nano-sized (biological or synthetic) and can perform preprogrammed tasks at an atomic level. They can be autonomous in nature and can interact at a nanoscale and help us understand and manipulate structures at that level.

Nanobots released into our blood streams can clean our arteries and repair organs damaged by age or trauma.

But what will really make you sit up is the fact that eventually, they could soon even restore our DNA to how it was when we were in our twenties. This can turn fragile senior citizens into healthy young individuals overnight. In short, the promise of eternal youth.

In the Puranas, Shiva grants the devout sage Mrikandu Rishi and his wife Marudmati a boon. They can choose to have a super-intelligent, righteous son destined to live a short life or a son of low intelligence with a long life. The couple chose the former and were blessed with Markandeya, destined to die at sixteen. But fate (and the gods) had other plans and Markandeya became immortal at sixteen.

Maybe that is what nanotechnology will bless our next generation with, super intelligence and immortal youth. All Markandeyas.

Stem-cell therapy is another development that is pushing us towards a better engineered human. Stem-cell therapy's ability to grow vital organs gives regenerative medicine magical capabilities.

Stem cells are the body's basic elements, from which all other cells with specialized functions are generated. Stem cells divide to form daughter cells which can become either new stem cells or cells with specific functions like brain cells, heart muscle, bone or blood cells.

Stem cells can be grown to become new tissues for transplant or regenerative medicine, a natural ability no other cell in the body has. Watching stem cells mature into specialized cells is also telling researchers a lot about how diseases and conditions develop.

I believe stem-cell therapy will soon make integrated and seamlessly regenerative medical practices accessible to all. Replacing damaged or diseased organs will be something everyone can do.

Stem-cell therapy, alongside genetic sciences and nanotechnology, can slow or even stop the inexorable march of biological time.

All of this reminds me of Oscar Wilde's *Dorian Gray*, who is young, handsome and cannot age; who, therefore, begins to believe that beauty is the only aspect of life worth striving for and descends into an amoral morass. What will we do with our science-granted beauty and science-granted youth? Will we misuse it?

That brings us to our last option. That of humans turning into cyborgs.

Humans Becoming Machines—Cyborg

Turing famously asked, 'Can machines think?'[10] But what if Turning had not asked this question? What if his question had been, 'can man be augmented?'

Would man's machine-ness and not the machine's human-ness have been our benchmark then? Would we then have looked at how to augment our already considerable abilities?

Ever since Turing asked this question, our endeavours have been to make the machine more and more 'human', its human-ness being our benchmark.

If we are to look at the AI destination as a machine-powered human and not as a conscious machine, the entire equation changes. The fact is that while machines indeed are becoming more artificially intelligent, we are also becoming more and more synthetic. At an equal or faster rate! Our environment is increasingly wired, sensor-filled, and digitally connected. With that smartphone in your hand, you are to some extent cyborg already.

Imagine and consider that your smartphone would soon be available as cellular-sized nanorobots. These can be inserted into your capillaries and the screen image will be projected on to your retina. All it requires is a brain-computer interface to operate the nanorobots in your blood stream.

The progress that is being made on brain-computer interfaces verges on science-fiction. This means that soon you will be able to operate the computer with thought, much the same way our thoughts control our speech, movements and feelings.

Stephen Hawking used a brain-computer interface.[11] Initially, he communicated using a spelling card, indicating letters and forming words by lifting his eyebrows. Later a company called Word Plus devised a computer programme called Equalizer which helped users like Hawking to select words and commands on a computer using a hand-clicker.

As the disease progressed, Hawking lost his ability to use the clicker. Eventually, after much trial and error, Intel devised a system whereby the interface would interpret Hawking's intention rather than the actual input—much like the algorithm used for natural language processing in your mobile phone. This technology also provided Hawking with various shortcuts to speak, search, email or deliver a lecture based on contextual menus.

Now we also have technology that uses electrical signals to stimulate the brain. Nathan Copeland, a paraplegic, was provided a prosthetic hand which he cannot just control with 'thought' but can also sense touch—he 'feels' when you touch him on his prosthetic.[12]

So far, brain-computer interfaces have been used for relatively simple tasks, mainly to restore motor control for paralyzed patients and enable communication for locked-in patients with brain injuries that prevent them from communicating effectively.

The day is not far when these will be used to augment our abilities. Not to aid the challenged but to make us smarter.

Neural engineering is another area that is seeing great interest. DARPA in the US is investing millions into their neural engineering systems design programme. The programme's purpose is to develop a cubic-centimetre-sized brain implant that can translate human thoughts into computer code, and vice versa.

Once implanted, this can enable data transfer to and from the brain (by communicating between a digital interface and over a million neurons). What this can do is the stuff of legend—it can make the blind see and the deaf hear. And, it can help humans communicate, without typing, speaking or moving.

Remember that this is a nanorobot that has integrated with your brain, expanding its power[n].

Shouldn't we then be looking at the new, improved human? A new being with all the consciousness of a human and the perfection of machine? (Instead of worrying about a machine takeover).

What Is the Next Storey to Climb?

Having looked at humanoids, engineered biology and cyborgs, I believe that what lies next for Homo sapiens is a coming together of artificial and natural intelligence and human consciousness to create a super-intelligent, conscious human.

As Arthur C. Clarke said:

> It may be that our role on this planet is not to worship God—but to create him.[13]

In *Homo Deus*, Harari predicts that humans will make an attempt, with these new-found powers at our command, to gain happiness, immortality and other God-like powers.

In *The Singularity is Near*, Kurzweil believes that evolution moves towards:

> . . . greater complexity, greater elegance, greater knowledge, greater intelligence, greater beauty, greater creativity, and greater levels of subtle attributes such as love.

Which he believes are generally the attributes we use to describe God.

I do not know if God awaits ahead or Homo sapiens 2.0. All I know is that this talk about gods makes me think about the chimpanzee.

Genetically speaking, nucleotide-to-nucleotide, we differ from the chimp by precisely 1.23 per cent.[14] About 6.5 million years ago, chimpanzees in the drier habitats of Africa, started standing to get closer to the tree and its fruits. The chimps in the denser forest had no advantage in standing up as the trees were much taller and the fruits much higher. That is where we began.

The moment we started walking, we had hands to carry tools. And from there, we have never looked back.

We have walked and climbed, bringing us to a stage where we can dictate how we need to evolve. Where we can artificially engineer evolution, make it deterministic and not random probabilistic.

That desire to stand, that 1.23 per cent, led to our cousins ending up in the zoo and man going on to conquer this world.

The next 1 per cent will be change we dictate, and I know it will lead to many new worlds being conquered.

This is a beginning. Not the end.

Behind us, is Homo sapiens.
Before us, is a whole new species.
We are the transitional generation.
What a great place and time to be in!

Bibliography

These books are a part of my collection at home, keenly read and preciously treasured. In some cases they are not the most authoritative of sources, or the best editions that have been put to print. Here, I simply list the books in my possession that I have read (and reread) to write this book. I acknowledge my debt to all writers for their original works, or for their contribution to secondary research in many cases.

Chapter 1: A Requiem for Alan Turing

1. B. Jack Copeland, ed., *The Essential Turing: Seminal Writings in Computing, Logic, Philosophy, Artificial Intelligence, and Artificial Life plus the Secrets of Enigma* (Clarendon Press, OUP; first edition, 2004).
2. George Dyson, *Turing's Cathedral* (Vintage Books, A Division of Random House, Inc., New York, 2012).
3. Andrew Hodges, *Alan Turing: The Enigma* (Vintage Publishing, United Kingdom, 2014).
4. Bertrand Russell, *Mysticism and Logic and Other Essays* (Project Gutenburg, updated 24 May 2012).
5. Stuart J. Russell and Peter Norvig, eds., *Artificial Intelligence: A Modern Approach* (global edition, Pearson Education Limited, Essex, UK, 2010).

Chapter 2: The Philosophy of AI

1. Isaac Asimov, 'Runaround' in *I, Robot* (Bantam Spectra Books, Bantam Dell, Random House, NY; mass market edition, 1991).
2. -----, *Foundation* (Bantam Spectra Books, Bantam Dell, Random House, NY; Mass Market Edition, 1991).

3. Yuval Noah Harari, *Homo Deus: A Brief History of Tomorrow* (Harvill Secker, an imprint of Vintage, Penguin Random House, UK, 2016).
4. Ray Kurzweil, *The Singularity Is Near: When Humans Transcend Biology* (Penguin Books, NY, 2006).
5. Ramana Maharishi, *Who am I?* (Sri Ramana Ashram, twenty-fourth edition, 8 January 2008).
6. Marvin Minsky, *The Emotion Machine: Commonsense Thinking, Artificial Intelligence, and the Future of the Human Mind* (Simon & Schuster, NY, paperback, 13 November 2007).
7. Michael Rescorla, *The Computational Theory of Mind*, The Stanford Encyclopedia of Philosophy (Spring 2017 Edition), Edward N. Zalta (ed.), https://plato.stanford.edu/archives/spr2017/entries/computational-mind/.
8. Herbert Alexander Simon, *Sciences of the* Artificial (The MIT Press, NY, 3rd Edition, Paperback).

Chapter 3: The Technology of AI

1. Stuart J. Russell and Peter Norvig, Artificial Intelligence.
2. Simon Haykin, Neural Networks and Learning Machines (Pearson India Education Services Pvt. Ltd, 2016).
3. Christopher D. Manning and Hinrich Schutze, 'Foundations of Statistical Natural Language Processing' (Massachusetts Institute of Technology, 1999).
4. Ian Goodfellow, Yoshua Bengio and Aaron Courville, Deep Learning (MIT Press, 2017).
5. Jeff Hawkins, *On Intelligence* (St. Martin's Griffin, NY, 2004).

Chapter 4: Nanotechnology

1. William Illsey Atkinson, *Nanocosm: Nanotechnology and the Big Changes Coming from the Inconceivably Small* (AMACOM; first edition, 7 May 2003).
2. K.K. Chattopadhyay and A.N. Banerjee, *Introduction to Nanoscience and Nanotechnology* (PHI, Kindle edition, 1 December 2009).

3. Eric Drexler, *Engines of Creation: The Coming Era of Nanotechnology* (Fourth Estate; new edition, 6 May 1996).
4. Richard P. Feynman, *Surely You're Joking Mr Feynman: Adventures of a Curious Character* (Vintage, Random House, UK; Paperback, 19 November 1992).
5. Osho, *Tao: The Pathless Path* (Renaissance Books; first edition, paperback, 22 February 2002).

Chapter 5: Quantum Computing

1. Jim Al-Khalili and Johnjoe McFadden, *Life on the Edge* (Random House, paperback, 1 October 2015).
2. Erwin Schrödinger, *What Is Life?: With Mind and Matter and Autobiographical Sketches* (Cambridge University Press; reprint edition, paperback, 26 March 2012).

Chapter 6: Genetics

1. George M. Church and Ed Regis, *Regenesis: How Synthetic Biology Will Reinvent Nature and Ourselves*, (Basic Books, Perseus Books Group, NY, paperback, 2014).
2. Francis S. Collins, *The Language of Life: DNA and the Revolution in Personalized Medicine* (Harper Perennial, HarperCollins Publishers, NY, paperback, 18 January 2011).
3. Juan Enriquez and Steve Gullans, *Evolving Ourselves: Redesigning the Future of Humanity—One Gene at a Time* (current, an imprint of Penguin Random House LLC, NY, revised edition, 15 November 2016).
4. Leland Hartwell, Michael L. Goldberg, Janice Fischer and Leroy Hood, *Genetics: From Genes to Genomes* (McGraw-Hill Education, NY; sixth edition, 2017).
5. Robin Marantz Henig, *The Monk in the Garden: The Lost and Found Genius of Gregor Mendel, the Father of Genetics* (Mariner Books, NY, paperback, 12 May 2001).
6. Siddhartha Mukherjee, *The Gene: An Intimate History* (Scribner, an imprint of Simon & Schuster, Inc., NY, paperback, 2017).

7. James D. Watson and Andrew Berry, *DNA: The Secret of* Life, (Alfred A. Knopf, USA, reprint edition, 2003).

Chapter 7: The Filter Bubble

1. Mary Aiken, *The Cyber Effect* (Hodder & Stoughton; paperback, 7 September 2016).
2. Sumitra M. Katre, *Astadhyayi of Panini* (Motilal Banarsidass; second reprint edition, hardcover, 1 January 2015).
3. Evgeny Morozov, *The Net Delusion* (Penguin, UK; paperback, 5 April 2012).
4. Eli Pariser, *The Filter Bubble: What the Internet Is Hiding from You* (Penguin, UK; paperback, 1 March 2012).

Chapter 8: Matchmaking

1. Aziz Ansari and Eric Klinenberg, *Modern Romance* (Penguin Books, reprint edition, 14 June 2016).
2. Italo Calvino, George Martin (translator), Italian Folktales [Series: Penguin Modern Classics] (Penguin Books, paperback, 24 February 2000).
3. Eli J. Finkel, *The All-or-Nothing Marriage: How the Best Marriages Work* (Dutton, 19 September 2017).
4. P.V.R. Rayudu, *How to Match Horoscopes for Marriage: A Scientific Model of Compatibility Points based on Moon and Other Aspects as per Hindu Astrology* (SAB, 2001).
5. Ram Babu Sao, *Perfect Astrology (Matchmaking): Muhurata for Venture and Matchmaking between Partners* (Amazon.in, paperback, first edition, 2016).
6. Dan Slater, *Love in the Time of Algorithms: What Technology Does to Meeting and Mating* (current, Penguin Group (USA) Inc., 24 January 2013).
7. Nassim Nicholas Taleb, *The Black Swan: The Impact of the Highly Improbable* (Random House Trade Paperbacks, an imprint of The Random House, Inc., New York, second edition, 2010).

Chapter 9: Electoral Math

1. Sasha Issenberg, *The Victory Lab* (Broadway Books, reprint edition, 17 September 2013).
2. Michael Lewis, *Moneyball: The Art of Winning an Unfair Game,* (W.W. Norton & Company; reprint edition, 13 July 2004).

Chapter 10: Blockchain and Cryptocurrency

1. Nathaniel Popper, *Digital Gold: Bitcoin and the Inside Story of the Misfits and Millionaires Trying to Reinvent Money* (Harper Paperbacks; reprint edition, May 2016).
2. Paul Vigna and Michael Casey, *Cryptocurrency: How Bitcoin and Digital Money are Challenging the Global Economic Order* (Vintage, Penguin Random House; paperback, 28 January 2016).

Chapter 12: Data Privacy

1. Aldous Huxley, *Brave New World* (Vintage, Penguin Random House, UK; paperback, 2 September 2004).
2. George Orwell, *1984* (Maple Press, paperback, 1 September 2013).

Chapter 13: Jobs and AI

1. Erik Brynjolfsson and Andrew McAfee, *The Second Machine Age: Work, Progress, and Prosperity in a Time of Brilliant Technologies* (W.W. Norton & Company; reprint edition, 26 January 2016).
2. Yuval Noah Harari, *Homo Deus: A Brief History of Tomorrow.*
3. Martin Ford, *The Rise of the Robots: Technology and the Threat of Mass Unemployment* (Oneworld Publications; paperback, 2 June 2016).
4. Malcom Frank, Paul Roehrig, and Ben Pring, *What to Do When Machines Do Everything: How to Get Ahead in a World of AI, Algorithms, Bots, and Big Data* (John Wiley & Sons; first edition, 10 February 2017).

5. Kevin Kelly, *The Inevitable* (Penguin; hardcover, first edition, 20 July 2016).

Chapter 14: Love, Sex and AI

1. David Levy, *Love and Sex with Robots: The Evolution of Human-Robot Relationships* (Harper Perennial; reprint edition, paperback, 4 November 2008).

Chapter 15: Ethics and AI

1. Isaac Asimov, 'Runaround' in *I, Robot*.

Chapter 16: The Periodic Table

1. Robert Boyle, *The Sceptical Chymist* (Sagwan Press, paperback, 7 February 2018).
2. Carl Huffman, 'The Role of Number in Philolaus' Philosophy' (essay published in 'Phronesis: A Journal of Ancient Philosophy' (ISSN   0031-8868),   [https://www.scribd.com/doc/19661208/Huffman-The-Role-of-Number-in-Philolaus-Philosophy].

Chapter 17: Math and Art

1. Benoit B. Mandelbrot, *The Fractal Geometry of Nature* (Times Books, updated edition, hardcover, 15 August 1982).
2. Jules Henri Poincare, *Science and Hypothesis* (Dover Publications Inc., underlining edition, 7 February 1998).
3. Tandalam Sundara Rao, *Geometrical Exercises in Paper Folding* (Nabu Press, primary source edition, paperback, 22 February 2014).

Chapter 18: The Idea of Math

1. Mario Livo, *Is God a Mathematician?* (Simon & Schuster, 19 January 2010).

Chapter 19: The Prediction of Neptune

1. Ian Stewart, *Calculating the Cosmos* (Profile Books Ltd., London, UK; export edition, 3 November 2016).

Chapter 21: The Happiness Pill

1. Aldous Huxley, *Brave New World* (Harper Perennial; reprint edition, 18 October 2006).

Chapter 22: On Extraterrestrial Life

1. Steven J. Dick. *Plurality of Worlds: The Origins of the Extraterrestrial Life Debate from Democritus to Kant* (Cambridge University Press; first edition, 31 March 1982).

Chapter 23: Simulation

1. Nick Bostrom, 'Are You Living in a Computer Simulation?', published in *Philosophical Quarterly* (2003), vol. 53, no. 211, pp. 243–55. (First Version: 2001), https://www.simulation-argument.com/simulation.pdf.
2. Rene Descartes and John Veitch (translator), *Meditations on First Philosophy* (Createspace Independent Pub, paperback, 10 October 2017).
3. Hilary Putnam, *Reason, Truth and History* (Cambridge University Press, hardcover, 31 December 1981).

Chapter 24: Transhumanism

1. Isaac Asimov, 'Runaround' in *I, Robot*.
2. Nick Bostrom, *Superintelligence: Paths, Dangers, Strategies* (Oxford University Press, UK; paperback, reprint edition, 14 July 2016).
3. Michio Kaku, *The Future of the Mind: The Scientific Quest to Understand, Enhance and Empower the Mind* (Penguin Group, UK; paperback, 26 February 2015).

4. Ray Kurzweil, *The Singularity Is Near: When Humans Transcend Biology.*

5. William Winwood Reade, *The Martyrdom of Man*, classic reprint (Forgotten Books, hardcover, 21 April 2018).

Chapter 25: Data Religion

1. Neil Gaiman, *American Gods* (Headline Book Publishing; paperback, 4 March 2002).

2. Robert G. Ingersoll, *On the Gods and Other Essays* (Prometheus Books; hardcover, 1 July 1990).

3. Nandalal Sinha, *The Samkhya Philosophy* (Munshirm Manoharlal pub. pvt. ltd; reprint edition 1 December 2003).

Chapter 26: The Upgrade to God

1. Ray Kurzweil, *The Singularity Is Near: When Humans Transcend Biology.*

2. Yuval Noah Harari, *Homo Deus: A Brief History of Tomorrow.*

Endnotes

Chapter 1: A Requiem for Alan Turing

1. From *The Imitation Game*, 2014.
2. 'Computing Machinery and Intelligence', Alan Turing, 1950, http://web.iitd.ac.in/~sumeet/Turing50.pdf, pp.1-2.
3. 'The Prelude', William Wordsworth, https://www.goodreads.com/quotes/168824-bliss-it-was-in-that-dawn-to-be-alive-but.
4. 'Computing Machinery and Intelligence', Turing.
5. 'The Chemical Basis of Morphogenesis', Turing, Philosophical Transactions of the Royal Society of London, series B, Biological Sciences, vol. 237, no. 641 (14 August 1952), pp. 37–72, https://www.jstor.org/stable/92463. In this paper, he described the way in which natural patterns such as stripes, spots and spirals may arise naturally out of a homogeneous, uniform state. The theory, which can be called a reaction–diffusion theory of morphogenesis, has served as a basic model in theoretical biology.
6. http://www.quotehd.com/quotes/ralph-waldo-emerson-nature-quotes-when-nature-has-work-to-be-done-she-creates-a.
7. Bertrand Russell, *Mysticism and Logic and Other Essays*, Project Gutenburg, updated 24 May 2012, pp. 61. A longer version of the quote is: 'Mathematics, rightly viewed, possesses not only truth, but supreme beauty—a beauty cold and austere, like that of sculpture, without appeal to any part of our weaker nature, without the gorgeous trappings of painting or music, yet sublimely pure, and capable of a stern perfection such as only the greatest art can show. The true spirit of delight, the exaltation, the sense of being more than Man, which is the touchstone of the highest excellence, is to be found in mathematics as surely as poetry.'

8. Holden Frith, 'Unraveling the Tale behind the Apple Logo', CNN. com, international edition, 7 October 2011, https://edition.cnn. com/2011/10/06/opinion/apple-logo/index.html.

Chapter 2: The Philosophy of AI

1. Isaac Asimov, 'Runaround', *I, Robot*, 1950.
2. 'South Korea Creates Ethical Code for Righteous Robots', *NewScientist*, 8 March 2007, https://www.newscientist.com/article/ dn11334-south-korea-creates-ethical-code-for-righteous-robots/.
3. Psychohistory is a fictional science in Isaac Asimov's Foundation universe which combines history, sociology and mathematical statistics to make general predictions about the future behaviour of very large groups of people, such as the Galactic Empire. It was first introduced in the four short stories (1942–44) which would later be collected for the 1951 novel, *Foundation*.
4. Neil deGrasse Tyson quotes. BrainyQuote.com, https://www. brainyquote.com/quotes/neil_degrasse_tyson_531089, accessed 3 November 2018.
5. 'The Ratio Club: A Melting Pot for British Cybernetics' Olivia Solon, *Wired*, 21 June 2012, https://www.wired.co.uk/article/ratio-club-turing.
6. 'Computing Machinery and Intelligence', Turing. The seminal paper is based on the topic of artificial intelligence. Published in 1950, it was the first to introduce Turing's concept of what is now known as the Turing Test to the general public.

 Further, Turing's paper considers the question 'Can machines think?' Since the words 'think' and 'machine' cannot be defined in a clear way that satisfies everyone, Turing suggests we 'replace the question by another, which is closely related to it and is expressed in relatively unambiguous words:' To do this, he must first find a simple and unambiguous idea to replace the word 'think', he must explain exactly which 'machines' he is considering, and finally, armed with these tools, he formulates a new question, related to the first, that he believes he can answer in the affirmative.

7. In computer science, a universal Turing machine (UTM) is a Turing machine that can simulate an arbitrary Turing machine based on arbitrary input. The universal machine essentially achieves this by reading both the description of the machine to be simulated as well as the input thereof from its own tape. Alan Turing introduced the idea of such a machine in 1936–37. This principle is considered to be the origin of the idea of a stored-programme computer used by John von Neumann in 1946 for the 'Electronic Computing Instrument' that now bears von Neumann's name: the von Neumann architecture. In terms of computational complexity, a multi-tape universal Turing machine need only be slower by a logarithmic factor compared to the machines it simulates.
    Refer to 'The Computational Theory of Mind', Michael Rescorla, The Stanford Encyclopedia of Philosophy (Spring 2017 Edition), Edward N. Zalta (ed.), https://plato.stanford.edu/archives/spr2017/entries/computational-mind/>.

8. 'What Marvin Minsky Still Means for AI', Will Knight, MIT Technology Review, 26 January 2016, https://www.technologyreview.com/s/546116/what-marvin-minsky-still-means-for-ai/#.

9. 'The Second-best Science Fiction Writer in the World Also Wrote Bawdy Verse and Crime Fiction', Gautham Shenoy, Factor Daily, 6 January 2017, https://factordaily.com/isaac-asimov-golden-age-science-fiction/.

10. *The Emotion Machine: Commonsense Thinking, Artificial Intelligence, and the Future of the Human Mind*, Marvin Minsky, Simon & Schuster, 2007.

11. 'The Computational Theory of Mind', Rescorla.

12. Ibid.

13. Ibid.

14. Ibid.

15. Ibid.

16. Herbert Alexander Simon, *Sciences of the Artificial*, MIT Press, New York, third edition, 1996)

17. 'Unthinking Machines', Stephen Class, MIT Technology Review, 4 May 2011, https://www.technologyreview.com/s/423917/unthinking-machines/.

18. 'Technology; The Computer as Translator', Andrew Pollack, *New York Times*, 28 April 1983, https://www.nytimes.com/1983/04/28/business/technology-the-computer-as-translator.html.

19. Ibid.

20. Read about the great match-up on Chess.com, 'Kasparov vs. Deep Blue: The Match That Changed History', 1 October 2018, https://www.chess.com/article/view/deep-blue-kasparov-chess.

21. http://www.doc.ic.ac.uk/~ad2816/index.html/page_1.html.

22. Read about The All new Roomba® i7 at https://www.irobot.com/for-the-home/vacuuming/roomba.

23. 'John McCarthy', blog by Bertrand Meyer in Blog@CACM of ACM.org, 28 October 2011, https://cacm.acm.org/blogs/blog-cacm/138907-john-mccarthy/fulltext.

24. *Homo Deus: A Brief History of Tomorrow,* Yuval Noah Harari, 2017.

25. *The Singularity Is Near: When Humans Transcend Biology* is a 2006 non-fiction book about AI and the future of humanity by inventor and futurist Ray Kurzweil.

26. Ibid.

27. *Who am I?,* Ramana Maharishi (Sri Ramana Ashram), twenty-fourth edition, 8 January 2008.

Chapter 3: The Technology of AI

1. 'Gartner on Blockchain, AI and Data: Hype or Hope?', Bruno Aziza, *Forbes*, 8 May 2018, https://www.forbes.com/sites/ciocentral/2018/05/08/gartner-on-blockchain-ai-and-data-hype-or-hope/#60b195c162cd.

2. More on the history at Atlas Obscura: *Object of Intrigue: The Turk, a Mechanical Chess Player that Unsettled the World,* Ella Morton, 18 August 2015, https://www.atlasobscura.com/articles/object-of-intrigue-the-turk.

3. 'Kasparov vs. Deep Blue: The Match That Changed History', https://www.chess.com/article/view/deep-blue-kasparov-chess.

4. 'The Brain's Last Stand', key-note address at DefCon 2017 by Garry Kasparov, 18 August 2017, http://www.kasparov.com/the-brains-last-stand-key-note-address-at-defcon-2017/.

5. For a brief history of the game, refer to the website of the British Go Association, https://www.britgo.org/intro/history.

6. 'Computer Learns to Play Go at Superhuman Levels "Without Human Knowledge"', Merrit Kennedy, NPR.org, 18 October 2017.

7. Ibid.

8. For a quick round-up on neural networks see: 'What Is an Artificial Neural Network?' Luke Dormehl, Digital Trends, 13 September 2018, https://www.digitaltrends.com/cool-tech/what-is-an-artificial-neural-network/.

9. 'AlphaGo: Using Machine Learning to Master the Ancient Game of Go', Demis Hassabis, CEO and co-founder of DeepMind, published 27 January 2016, https://www.blog.google/technology/ai/alphago-machine-learning-game-go/.

10. 'DeepMind's Social Agenda Plays to Its AI Strengths', Madhumita Murgia, *Financial Times*, 17 March 2017, https://www.ft.com/content/cada14c4-d366-11e6-b06b-680c49b4b4c0.

11. 'The Divine Move', Rafael Jimenez, Medium.com, 11 March 2016, https://medium.com/@rafael_j/the-divine-move-a444229c2e64.

12. Definition at whatis.com, 'Infinite Monkey Theorem', Margaret Rouse, October 2013, https://whatis.techtarget.com/definition/Infinite-Monkey-Theorem.

Chapter 4: Nanotechnology

1. For further reading, refer to https://www.scholastic.com/teachers/articles/teaching-content/daoism-taoism/.

2. 'There's Plenty of Room at the Bottom', Richard P. Feynman, http://calteches.library.caltech.edu/1976/1/1960Bottom.pdf.

3. 'Tiny Machines', Richard Feynman's lecture on nanotechnology, https://cosmolearning.org/courses/richard-feynman-lecture-on-nanotechnology-tiny-machines-473/.

4. 'Nanotechnology, Nanoparticles and Nanononsense', Mark Bumiller, Horiba.com, 2017, http://www.horiba.com/fileadmin/uploads/Scientific/Documents/PSA/AP003.pdf.

5. 'Press Release: The Nobel Prize in Chemistry 2017', https://www.nobelprize.org/prizes/chemistry/2017/press-release/.

6. 'How Nanotechnology Works', Kevin Bonsor and Jonathan Strickland, howstuffworks.com, https://science.howstuffworks.com/nanotechnology.htm.

7. *Nanocosm: Nanotechnology and the Big Changes Coming from the Inconceivably Small*, William Illsey Atkinson, AMACOM, 2014.

8. 'Wootz Steel: The Mysterious Metal That Was Used in Deadly Damascus Blades', Dhwty, Ancient-origins.net, 2 June 2018, https://www.ancient-origins.net/artifacts-ancient-technology/wootz-steel-damascus-blades-0010148.

9. https://en.wikipedia.org/wiki/Damascus_steel.

10. Luke 23:34, https://biblehub.com/luke/23-34.htm.

11. 'The History of Bulletproof Vests', Aaron Spuler, Weapon-blog.com, 30 July 2015.

12. 'Carbon Nanotube Membranes: Synthesis, Properties, and Future Filtration Applications', paper in Nanomaterials (Basel), Md. Harun-Or Rashid and Stephen F. Ralph, Yuan Chen (academic editor), published online 1 May 2017, https://www.ncbi.nlm.nih.gov/pmc/articles/PMC5449980/.

13. 'How Nanotechnology Works', Kevin Bonsor and Jonathan Strickland.

14. 'Enhancement of Tumor Thermal Therapy Using Gold Nanoparticle-Assisted Tumor Necrosis Factor-Alpha Delivery', R.K. Visaria, R.J. Griffin, B.W. Williams, E.S. Ebbini, G.F. Paciotti, C.W. Song CW and J.C. Bischof, NCBI (Mol Cancer Ther. 2006 Apr; 5(4):1014), https://www.ncbi.nlm.nih.gov/pubmed/16648573.

15. See 'Nanotechnology in Cancer Treatment', http://www.understandingnano.com/cancer-treatment-nanotechnology.html.

Chapter 5: Quantum Computing

1. 'The First Computer Comes To India . . .', Dataquest, 30 December 2006, https://www.dqindia.com/the-first-computer-comes-to-india/.

2. 'Inside Apple's new A11 Bionic processor', Adrian Kingsley-Hughes, ZD Net, for Hardware 2.0, 12 September 2017, https://www.zdnet.com/article/inside-apples-new-a11-bionic-processor/.

3. 'Electronics Are about to Reach Their Limit in Processing Power—But There's a Solution', Arnab Hazari, Quartz, 5 January 2017, https://qz.com/852770/theres-a-limit-to-how-small-we-can-make-transistors-but-the-solution-is-photonic-chips/.

4. Ibid.

5. For more, refer to http://www.mooreslaw.org/.

6. For a relatively easy explanation see 'What Is Superposition', Physics.org, http://www.physics.org/article-questions.asp?id=124.

7. See Science Daily's 'Reference Terms: Quantum Entanglement' (from Wikipedia, the free encyclopedia), https://www.sciencedaily.com/terms/quantum_entanglement.htm.

8. 'Einstein's "Spooky Action at a Distance" Spotted in Objects Almost Big Enough to See', Gabriel Popkin, 25 April 2018, https://www.sciencemag.org/news/2018/04/einstein-s-spooky-action-distance-spotted-objects-almost-big-enough-see.

9. '2017 Founders' Letter', Alphabet Investor Relations, https://abc.xyz/investor/founders-letters/2017/.

10. 'Microsoft Wants to Save the World with Quantum Computing', Barb Darrow, *Fortune*, 25 September 2017, http://fortune.com/2017/09/25/microsoft-quantum-computing/.

11. *Life on the Edge*, Jim Al-Khalili and Johnjoe McFadden, Broadway Books.

12. 'Philosopher David Chalmers on Consciousness, the Hard Problem and the Nature of Reality', Daniel Keane, Abc.net.au, 7 July 2017, https://www.abc.net.au/news/2017-07-07/david-chalmers-and-the-puzzle-of-consciousness/8679884.

13. 'Why a "Genius" Scientist Thinks Our Consciousness Originates at the Quantum Level', Paul Ratner, 15 January 2018, https://bigthink.com/paul-ratner/why-a-genius-scientist-thinks-our-consciousness-originates-at-the-quantum-level.

14. 'Discovery of Quantum Vibrations in "Microtubules"', Elsevier, inside brain neurons supports controversial theory of consciousness, ScienceDaily, 16 January 2014, www.sciencedaily.com/releases/2014/01/140116085105.htm.

15. 'Quantum Simulation', Andreas Trabesinger, *Nature Physics*, 2 April 2012, vol. 8, pp. 263 (2012), https://www.nature.com/articles/nphys2258.

Chapter 6: Genetics

1. 'Nobel Scientist Happy to "Play God" with DNA', Steve Connor, Independent, 17 May 2000, https://www.independent.co.uk/news/science/nobel-scientist-happy-to-play-god-with-dna-277364.html.

2. 'Charles in GM "Disaster" Warning', BBC News, page updated on 13 August 2008, http://news.bbc.co.uk/2/hi/uk/7557644.stm], comments made on 19 May 2000.

3. 'Don't Turn Your Back on Science', *Guardian*, an open letter from biologist Richard Dawkins to Prince Charles, 21 May 2000, https://www.theguardian.com/science/2000/may/21/gm.food1.

4. 'Potato Introductions and Breeding up to the Early 20th Century', D.R. Glendenning, *New Phytologist* (1983) 94, pp. 479-505, https://nph.onlinelibrary.wiley.com/doi/pdf/10.1111/j.1469-8137.1983.tb03460.x.

5. For a more detailed discussion, read *The Gene: An Intimate History* by Siddhartha Mukherjee.

6. Ibid.

7. For a detailed explanation of the experiments, read *The Monk in the Garden: The Lost and Found Genius of Gregor Mendel, the Father of Genetics* by Robin Marantz Henig.

8. Ibid.

9. Oppenheimer spoke these words in the NBC television documentary titled *The Decision to Drop the Bomb* (prod. Fred Freed, 1965). Oppenheimer read the original text in Sanskrit and the translation is his own. In the literature, the quote usually appears in the form 'shatterer of worlds', because this was the form in which it first appeared in print, in *Time* magazine on 8 November 1948. It later appeared in Robert Jungk's *Brighter Than a Thousand Suns: A Personal History of the Atomic Scientists* (1958) based on an interview with Oppenheimer.

10. 'Beyond the Bomb: Atomic Research Changed Medicine, Biology';
    Michael Hotchkiss, Princeton University News (online), 27
    February 2014, https://www.princeton.edu/news/2014/02/27/
    beyond-bomb-atomic-research-changed-medicine-biology.
11. A free online copy of Erwin Schrödinger's *What Is Life?* (first
    published 1944) is available here: http://www.whatislife.ie/
    downloads/What-is-Life.pdf.
12. Ibid.
13. For an elaborate discussion, please read *DNA: The Secret of* Life,
    James D. Watson and Andrew Berry, Knopf.
14. Watson, Crick and Maurice Wilkins have all stated that they were
    inspired to study DNA by Schrödinger's book *What Is Life?*, http://
    www.whatislife.ie/schrodinger.htm.
15. Read *DNA, Watson and Berry.*
16. Ibid.
17. Ibid.
18. Those seeking a comprehensive understanding of the Human
    Genome Project, please read 'An Overview of the Human Genome
    Project' on the NIH (National Human Genome Research Institute)
    website, https://www.genome.gov/12011238/an-overview-of-the-
    human-genome-project/.
19. For commercial details and other specifics, please visit the 23andMe
    website, https://www.23andme.com/en-int/dna-ancestry/.
20. Ibid.
21. 'Angelina Jolie, Inherited Breast Cancer and the BRCA1 Gene',
    science blog of Cancer Research, UK, 14 May 2013, https://
    scienceblog.cancerresearchuk.org/2013/05/14/angelina-jolie-
    inherited-breast-cancer-and-the-brca1-gene/.
22. Read more about CRISPR-Cas in the news item 'DuPont
    Scientist Philippe Horvath Receives Franklin Institute Science
    Prize 2018 Bower Award for Groundbreaking Research on
    CRISPR-Cas', Danisco.com (Dupont), websitehttp://www.
    danisco.com/about-dupont/news/news-archive/2017/dupont-
    scientist-philippe-horvath-receives-franklin-institute-science-
    prize-2018-bower-award-for-groundbreaking-research-on-
    crispr-cas/.

23. Cas9 (CRISPR associated protein 9) is an RNA-guided DNA endonuclease enzyme associated with the CRISPR adaptive immunity system, https://en.wikipedia.org/wiki/Cas9.

24. https://www.youtube.com/watch?v=hVI_y0WhtXw.

Chapter 7: The Filter Bubble

1. From Kasika (online), http://shodhganga.inflibnet.ac.in/bitstream/10603/67967/15/15_chapter%208.pdf.

2. *The Filter Bubble: What the Internet Is Hiding from You*, Eli Pariser, Penguin, 2012.

3. Ibid.

4. 'One Small Step for the Web', Tim Berners-Lee, Medium (Technology), 29 September 2018, https://medium.com/@timberners_lee/one-small-step-for-the-web-87f92217d085.

5. Quote attributed to Henry David Thoreau. However, the *New York Times* contends that it is misattributed, as per Poynter.org, https://www.poynter.org/news/new-york-times-corrects-misquote-thoreaus-quiet-desperation-line.

6. From the poem 'Lady, I Will Touch You with My Mind', E.E. Cummings, https://allpoetry.com/lady-i-will-touch-you-with-my-mind.

7. 'What Democrats Must Do', Josh Mound, *Jacobin*, 30 September 2017, https://jacobinmag.com/2017/09/democratic-party-2016-election-working-class.

8. Definition of 'cyberbalkanization' in Technopedia.com, https://www.techopedia.com/definition/28087/cyberbalkanization.

9. 'No Man Is an Island', John Donne, https://www.poemhunter.com/poem/no-man-is-an-island/.

10. 'When the Internet Thinks It Knows You', opinion section of the *New York Times*, Eli Pariser, 22 May 2011, https://www.nytimes.com/2011/05/23/opinion/23pariser.html.

11. 'Filter Bubbles Are a Serious Problem with News, Says Bill Gates', Kevin J. Delaney, reprinted from Quartz, 21 February 2017, https://finance.yahoo.com/news/filter-bubbles-serious-problem-news-161323398.html.

12. 'Agents of Alienation', Jaron Lanier, http://www.jaronlanier.com/agentalien.html.

13. Proverbs 16–18 discussed in BibleHub, https://biblehub.com/proverbs/16-18.htm.

14. 'Donald Trump's Presidential Counsellor Kellyanne Conway Says Sean Spicer Gave "Alternative Facts" at First Press Briefing', Rachael Revesz, Independent, 22 January 2017, https://www.independent.co.uk/news/world/americas/kellyanne-conway-sean-spicer-alternative-facts-lies-press-briefing-donald-trump-administration-a7540441.html.

15. This classic tale can be accessed at Chabad.org, 'A Pillow Full of Feathers' by Shoshannah Brombacher.

16. 'On Twitter, False News Travels Faster than True Stories', Peter Dizikes, MIT News, 8 March 2018, http://news.mit.edu/2018/study-twitter-false-news-travels-faster-true-stories-0308.

17. 'News Use Across Social Media Platforms 2017', Elisa Shearer and Jeffrey Gottfried, Pew Research Center, 7 September 2017, http://www.journalism.org/2017/09/07/news-use-across-social-media-platforms-2017/.

18. 'A New Book Details the Damage Done by the Right-Wing Media in 2016', Jeffrey Toobin, New Yorker, 28 August 2018, https://www.newyorker.com/news/daily-comment/a-new-book-details-the-damage-done-by-the-right-wing-media-in-2016.

19. 'A Software Developer Created a Way for You to Escape Your Political Bubble on Facebook', Chris Sanchez, Business Insider, 3 December 2016, https://www.businessinsider.com/escape-your-bubble-facebook-news-feed-2016-12?IR=T.

20. Read more on https://www.hifromtheotherside.com/.

21. 'Social Media Algorithm Pops Filter Bubbles by Presenting Ideas You Disagree with', Luke Dormehl, Digital Trends, 12 June 2017, https://www.digitaltrends.com/cool-tech/filter-bubble-algorithm-pop/.

22. 'WVU students experiment with artificial intelligence to detect fake news', WVUtoday, 27 March 2017,[https://wvutoday.wvu.edu/stories/2017/03/27/wvu-students-experiment-with-artificial-intelligence-to-detect-fake-news.

23. Quote by Junot Diaz at https://www.azquotes.com/quote/77736.

24. 'Donald Trump Wants to "Close Up" the Internet', David Goldman, CNN Business, 8 December 2015, https://money.cnn.com/2015/12/08/technology/donald-trump-internet/index.html.

Chapter 8: Matchmaking

1. Italian Folktales (*Fiabe Italiane*) is a collection of 200 Italian folktales published in 1956 by Italo Calvino.

2. *The Black Swan: The Impact of The Highly Improbable* is a book that focuses on what has now come to be known as the Black Swan theory. Through a number of examples, the author aims to show his readers how rare and unpredictable events have a deep and lasting impact on a person's life.

3. Read about Jewish matchmaking customs in 'What Is a "Shadchan"?' at Chabad.org, https://www.chabad.org/library/article_cdo/aid/160984/jewish/What-Is-a-Shadchan.htm.

4. Ram Babu Sao explains this well in *Perfect Astrology (Matchmaking): Muhurata for Venture and Matchmaking between Partners*.

5. Read more about Operation Match in *The Originals*, Nell Porter Brown, *Harvard Magazine*, March–April 2003, https://harvardmagazine.com/2003/03/the-originals-html.

6. There are some good examples in *Modern Romance* by Aziz Ansari and Eric Klinenberg.

7. For a more detailed discussion, read *The All-or-Nothing Marriage: How the Best Marriages Work* by Eli J. Finkel.

8. 'The Sociometer: A Wearable Device for Understanding Human Networks', paper by Tanzeem Choudhury and Alex Pentland (Human Design Group, Cambridge, Mass.), https://alumni.media.mit.edu/~tanzeem/shortcuts/workingpaper.pdf.

9. 'Jerk-O-Meter Rates Phone Chatter', *Wired* (Associated Press, Business, 8 November 2005), https://www.wired.com/2005/08/jerk-o-meter-rates-phone-chatter/.

10. Refer to the book *Love in the Time of Algorithms: What Technology Does to Meeting and Mating* by Dan Slater.

Chapter 9: Electoral Math

1. 'Facebook and Cambridge Analytica: What Just Happened?', Eric Johnson, Recode.net, 23 March 2018, https://www.recode. net/2018/3/23/17153368/facebook-cambridge-analytica-mark-zuckerberg-lauren-goode-kara-swisher-kurt-wagner-recode-podcast.

2. Read more about Cleisthenes at ancient-origins.net: 'Cleisthenes, Father of Democracy, Invented a Form of Government That Has Endured for Over 2,500 Years', Theodoros Karasavvas, 28 February 2017, https://www.ancient-origins.net/history-famous-people/cleisthenes-father-democracy-invented-form-government-has-endured-over-021247.

3. 'When the Nerds Go Marching In;, Alexis C. Madrigal, *Atlantic*, 16 November 2012, https://www.theatlantic.com/technology/archive/2012/11/when-the-nerds-go-marching-in/265325/.

4. 'Killer Fail: How Romney's Broken Orca App Cost Him Thousands of Votes', Adi Robertson, 9 November 2012, https://www.theverge.com/2012/11/9/3624636/killer-fail-how-romneys-broken-orca-app-cost-him-thousands-of-votes.

5. 'The Science Behind Cambridge Analytica: Does Psychological Profiling Work?', Edmund L. Andrews, Stanford GSB, 12 April 2018, https://www.gsb.stanford.edu/insights/science-behind-cambridge-analytica-does-psychological-profiling-work.

6. 'Statement from the University of Cambridge about Dr Aleksandr Kogan', 23 March 2018, https://www.cam.ac.uk/notices/news/statement-from-the-university-of-cambridge-about-dr-aleksandr-kogan.

7. 'Mathematics of Politics Talks Data Analysis, Campaigns', Alex Torpey, Dailybruin.com, 23 April 2014, https://dailybruin.com/2014/04/23/mathematics-of-politics-talks-data-analysis-campaigns/.

8. *Moneyball: The Art of Winning an Unfair Game,* Michael Lewis, W.W. Norton & Company.

9. 'Why FiveThirtyEight Gave Trump a Better Chance than Almost Anyone Else', Nate Silver, 11 November 2016, https://

fivethirtyeight.com/features/why-fivethirtyeight-gave-trump-a-better-chance-than-almost-anyone-else/.

10. 'White and Wealthy Voters Gave Victory to Donald Trump, Exit Polls Show', Jon Henley, *Guardian*, 9 November 2016, https://www.theguardian.com/us-news/2016/nov/09/white-voters-victory-donald-trump-exit-polls.

11. Study by Kosinski et al., titled 'Private Traits and Attributes are Predictable from Digital Records of Human Behavior', http://www.pnas.org/content/pnas/110/15/5802.full.pdf.

12. 'Obama Hope Poster—Shepard Fairey (2008)', Mac Scott, Medium.com, 16 October 2017, https://medium.com/fgd1-the-archive/obama-hope-poster-by-shepard-fairey-1307a8b6c7be.

13. 'Hope and Glory', Peter Schjeldahl, *New Yorker*, 23 February 2009, https://www.newyorker.com/magazine/2009/02/23/hope-and-glory.

14. 'Obama's On-the-Wall Endorsement', William Booth, *Washington Post,* 18 May 2008, http://www.washingtonpost.com/wp-dyn/content/article/2008/05/16/AR2008051601017.html?noredirect=on.

15. 'Big Data Meets Presidential Politics', Jim Battey, CSC World Magazine, 2013, https://vdocuments.mx/csc-world-magazinemarch-2013.html.

16. Article in Medium.com, 'How We Used Neural Networks to Understand Congress', Anastassia Kornilova, 10 July 2018, https://medium.com/fiscalnote-in-depth/how-we-used-neural-networks-to-understand-congress-c6aec3069594.

Chapter 10: Blockchain and Cryptocurrency

1. Read about it in *USA Today*, 'How FBI Brought Down Cyber-Underworld Site Silk Road', Donna Leinwand Leger, 21 October 2013, 15 May 2014, https://www.usatoday.com/story/news/nation/2013/10/21/fbi-cracks-silk-road/2984921/.

2. *Digital Gold: Bitcoin and the Inside Story of the Misfits and Millionaires Trying to Reinvent Money,* Nathaniel Popper, Harper paperbacks.

3. 'The Invention of Paper Money', Kallie Szczepanski, ThoughtCo. com, 22 October 2018, https://www.thoughtco.com/the-invention-of-paper-money-195167.
4. Sir Isaac Newton was 'Warden and then Master of the Royal Mint 1696-1727' (The Royal Mint Museum website), http://www. royalmintmuseum.org.uk/history/people/mint-officials/isaac-newton/index.html.
5. Read *An Inquiry into John Nash's Proposal For Ideal Money* by Juice, 9 August 2017, https://medium.com/@rextar4444/an-inquiry-into-john-nashs-proposal-for-ideal-money-f1551c46da31.
6. https://monetary-metals.com/why-did-jp-morgan-say-money-is-gold-nothing-else/, Addison Quale, MonetaryMetals, 3 August 2018.
7. Read the original lecture by John F. Nash Jr., 'Ideal Money and Asymptotically Ideal Money', http://personal.psu.edu/gjb6/nash/money.pdf.
8. Ibid.
9. Read the original paper: 'Bitcoin: A Peer-to-Peer Electronic Cash System', Satoshi Nakamoto, 31 October 2008, https://nakamotoinstitute.org/bitcoin/#selection-7.4-19.27.
10. Read 'Hal Finney, RIP', Prof. Bill Buchanan OBE, Medium.com, https://medium.com/coinmonks/hal-finney-rip-8ee30a8998e4.
11. Ibid.
12. 'Bitcoin: A Peer-to-Peer Electronic Cash System', Nakamoto.
13. Read more about Sterling Lujan at https://sterlinlujan.com/.
14. 'Hungry Venezuelans Break into Caracas Zoo and Butcher a Horse', Harriet Alexander, *Telegraph*, 19 August 2016, https://www.telegraph.co.uk/news/2016/08/19/hungryvenezuelans-break-into-caracas-zoo-and-butcher-a-horse/.
15. 'The Byzantine Generals' Problem', Kiran Vaidya, Medium.com, 11 November 2016, https://medium.com/all-things-ledger/the-byzantine-generals-problem-168553f31480.
16. 'Luca Pacioli: The Father of Accounting', Murphy Smith, revised 8 March 2018, https://papers.ssrn.com/sol3/papers.cfm?abstract_id=2320658.
17. Goldman Sachs is heavily invested in blockchain technology: https://www.goldmansachs.com/insights/pages/blockchain/.

Chapter 11: Personal Data Ownership

1. 'Facebook Scandal "Hit 87 Million Users"', BBC, 4 April 2018, https://www.bbc.com/news/technology-43649018/.
2. 'Mark Zuckerberg Says Facebook Collects Data on Non-Users for "Security": Here's the Whole Story', Rob Price, Business Insider (India), 12 April 2018, https://www.businessinsider.in/Mark-Zuckerberg-says-Facebook-collects-data-on-non-users-for-security-heres-the-whole-story/articleshow/63721336.cms.
3. See Encyclopædia Britannica's, 'Faustian Bargain' by The Editors of Encyclopædia Britannica (Encyclopædia Britannica, inc.; Pub. July 19, 2016, accessed on 18 November 2018), https://www.britannica.com/topic/Faustian-bargain.
4. See the full description at The Myers & Briggs Foundation: *MBTI® Basics,* https://www.myersbriggs.org/my-mbti-personality-type/mbti-basics/home.htm?bhcp=1.
5. Read the actual keynote speech 'Roundtable on Online Data Collection, Targeting and Profiling', Meglena Kuneva, European Consumer Commissioner, Brussels, 31 March 2009, http://europa.eu/rapid/press-release_SPEECH-09-156_en.htm.
6. The quote is also credited to Jomo Kenyatta, as it is to Rolf Hochhuth. See discussion thread on skeptics, 'Did Desmond Tutu criticize African missionaries for stealing land?', https://skeptics.stackexchange.com/questions/8644/did-desmond-tutu-criticize-african-missionaries-for-stealing-land/8648#8648.
7. Read *Oliver Twist* online at charlesdickenspage.com, 'Oliver Asks for More' (condensed from Chapter 2), https://charlesdickenspage.com/twist_more.html.

Chapter 12: Data Privacy

1. You can read an introduction (by the editor) of the classic text *History of the Decline and Fall of the Roman Empire, Volume I.* by Edward Gibbon in the University of Oxford Text Archive, http://ota.ox.ac.uk/text/3169.html.

2. See the definition of the term 'surveillance' on the Military Factory website, https://www.militaryfactory.com/dictionary/military-terms-defined.asp?term_id=5219.

3. See theinnovationenterprise.com, 'Palantir: How Big Data Is Used to Help the CIA and to Detect Bombs in Afghanistan' (extract of: Bernard Marr's book *Big Data In Practice: How 45 Successful Companies Used Big Data Analytics to Deliver Extraordinary Results*), https://channels.theinnovationenterprise.com/articles/how-big-data-is-used-to-help-the-cia-and-to-detect-bombs-in-afghanistan.

4. 'You Have Zero Privacy Anyway: Get Over It', Marcel Warmerdam, The Metis Files website, 14 May 2015, https://www.themetisfiles.com/2015/05/you-have-zero-privacy-anyway-get-over-it/.

5. Learn about the FICO® score and its long history at https://www.fico.com/25years/.

6. 'Big Data Meets Big Brother as China Moves to Rate Its Citizens' Rachel Botsman, *Wired*, 21 October 2017, https://www.wired.co.uk/article/chinese-government-social-credit-score-privacy-invasion.

7. Ibid.

8. Ibid.

9. 'Journey of Aadhaar', posted on 21 May 2016, https://sflc.in/journey-aadhaar.

10. Quote by former Prime Minister Rajiv Gandhi, 'Rahul Echoes Rajiv Gandhi's Comment on Public Funds', Santosh K. Joy, 17 January 2008, https://www.rediff.com/news/2008/jan/17rahul.htm.

11. For a more extensive discussion on the Australian welfare system read 'The Rise and Fall of Welfare Dependency in Australia', Peter Whiteford, Crawford School of Public Policy, Australian National University, https://crawford.anu.edu.au/pdf/events/2012/20121023-welfare-dependency-in-australia.pdf.

12. 'Amazon Consumer Tracking with an Orwellian Twist', Samuel Wade, Chinadigitaltimes.net, 2 May 2015, https://chinadigitaltimes.net/2015/05/china-pursues-amazon-consumer-tracking-with-orwellian-twist/.

13. See the '2018 Reform of EU Data Protection Rules' on https://ec.europa.eu/commission/priorities/justice-and-fundamental-rights/data-protection/2018-reform-eu-data-protection-rules_en.
14. 'The Personal Data Protection Bill 2018 Does Everything but Protect Personal Data', Bhumika Khatri, Inc42.com, 29 July 2018, https://inc42.com/features/the-personal-data-protection-bill-2018-does-everything-but-protect-personal-data/.
15. Lyrics from John Lennon's 'Imagine'.
16. Full citation: Chander, Anupam and Le, Uyen P., *Data Nationalism* (13 March 2015). Emory Law Journal, vol. 64, no. 3, 2015. Available at SSRN: https://ssrn.com/abstract=2577947, https://papers.ssrn.com/sol3/papers.cfm?abstract_id=2577947.
17. 'Zamyatin's We and The Power of Words', Hung Te Tjia, Science Fiction & the City, 23 February 2009, https://blogs.ubc.ca/sciencefictionandthecity/2009/02/23/zamyatins-we-and-the-power-of-words/.

Chapter 13: Jobs and AI

1. Read the entire text at http://faculty.econ.ucdavis.edu/faculty/gclark/papers/FTA20061.pdf.
2. 'The True Meaning of "In the Long Run We Are All Dead"', blog by Simon Taylor, 5 May 2013, https://www.simontaylorsblog.com/2013/05/05/the-true-meaning-of-in-the-long-run-we-are-all-dead/.
3. See bibliography.
4. 'The Fixed Pie Fallacy', Mark J. Perry, AEI.com, 23 December 2006, http://www.aei.org/publication/the-fixed-pie-fallacy/.
5. *The Rise of the Robots: Technology and the Threat of Mass Unemployment,* Martin Ford, Oneworld Publications.
6. 'Why Has Inequality Been Growing?', Robert H. Frank, Slate.com, 6 December 2011, https://slate.com/business/2011/12/how-technology-and-winner-take-all-markets-have-made-income-inequality-so-much-worse.html.
7. 'Rich and Poor: The Unequal Struggle', Michael Marmot, *NewScientist*, 24 May 2006.

8. 'Switzerland: Swiss Vote "No" on Basic Income Referendum', Josh Martin, Basicincome.org, 5 June 2016, https://basicincome. org/news/2016/06/switzerland-swiss-vote-no-on-basic-income-referendum/.

9. See the February 2018 numbers on the Bureau of Labor Statistics site: 'Unemployment Rate at 4.1 per cent in February 2018', 14 March 2018, https://www.bls.gov/opub/ted/2018/ unemployment-rate-at-4-point-1-percent-in-february-2018. htm?view_full.

10. *Homo Deus: A Brief History of Tomorrow,* Yuval Noah Harari.

11. Genesis 3:19 (New International Version), https://biblehub.com/ genesis/3-19.htm.

12. *The Inevitable,* Kevin Kelly.

13. '5 Predictions from Marvin Minsky as "father of AI" Dies Aged 88', Colm Gorey, Silicon Republic, 26 January 2016, https://www. siliconrepublic.com/machines/marvin-minsky-ai-predictions.

14. 'Economic Possibilities for Our Grandchildren', John Maynard Keynes, written in 1930 (source: scanned from John Maynard Keynes, Essays in Persuasion, New York: W.W. Norton & Co., 1963, pp. 358–73. Transcribed by Viola Wilkins), https://www. marxists.org/reference/subject/economics/keynes/1930/our-grandchildren.htm.

Chapter 14: Love, Sex and AI

1. 'Porn, the Low-Slung Engine of Progress', John Tierney, *New York Times*, 9 January 1994, https://www.nytimes.com/1994/01/09/ arts/porn-the-low-slung-engine-of-progress.html.

2. 'Europe's First Pornographic Blockbuster Was Made in the Vatican', Esther Inglis-Arkell, Atlasobscura.com, 13 June 2016, https://www.atlasobscura.com/articles/europes-first-pornographic-blockbuster-was-made-in-the-vatican.

3. Accepted quote in general: 'greatest invention of the 19th century'. See article on Medicnenet.com, 'A History of Birth Control', Daniel DeNoon, 6 August 2001, https://www.medicinenet.com/ script/main/art.asp?articlekey=51170.

4. See the Wikipedia entry for 'The Kiss', https://en.wikipedia.org/wiki/The_Kiss_(1896_film).

5. Read 'The Story of Pygmalion from Ovid's *Metamorphoses*', translated by Rolfe Humphries (1954), http://www.victorianweb.org/painting/classical/humphries1.html.

6. 'The "Dutch Wife" Sex Doll Is So Realistic, Who Needs A Girlfriend?', Pamela J. Hobart, Bustle.com, 13 August 2014, https://www.bustle.com/articles/35527-the-dutch-wife-sex-doll-is-so-realistic-who-needs-a-girlfriend.

7. See quotes from the movie at https://www.imdb.com/title/tt1798709/quotes.

8. *Love and Sex with Robots: The Evolution of Human-Robot Relationships,* David Levy, Harper Perennial, 2008.

9. 'Hiroshi Ishiguro: The Man Who Made a Copy of Himself', Erico Guizzo, IEEE Spectrum, 23 April 2010, https://spectrum.ieee.org/robotics/humanoids/hiroshi-ishiguro-the-man-who-made-a-copy-of-himself.

10. See the Internet Encyclopedia of Philosophy: *Xenophanes (c. 570—c. 478 BCE)* by Michael Patzia, https://www.iep.utm.edu/xenoph/.

11. 'How Computers Change the Way We Think', Sherry Turkle, 16 April 2008, http://web.mit.edu/sturkle/www/pdfsforstwebpage/Turkle_how_computers_change_way_we_think.pdf.

12. Read the position paper titled 'The Asymmetrical "Relationship": Parallels Between Prostitution and the Development of Sex Robots', Kathleen Richardson, published on the ACM Digital Library as a special issue of the ACM SIGCAS newsletter, SIGCAS Computers and Society, vol. 45, no. 3, pp. 290–93, September 2015, https://campaignagainstsexrobots.org/the-asymmetrical-relationship-parallels-between-prostitution-and-the-development-of-sex-robots/.

13. 'Hello Harmony: RealDoll Sex Robots with "X-Mode" Ship in September', Ry Crist, 25 August 2018, https://www.cnet.com/news/realdoll-sex-robots-with-x-mode-from-abyss-creations-ship-in-september/.

14. 'Engineer "Marries" Robot He Built And It's Totally Not Creepy At All', David Moye, HuffPost, 4 April 2017, https://

www.huffingtonpost.in/entry/zheng-jiajia-robot-marriage_
us_58e3c701e4b0d0b7e1651098.

15. 'Everything You Need to Know about Sophia, The World's First
Robot Citizen', Zara Stone, *Forbes*, 7 November 2017, https://www.
forbes.com/sites/zarastone/2017/11/07/everything-you-need-to-
know-about-sophia-the-worlds-first-robot-citizen/#6cb7df7046fa.

16. 'Meet Erica, Japan's Next Robot News Anchor', Brandon Specktor,
LiveScience, 30 January 2018, https://www.livescience.com/61575-
erica-robot-replace-japanese-news-anchor.html.

17. 'The Uncanny Valley: The Original Essay by Masahiro Mori',
translated by Karl F. MacDorman and Norri Kageki, IEEE.org,
12 June 2012, https://spectrum.ieee.org/automaton/robotics/
humanoids/the-uncanny-valley.

Chapter 15: Ethics and AI

1. 'Everything You Need to Know about Sophia', *Forbes*.

2. 'Tesla Death Smash Probe: Neither Driver nor Autopilot Saw the
Truck', Gareth Corfield, Register, 20 June 2017, https://www.
theregister.co.uk/2017/06/20/tesla_death_crash_accident_report_
ntsb/.

3. 'Self-driving Uber Kills Arizona Woman in First Fatal Crash
Involving Pedestrian', Sam Levin and Julia Carrie Wong, *Guardian*,
19 March 2018, https://www.theguardian.com/technology/2018/
mar/19/uber-self-driving-car-kills-woman-arizona-tempe.

4. Definition from English Oxford Living Dictionaries, https://
en.oxforddictionaries.com/definition/law.

5. See the open letter on the Future of Life Institute website, so far
'3978 AI/Robotics researchers and 22,540 others' have signed the
letter: 'Autonomous Weapons: An Open Letter from AI & Robotics
Researchers, This open letter was announced 28 July at the opening
of the IJCAI 2015 conference, https://futureoflife.org/open-letter-
autonomous-weapons/.

6. 'Background Guide: Un Human Rights Council', GDGIMUN.
org, https://www.gdgimun.org/uploads/7/2/7/0/7270117/hrc_
background_guide.pdf.

7. For more quotes from *Alice in Wonderland*, see http://www.alice-in-wonderland.net/resources/chapters-script/alice-in-wonderland-quotes/.

8. See the IOActive.com site, 'Hacking Robots before Skynet', Cesar Cerrudo and Lucas Apa, https://ioactive.com/pdfs/Hacking-Robots-Before-Skynet.pdf.

9. See quote on the Prezi site, '2010: Odyssey Two', David Johnson, 10 November 2013, https://prezi.com/lt5fyhrwtart/2010-odyssey-two/.

10. 'Olympics: Blade Jumper Markus Rehm Sees Rio Dreams Fade', *Straits Times*, 18 June 2016, https://www.straitstimes.com/sport/olympics-blade-jumper-markus-rehm-sees-rio-dreams-fade.

11. 'The Trolley Dilemma: Would You Kill One Person to Save Five?', Laura D'Olimpio, Conversation, 3 June 2016, https://theconversation.com/the-trolley-dilemma-would-you-kill-one-person-to-save-five-57111.

12. 'Stanford Scholars, Researchers Discuss Key Ethical Questions Self-driving Cars Present', Alex Shashkevich, Stanford News, 22 May 2017, https://news.stanford.edu/2017/05/22/stanford-scholars-researchers-discuss-key-ethical-questions-self-driving-cars-present/.

13. 'Nietzsche's Idea of an Overman and Life from His Point of View', https://ccrma.stanford.edu/~pj97/Nietzsche.htm.

14. See Lennon's quote on Philipjonesgriffiths.org, http://philipjonesgriffiths.org/photography/selected-work/the-beatles/.

Chapter 16: The Periodic Table

1. 'In Retrospect: The Sceptical Chymist', Lawrence Principe, *Nature*, vol. 469, pp. 30–31, 6 January 2011, https://www.nature.com/articles/469030a.

2. 'Aristotelian Aether and Void in the Universe', Konstantinos Kalachanis, Efstratios Theodosiou and Milan Dimitrijevic, 1 January 2016, https://www.researchgate.net/publication/318943230_ARISTOTELIAN_AETHER_AND_VOID_IN_THE_UNIVERSE.

3. *The Role of Number in Philolaus' Philosophy*, Carl Huffman.

4. You can read a summary of Hennig Brand's life and the discovery of phosphorous at https://www.famousscientists.org/hennig-brand/.

5. 'Here's What It Was Like to Discover Laughing Gas', Rose Eveleth, *Smithsonian*, 27 March 2014, https://www.smithsonianmag.com/smart-news/heres-what-it-was-discover-laughing-gas-180950289/.

6. 'Antoine Laurent Lavoisier, 1743–1794', J.R. Partington, *Nature*, vol. 152, pp. 207–08, 21 August 1943, https://www.nature.com/articles/152207a0.

7. '1794: Antoine Laurent Lavoisier, Father of Modern Chemistry', ExecutedToday.com, 8 May 2010, http://www.executedtoday.com/2010/05/08/1794-antoine-laurent-lavoisier-father-of-modern-chemistry/.

8. From 'Engines of Our Ingenuity' programme on University of Houston: *Marie Lavoisier*, John H. Lienhard (Original essay: Hoffmann, R., Mme Lavoisier. *American Scientist*, vol. 90, Jan-Feb 2002, pp. 22–24), https://www.uh.edu/engines/epi1673.htm.

9. 'How Mendeleev Invented his Periodic Table in a Dream, Maria Popova, Brainpickings.com, 8 February 2016, https://www.brainpickings.org/2016/02/08/mendeleev-periodic-table-dream/.

10. Entry in 'Bitesize' on bbc.com: 'The Periodic Table', https://www.bbc.com/bitesize/guides/zxmmsrd/revision/1.

11. Quote by Michael Shermer at https://www.goodreads.com/quotes/43622-humans-are-pattern-seeking-story-telling-animals-and-we-are-quite-adept.

12. 'Julius Lothar Meyer and Dmitri Ivanovich Mendeleev', Sciencehistory.org, updated on 12 December 2017, https://www.sciencehistory.org/historical-profile/julius-lothar-meyer-and-dmitri-ivanovich-mendeleev.

13. More on Philip Ball at https://www.philipball.co.uk/.

14. You can read a summary of Henry Moseley's life and achievements at https://www.famousscientists.org/henry-moseley/.

15. 'Terry Pratchett Fans Sign Petition to Name Element 117 After Discworld's Octarine', Natalie Zutter, Tor.com, 12 January 2016, https://www.tor.com/2016/01/12/terry-pratchett-octarine-element-117-petition-discworld-magic/.

Chapter 17: Math and Art

1. 'Mathematical Concepts Illustrated by Hamid Naderi Yeganeh' at the American Mathematical Society, https://www.ams.org/mathimagery/thumbnails.php?album=40.

2. https://www.ams.org/mathimagery/displayimage.php?album=40&pid=678.

3. You can read more about kolam at https://en.wikipedia.org/wiki/Kolam.

4. View the University of St Andrews, Scotland: MacTutor History of Mathematics archive's quotations page, http://www-history.mcs.st-andrews.ac.uk/Quotations/Dirac.html.

5. http://www-history.mcs.st-and.ac.uk/Quotations/Aristotle.html.

6. 'Polyclitus' by the editors of Encyclopædia Britannica, Encyclopædia Britannica Inc., pub. 4 May 2016, accessed on 14 November 2018, https://www.britannica.com/biography/Polyclitus.

7. See the illustration courtesy https://www.leonardodavinci.net/the-vitruvian-man.jsp.

8. 'On Art and Aesthetics', *Da Divina Proportione*, 2 March 2016, https://onartandaesthetics.com/2016/03/02/de-divina-proportione/.

9. 'Quotes Related to Phi', Gary Meisner, Goldennumber.net, 13 May 2012, https://www.goldennumber.net/phi-quotations/.

10. 'What is the Golden Ratio?', Elaine J. Hom, LiveScience, 24 June 2013, https://www.livescience.com/37704-phi-golden-ratio.html.

11. 'Michelangelo and the Art of the Golden Ratio in Design and Composition', Gary Meisner, 18 January 2016, https://www.goldennumber.net/michelangelo-sistine-chapel-golden-ratio-art-design/.

12. 'Parmigianino, Self-Portrait in a Convex Mirror', Beth Harris and Steven Zucker, Smarthistory, 9 December 2015, accessed 14 November 2018, https://smarthistory.org/parmigianino-self-portrait-in-a-convex-mirror/.

13. *Science and Hypothesis,* Jules Henri Poincare.

14. 'Perspective: Geometric Games: A Brief History of the Not-so Regular Solids', Kim H. Veltman, academic paper at Virtual Maastrict Macluhan Institute, http://www.sumscorp.com/perspective/geometric_games/.

15. Read more about Dadaism on Artyfactory, http://www.artyfactory. com/art_appreciation/art_movements/dadaism.htm.
16. View the famous illustration on The Famous Artists, http://www. thefamousartists.com/paolo-uccello/study-of-a-chalice.
17. Download a copy of the original book from (courtesy OUP) https://fadingtheaesthetic.files.wordpress.com/2014/08/michael-baxandall-painting-and-experience-in-fifteenthcentury-italy-a-primer-in-the-social-history-of-pictorial-style-1.pdf.
18. See the quote in Metamorphite's blog, 'Plato said God Geometrizes Continually', Noah Haalilio Solomon, 29 June 2010, https:// metamorphite.wordpress.com/2010/06/29/plato-said-god-geometrizes-continually/.
19. Definition and symbolism of 'mandala' at Ancient History Encyclopedia, https://www.ancient.eu/mandala/.
20. See 'Finding π from Pythagoras's Theorem' at http://www. physicsinsights.org/pi_from_pythagoras-1.html.
21. 'A Bigger Altar: Geometry & Ritual', Lawrence Brenton, Mathematical Association of America's Math Horizons, November 2017, pp. 8–9, http://digitaleditions. walsworthprintgroup.com/publication/?i=446441&article_id=2913291&view=articleBrowser&ver=html5#%22{%22.
22. Read 'Brunelleschi: Life, Facts, Curiosities and Art', https:// www.visittuscany.com/en/ideas/brunelleschi-life-facts-curiosities-and-art/.
23. View the University of St Andrews, Scotland: 'MacTutor History of Mathematics Archive's Quotations Page', http://www-history.mcs. st-andrews.ac.uk/Quotations/Galileo.html.
24. *Geometrical Exercises in Paper Folding*, Tandalam Sundara Rao.
25. Visit the msescher website, https://www.mcescher.com/.
26. See examples of 'tessellation' at http://www.tessellations.org/tess-escher1.shtml.
27. View the *Circle Limit III* at https://www.mcescher.com/gallery/recognition-success/circle-limit-iii/.
28. Read this great article by Mandelbrot himself: 'How Long Is the Coast of Britain? Statistical Self-similarity and Fractional Dimension' by B.B. Mandelbrot (Science: 156, 1967, 636-638)

29. See 'fractal art' on Wikipedia, https://en.wikipedia.org/wiki/ Fractal_art.

30. 'Peek into the Weird and Wonderful Age of AI (Yes, There's a Chatbot): AI Could Mean Artistic Intelligence', Klint Finley, *Wired*, 17 May 2016, https://www.wired.com/2016/05/what-is-ai-artificial-intelligence/.

31. 'Hardy's Apology', Thatsmaths.com, 8 February 2018, https:// thatsmaths.com/2018/02/08/hardys-apology/.

Chapter 18: The Idea of Math

1. 'Mathematical Platonism', see IEP (Internet Encyclopedia of Philosophy), https://www.iep.utm.edu/mathplat/.

2. 'Closer to Truth' interview, 'Roger Penrose: Is Mathematics Invented or Discovered?', http://www.yousubtitles.com/Roger-Penrose-Is-Mathematics-Invented-or-Discovered-id-766611.

3. Scotland: 'MacTutor History of Mathematics Archive's Quotations Page', http://www-history.mcs.st-andrews.ac.uk/Quotations/ Ramanujan.html.

4. Øystein Linnebo, 'Platonism in the Philosophy of Mathematics', The Stanford Encyclopedia of Philosophy (Spring 2018 Edition), Edward N. Zalta (ed.), https://plato.stanford.edu/archives/spr2018/ entries/platonism-mathematics/.

5. 'The Evolution of the Physicist's Picture of Nature', Paul Dirac, republished in *Scientific American*, originally published in the May 1963 issue of *Scientific American*, 25 June 2010, https://blogs. scientificamerican.com/guest-blog/the-evolution-of-the-physicists-picture-of-nature/.

6. 'Why a Course in the Mathematics of Music?', Johns Hopkins University (Department of Applied Mathematics and Statistics), https://www.ams.jhu.edu/dan-mathofmusic/.

7. See quote in mathforum.org, *Proclus: 410 –485 AD,* http:// mathforum.org/geometry/wwweuclid/proclus.htm.

8. 'Pythagoras & Music of the Spheres', see the Dartmouth College math page, https://www.math.dartmouth.edu/~matc/math5. geometry/unit3/unit3.html.

9. Ibid.

10. Read the 'Full Text of Portraits From Memory And Other Essays', section on 'Beliefs: Discarded and Retained', pp. 41, Archive. org, https://archive.org/stream/portraitsfrommem011249mbp/ portraitsfrommem011249mbp_djvu.txt.

11. 'How Math Unraveled the "Hard Day's Night" Mystery', Eliot Van Buskirk, *Wired*, 31 October 2008, https://www.wired. com/2008/10/how-a-professor/.

12. 'Fibonacci or Hemachandra Numbers', Jayakrishnan Nair, Varnam. org, 20 October 2004, http://varnam.org/2004/10/fibonacci_or_ hemachandra_numbe/.

13. Ibid.

14. See this quote in the University of Michigan (quod.lib) Emerson page: 'The Complete Works of Ralph Waldo Emerson: Society and Solitude', vol. 7, p. 179, https://quod.lib.umich.edu/e/ emerson/4957107.0007.001/1:11?rgn=div1;view=fulltext.

15. 'What Did the Big Bang Sound Like?', Melanie Radzicki McManus, HowStuffWorks.com, 10 January 2018, https://science. howstuffworks.com/what-did-big-bang-sound-like.html.

16. Scotland: MacTutor History of Mathematics archive's quotations page, http://www-history.mcs.st-andrews.ac.uk/Quotations/ Einstein.html.

17. Tweet at 5:41 a.m. on 15 June 2016, https://twitter.com/neiltyson/ status/743060864530448384?lang=en.

18. Reference to this accuracy made in paper titled 'Calculation of the Anomalous Magnetic Moment of the Electron, Dan Styer, 21 June 2012, http://www2.oberlin.edu/physics/dstyer/StrangeQM/ Moment.pdf.

19. '19th Century Mathematics: Gauss', Storyofmathematics.com, https://www.storyofmathematics.com/19th_gauss.html.

20. Scotland: MacTutor History of Mathematics Archive's Quotations Page, http://www-history.mcs.st-andrews.ac.uk/Quotations/Bacon.html.

Chapter 19: The Prediction of Neptune

1. 'Le Verrier, Urbain Jean Joseph (1811–1877)', daviddarling.info. info encyclopedia, http://www.daviddarling.info/encyclopedia/L/ Leverrier.html.

2.   See Encyclopædia Britannica's 'Kepler's Laws of Planetary Motion', Encyclopædia Britannica Inc., pub. 17 October 2018, accessed on 15 November 2018, https://www.britannica.com/science/Keplers-laws-of-planetary-motion.

3.   'Why Doesn't the Earth Fall Towards the Sun?', Gatot Soedarto, Medium.com, 13 July 2017, https://medium.com/@GatotSoedarto/why-doesnt-the-earth-fall-towards-the-sun-9a8a5e3fb8ab.

4.   *Calculating the Cosmos: How Mathematics Unveils the Universe,* Ian Stewart, 2016.

5.   'Today in Science: Discovery of Uranus', EarthSky in Space, 13 March 2017, https://earthsky.org/space/this-date-in-science-uranus-discovered-completely-by-accident.

6.   'The German Astronomer Who Found Neptune', Thelocal.de, 25 September 2015, https://www.thelocal.de/20150925/how-german-astronomers-expanded-the-solar-system.

7.   'Spotting Neptune, "with the Point of His Pen"', A.S. Ganesh, *The Hindu,* 23 September 2014, updated 20 April 2016, https://www.thehindu.com/in-school/sh-science/spotting-neptune-with-the-point-of-his-pen/article6438871.ece.

Chapter 20: Astrology

1.   Quote from the Messianic Prophecies (numbers 24:17), https://theoldtestamentandthenewtestament.com/2013/03/15/messianic-prophecy-number-29-numbers-24-17-a-king/.

2.   In the newer, narrower sense, collaborative filtering is a method of making automatic predictions (filtering) about the interests of a user by collecting preferences or taste information from many users (collaborating).

Chapter 21: The Happiness Pill

1.   Read and watch this interesting version of the story, 'The Happy Man's Shirt' as re-told by Shirin Sabri on Choraltales.org, http://www.choraltales.org/happy/.

2. Nietzsche talks about the contrast between what is 'noble' and 'contemptible'. You can read more in the summary section of 'Beyond Good and Evil' on Sparknotes, https://www.sparknotes. com/philosophy/beyondgood/section11/.

3. See the section on 'Happiness' on https://community.plu. edu/~nelsoned/Courses/115/StudyGuides/Aristotle.html.

4. 'Information in Living Organisms', Dr Werner Gitt, Answersingenesis.org, 2 April 2009, https://answersingenesis.org/ genetics/information-theory/information-in-living-organisms/.

5. Refer to the BMJ website, BMJ 2008, 337:a2338, https://www. bmj.com/content/337/bmj.a2338.

6. 'Salinger Caught the Attention of the World—Then Hid from It', David Usborne, *Independent*, 29 January 2010, https:// www.independent.co.uk/news/people/news/salinger-caught-the-attention-of-the-world-ndash-then-hid-from-it-1882551.html.

7. *Brave New World*, Aldous Huxley, 1931.

Chapter 22: On Extraterrestrial Life

1. 'How Many Stars Are There in the Milky Way?', Matt Williams Universetoday.com, 16 December 2008, https://www. universetoday.com/123225/how-many-stars-are-in-the-milky-way-2/.

2. See the definition on https://en.wikipedia.org/wiki/Mediocrity_ principle.

3. 'Fermi Paradox: Where Are the Aliens?', Elizabeth Howell, Space. com, 26 April 2018, https://www.space.com/25325-fermi-paradox. html.

4. Ibid.

5. 'Cosmic Search Vol. 1 No. 2: The Case for SETI', Richard Berendzen, Article Bigear.org, 19 September 1978, http://www. bigear.org/vol1no2/case.htm.

6. Article in Astronomy.com, 'Table for One? How the Fermi Paradox Attempts to Settle the Issue of Our Apparent Aloneness in the Universe', Doug Adler, published 18 May 2018, http://www. astronomy.com/news/2018/05/table-for-one.

7. 'Edward Snowden: We May Never Spot Space Aliens Thanks to Encryption' Nicky Woolf, *Guardian*, 19 September 2015, https://www.theguardian.com/us-news/2015/sep/19/edward-snowden-aliens-encryption-neil-degrasse-tyson-podcast.

8. 'Shermer's Last Law', published January 2002, https://michaelshermer.com/2002/01/shermers-last-law/.

9. 'Calvin and Hobbes Has Had It Right for a Long Time', https://www.reddit.com/r/funny/comments/1kvxs5/calvin_and_hobbes_has_had_it_right_for_a_long_time/.

10. Refer to http://www.heavensgate.com/.

11. 'John Zogby's Creative Polls', Chris Mooney, American Prospect, 17 January 2003, http://prospect.org/article/john-zogbys-creative-polls.

12. 'Far Out Friday: Alien Abduction Insurance on Sale for $9.99', Caitlin Bronson, Insurancebusinessmag.com, 16 October 2015, https://www.insurancebusinessmag.com/us/news/breaking-news/far-out-friday-alien-abduction-insurance-on-sale-for-9-99-25836.aspx.

13. 'Are We Not the Only Earth Out There?', William Harris and Jacob Silverman, HowStuffWorks.com, 30 August 2007, https://science.howstuffworks.com/other-earth.htm> 12 November 2018.

14. 'Exoplanet Hunting with Machine Learning and Kepler Data -> Recall 100%', Gabriel Garza, Medium.com, 15 March 2018, https://medium.com/@gabogarza/exoplanet-hunting-with-machine-learning-and-kepler-data-recall-100-155e1ddeaa95.

15. 'Cosmic Search Vol. 1 No. 2: The Quest for Extraterrestrial Intelligence', Carl Sagan, originally published in May 1978, http://www.bigear.org/vol1no2/case.htm.

16. 'Alien Search Detects Radio Signals from Dwarf Galaxy 3bn Light Years from Earth', Hannah Devlin, 1 September 2017, https://www.theguardian.com/science/2017/sep/01/alien-search-detects-radio-signals-from-dwarf-galaxy-3bn-light-years-from-earth.

17. Read the guidebook to The Green Bank Telescope on http://www.gb.nrao.edu/scienceDocs/GBTog.pdf.

18. 'Stephen Hawking's Most Intriguing Quotes on Aliens, Women and the Future of Humanity', Jeanna Bryner, LiveScience, 14

March 2018, https://www.livescience.com/62015-stephen-hawking-quotes.html.

Chapter 23: Simulation

1. http://www.svbf.org/journal/vol7no1-2/6_dakshina.pdf.
2. 'The Allegory of the Cave', S. Marc Cohen, https://faculty.washington.edu/smcohen/320/cave.htm.
3. 'Zhuangzi And That Bloody Butterfly', Raymond Tallis, Philosophy Now, 2009, https://philosophynow.org/issues/76/Zhuangzi_And_That_Bloody_Butterfly.
4. See the Philosophical Films site for a discussion on *The Matrix* (1999), http://www.philfilms.utm.edu/1/matrix.htm.
5. 'Unreal Truths: Matter Waves and the Bohr Model of the Atom', Jonah, The Physics Mill, 24 December 2012, http://www.thephysicsmill.com/2012/12/24/unreal-truths-the-bohr-model-of-the-atom/.
6. View on YouTube, 'Double Slit Experiment Explained!', Jim Al-Khalili, https://www.youtube.com/watch?v=A9tKncAdlHQ.
7. 'Is the Moon There When Nobody Looks? Reality and the Quantum Theory', N. David Mermin, *Physics Today*, April 1985, pp. 38–47, https://cp3.irmp.ucl.ac.be/~maltoni/PHY1222/mermin_moon.pdf.
8. 'Do Extraordinary Claims Require Extraordinary Evidence?', David Deming, https://www.researchgate.net/publication/309305745_Do_Extraordinary_Claims_Require_Extraordinary_Evidence.
9. 'Three Experiments That Show Quantum Physics Is Real', Chad Orzel, *Forbes*, 20 July 2015 (with embedded videos on 'Non-locality' and other subjects), https://www.forbes.com/sites/chadorzel/2015/07/20/three-experiments-that-show-quantum-physics-is-real/#13820df61ae5.
10. Ibid.
11. 'Sidebar: The Holographic Principle', J.R. Minkel, *Scientific American*, https://www.scientificamerican.com/article/sidebar-the-holographic-p/.
12. 'Neurons and Synapses', Human-memory.net, http://www.human-memory.net/brain_neurons.html.

13. 'See Our Universe Is a Gigantic and Wonderfully Detailed Holographic Illusion', MessageToEagle.com, 5 August 2015, http://www.messagetoeagle.com/our-universe-is-a-gigantic-and-wonderfully-detailed-holographic-illusion/.

14. 'How Do You Know You're Not in a Simulation?', Laura D'Olimpio, Realclearscience.com, 1 August 2016, https://www.realclearscience.com/articles/2016/08/02/how_do_you_know_youre_not_in_a_simulation_109706.html.

Chapter 24: Transhumanism

1. 'Ray Kurzweil Pulls Out All the Stops (And Pills) to Survive to the Singularity', Gary Wolf, Wired, 24 March 2008.

2. Read about it on the NASA site for the WMAP (Wilkinson Microwave Anisotropy Probe project, https://map.gsfc.nasa.gov/.

3. 'The Coming Technological Singularity' by Vernor Steffen Vinge. He taught mathematics and computer science at San Diego State University and is also a sci-fi author.

4. These evolutionary systems include but are not limited to the growth of technologies.

5. Gordon Earle Moore, American engineer and co-founder of Intel Corporation.

6. DARPA's former boss, Arati Prabhakar's, article in Wired, *The Merging of Humans and Machines Is Happening Now*, 27 January 2017.

7. DARPA. This department of defense agency creates emerging technologies for use by the US military.

8. Refer to *Superintelligence: Paths, Dangers, Strategies* by Nick Bostrom.

9. 'Elon Musk: Killer Robots Will Be Here Within Five Years', James Cook, Business Insider, 17 November 2014, https://www.businessinsider.in/ELON-MUSK-Killer-Robots-Will-Be-Here-Within-Five-Years/articleshow/45177105.cms.

10. Sir Julian Sorrel Huxley, British biologist and eugenicist. Interestingly, he is the brother of Aldous Huxley, author of *Brave New World*. This quote and the article can be viewed on https://

the-eye.eu/public/concen.org/The%20Omega%20Point%20
Transhumanism%20Video%20Collection%20%281975-
2017%29/ebooks/Transhumanism%20by%20Julian%20
Huxley%20%281957%29.pdf.

11. 'Stephen Hawking: Will AI Kill or Save Humankind?', Rory Cellan-Jones, BBC News, 20 October 2016.

12. William Winwood Reade was a British explorer and philosopher. This quote is from his 1872 book, *The Martyrdom of Man*, which created much controversy and was banned by William Gladstone as an irreligious book. His idea of 'social Darwinism', "while war, slavery, and religion had once been necessary, they would not always be so; in the future only science could guarantee human progress", did not go down very well with the establishment.

13. Issac Asimov, professor of biochemistry at Boston University. But of course, more famous as one of the world's most favourite writers of science fiction and popular science. In his 1942 short story 'Runaround' (later included in *I, Robot*), Asimov proposed the Three Laws of Robotics, ostensibly from the *Handbook of Robotics, 56th Edition, 2058 AD.*

14. Dr Michio Kaku, professor of theoretical physics in the City College of New York, is a theoretical physicist, futurist and a popular popularizer of science.

15. Are you not a James Bond fan?

16. 'Artificial Intelligence as a Threat', Nick Bilton, New York Times, 5 November 2014, https://www.nytimes.com/2014/11/06/fashion/artificial-intelligence-as-a-threat.html?rref=collection%2Fbyline%2Fnick-bilton&action=click&contentCollection=undefined&region=stream&module=stream_unit&version=search&contentPlacement=5&pgtype=collection.

17. 'Stephen Hawking: Brain Could Exist Outside Body', *Guardian*, 21 September 2013, https://www.theguardian.com/science/2013/sep/21/stephen-hawking-brain-outside-body.

18. The Blue Brain is a project at the Brain and Mind Institute of the *École* Polytechnique Féderalè de Lausanne in Switzerland. Founded by Henry Markram, it is believed that this project will eventually help us understand consciousness.

19. Sir Roger Penrose OM FRS is an English mathematical physicist, mathematician and philosopher of science. It was in his 1989 book, *The Emperor's New Mind*, that he proposed the quantum effects feature in human cognition. He wrote about the possibility of molecular structures in the brain that could have the ability to alter their state in response to quantum events. It would then be possible for these structures to assume a superposition state (like in the famous double-slit experiment). And these quantum superpositions could show up in the way neurons are triggered to communicate via electrical signals.

    This, according to Dr Penrose, explains our ability to sustain seemingly incompatible mental states is no quirk of perception, but a real quantum effect.

20. *Altered Carbon* is an American dystopian science-fiction television series created by Laeta Kalogridis and based on the 2002 novel of the same title by Richard K. Morgan. The series takes place over 300 years in the future, in the year 2384.

Chapter 25: Data Religion

1. Read 'Uranus' and other interesting stories from Greek mythology at https://greekgodsandgoddesses.net/gods/uranus/.
2. From *On the Gods and Other Essays* by Robert G. Ingersoll.
3. *American Gods* is a novel by English author Neil Gaiman. It is a blend of Americana, fantasy, and various strands of ancient and modern mythology, all centering on the mysterious and taciturn Shadow.
4. 'Vladimir Lenin, Report on the Work of the Council of People's Commissars. December 22, 1920', http://soviethistory.msu.edu/1921-2/electrification-campaign/communism-is-soviet-power-electrification-of-the-whole-country/.
5. 'Why Putin's Economy Survives', Chris Miller, *Wall Street Journal,* 29 December 2016, https://www.wsj.com/articles/why-putins-economy-survives-1483020001.
6. Read more about this school of Hinduism in *The Samkhya Philosophy* by Nandalal Sinha.

7. 'The Philosophy of Data', David Brooks, *New York Times*, 4 February 2013, https://www.nytimes.com/2013/02/05/opinion/brooks-the-philosophy-of-data.html.

8. Please refer to the chapter on *Simulation* in this book.

9. Ibid.

10. See the website for the *First United Church of Kopism, US*, https://kopimistsamfundetus.wordpress.com/about/.

11. 'God Is a Bot, and Anthony Levandowski Is His Messenger', Mark Harris, *Wired*, 27 September 2017, https://www.wired.com/story/god-is-a-bot-and-anthony-levandowski-is-his-messenger/.

12. 'Deus Ex Machina: Former Google Engineer is Developing an AI God', Olivia Solon, *Guardian*, 28 September 2017, https://www.theguardian.com/technology/2017/sep/28/artificial-intelligence-god-anthony-levandowski.

13. Read more about this church at https://www.venganza.org/about/.

Chapter 26: The Upgrade to God

1. 'Climbing White Stork Tower', *Poems of the Masters, China's Classic Anthology of Tang and Song Dynasty Verse,* Wang Zhi Huan, trans. Red Pine-Bill Porter, http://www.mountainsongs.net/poem_.php?id=804.

2. 'Where Do Humans Really Rank on the Food Chain?', Joseph Stromberg, Smithsonian.com, 2 December 2013, based on a study led by Sylvain Bonhommeau of the French Research Institute for Exploitation of the Sea, published in the Proceedings of the Natural Academy of Sciences.

3. An inappropriate quote from Thomas Hobbes' *The Leviathan*, on man's life outside society, https://www.phrases.org.uk/meanings/254050.html.

4. See webpage created by Yvonne A. Williams, 'Olympia and her sisters: Gynoids, Fembots, and Cyborgs', http://academic.depauw.edu/aevans_web/HONR101-02/WebPages/Spring2006/Williams(Yvonne)/Home.html.

5. The Copenhagen interpretation was largely devised by Niels Bohr and Werner Heisenberg. According to the Copenhagen interpretation, physical systems generally do not have definite

properties prior to being measured. The act of measurement affects the system, causing the set of probabilities to reduce to only one of the possible values immediately after the measurement.

6. A wormhole is a theoretical passage through space-time that is a shortcut for long journeys across the universe. Einstein's theory of general relativity predicts wormholes.

7. Through crossovers and mutations. A crossover usually occurs when matching regions on matching chromosomes break and then reconnect to the other chromosome. Mutation usually occurs when there is an error in cell division.

8. CRISPR-Cas9 is a unique technology that helps geneticists remove, add or alter sections of the DNA sequence. Think of it like molecular scissors snipping of and gluing precise parts of the genome to create a sequence you wish.

9. 'Angelina Jolie Inherited Breast Cancer and the BRCA1 Gene', Cancer Research, UK, 14 May 2013, https://scienceblog. cancerresearchuk.org/2013/05/14/angelina-jolie-inherited-breast-cancer-and-the-brca1-gene/.

10. For an annotated paper read: Turing, A.M. 'Computing Machinery and Intelligence.' *Mind: A Quarterly Review of Psychology and Philosophy*, October 1950: 433–60, annotation by David Whitehead (Theories of Media, Winter 2004), http://csmt.uchicago.edu/ annotations/turing.htm.

11. Stephen Hawking (1942–2018) suffered from ALS (Amyotrophic Lateral Sclerosis), a progressive neurodegenerative disease, and lost his ability to speak and write in 1985.

12. 'Quadriplegic Man Feels Touch on Robotic Hand with Brain Implant', Andy Coghlan, *NewScientist*, 13 October 2016, https:// www.newscientist.com/article/2109005-quadriplegic-man-feels-touch-on-robotic-hand-with-brain-implant/.

13. Read 'Yet Another Tribute to Sir Arthur C. Clarke', Giulio Prisco 1 November 2016, https://turingchurch.net/yet-another-tribute-to-sir-arthur-c-clarke-130b56549226.

14. 'Chimps vs. Humans: How Are We Different?', Natalie Wolchover, LiveScience, 29 July 2011, https://www.livescience.com/15297-chimps-humans.html.